Islamophobia in Muslim Majority Societies

In the last decade, Islamophobia in Western societies, where Muslims constitute the minority, has been studied extensively. However, Islamophobia is not restricted to the geography of the West, but rather constitutes a global phenomenon. It affects Muslim societies just as much, due to various historical, economic, political, cultural and social reasons.

Islamophobia in Muslim Majority Societies constitutes a first attempt to open a debate about the understudied phenomenon of Islamophobia in Muslim majority societies. An interdisciplinary study, it focuses on socio-political and historical aspects of Islamophobia in Muslim majority societies.

This volume will appeal to students, scholars and general readers who are interested in Racism Studies, Islamophobia Studies, the Middle East and North Africa (MENA) region, Islam and Politics.

Enes Bayraklı is a faculty member in the Department of Political Science at Turkish–German University, Istanbul, and Director of European Studies at the Foundation for Political, Economic and Social Research – Turkey (SETA).

Farid Hafez is currently Senior Researcher in the Department of Political Science and Sociology, University of Salzburg, Austria, and Senior Researcher at Georgetown University, USA.

Routledge Advances in Sociology

For more information about this series, please visit:
www.routledge.com/Routledge-Advances-in-Sociology/book-series/SE0511

Islamophobia in Muslim Majority Societies

**Edited by
Enes Bayraklı
and Farid Hafez**

LONDON AND NEW YORK

First published 2019
by Routledge
2 Park Square, Milton Park, Abingdon, Oxon OX14 4RN

and by Routledge
52 Vanderbilt Avenue, New York, NY 10017

First issued in paperback 2020

Routledge is an imprint of the Taylor & Francis Group, an informa business

British Library Cataloguing-in-Publication Data
A catalogue record for this book is available from the British Library

Library of Congress Cataloging-in-Publication Data
A catalog record has been requested for this book

ISBN 13: 978-0-367-58213-5 (pbk)
ISBN 13: 978-1-138-61300-3 (hbk)

Typeset in Times New Roman
by Wearset Ltd, Boldon, Tyne and Wear

Contents

Contributors

Deina Abdelkader is Associate Professor in the Political Science Department, a Visiting Scholar at the Centre for Middle Eastern Studies, Harvard University (2016–current), previously a Visiting Scholar at Alwaleed Islamic Studies Program, Harvard University (2014–2016). She is the author of *Social Justice in Islam* (IIIT, 2000) and *Islamic Activists: The Anti-Enlightenment Democrats* (Pluto Press, 2011). She has also authored a number of articles, including 'Coercion, Peace and the Issue of Jihad' in the *Digest of Middle East Studies*, and a book chapter, 'Modernity, Islam and Religious Activism', in *The New Global Order and the Middle East* (Routledge, 2016). She served as the chair of the Religion and International Relations Book Award for the Religion and International Relations Section of the International Studies Association (2015), and she is one of two women on the North American Muslim Jurisprudential Council. She is a co-founder and co-director of the Cohort for the Study of Islam and International Relations (COIRIS). Her areas of foci are democratic transitions in the Muslim world and Islamic Political Activism.

Ali Aslan studied Political Science and International Relations at the University of Delaware, USA, where he received his PhD in 2012. He is a member of faculty at Ibn Haldun University, and works as a researcher at Society and Media Directorate at SETA Istanbul. His academic interests include Political Theory and Turkish politics.

Enes Bayraklı earned his BA, MA and PhD from the Department of Political Science at the University of Vienna, and conducted research for his PhD thesis at the University of Nottingham in UK between 2009 and 2010. He took office as a Deputy Director at Yunus Emre Turkish Cultural Centre in London in 2011–2013. He also served as the founding Director of Yunus Emre Turkish Cultural Centres in Constanta and Bucharest during the period of August–December 2012. He has been a faculty member in the Department of Political Science at Turkish–German University since 2013. He is also director of European Studies at the Foundation for Political, Economic and Social Research (SETA). Since 2015 he is the co-editor of annual European Islamophobia Report. He also has appeared on Turkish national and international media on numerous occasions to discuss various issues such as anti-Muslim racism and Turkish Foreign Policy. His fields of research include the Transformation of Turkish Foreign Policy, Foreign Policy Analysis and Islamophobia.

Hatem Bazian is Provost, Co-founder and Professor of Islamic Law and Theology at Zaytuna College, the 1st Accredited Muslim Liberal Arts College in the United States. He is a teaching Professor in the Departments of Near Eastern and Ethnic Studies at the University of California, Berkeley. Between 2002 and 2007, he also served as an adjunct Professor of law at Boalt Hall School of Law at the University of California, Berkeley. In addition to Berkeley, he served as a visiting Professor in Religious Studies at Saint Mary's College of California 2001–2007 and adviser to the Religion, Politics and Globalization Centre at University of California, Berkeley. He is prolific writer having authored four books (two more are underway), numerous chapters in edited volumes, hundreds of articles and published studies on various subjects. In spring 2009, he founded at Berkeley the Islamophobia Research and Documentation Project at the Centre for Race and Gender, a research unit dedicated to the systematic study of Othering Islam and Muslims. In spring 2012, he launched the *Islamophobia Studies Journal*, the only academic journal dedicated to the Islamophobia Studies field, which is published bi-annually through Pluto Press.

Rezart Beka is currently a PhD student in Arabic and Islamic Studies at Georgetown University. He obtained his first MA (with summa cum laude) in Interdisciplinary Studies of Religions and Cultures from the Pontifical Gregorian University, Rome, Italy in 2011 and his second MA (with summa cum laude) in the Study of Contemporary Muslim Thought and Societies at Faculty of Islamic Studies (FIS) of Hamad Bin Khalifa University (HBKU), Doha, Qatar in 2016. He holds a BA in Sociology from University of Tirana, Albania. He has authored three books in Albanian, *The Pontifical Man*, (Erasmus Publishing, 2007) and 'Critical Commentary' (with footnotes) on *Rahmatullah Al-Hindi's Work Truth Revealed* (Erasmus Publishing, 2004) and a number of articles such as 'Comunione Matrimoniale Secondo i Testi Fondanti del Islam' (in Italian) *Periodica de Re Canonica*, Vol. 100, No. 3–4 2011, 'Jesus and Muhammad: The New Convergences' (in Albanian) *Një* No. 2 2010, 'The Development of Islamic Medicine' (in Albanian) *Pena* No. 1 2008.

Amina Easat-Daas earned her PhD at Aston University, Birmingham, UK and studied Muslim women's political participation in France and Belgium. She is currently part of the European Commission-funded Counter-Islamophobia Kit research project team at the University of Leeds. Her research interests include the study of Muslim women, Muslim youth, Islamophobia and countering-Islamophobia in Europe, 'European–Islam'. She has presented her research findings to the European Parliament, The Carter Centre and the

Organisation for Security and Co-operation in Europe (OSCE) among others and has appeared on international media on numerous occasions to discuss anti-Muslim current affairs.

Sahar El Zahed is a Candidate of Philosophy in Islamic Studies at University of California, Los Angeles (UCLA). She is interested in Islamophobia, Orientalism, the media representation of Islam and Muslims in countries with a Muslim majority and social media.

Léonard Faytre graduated from Sciences Po Paris University with degrees in both Political Science (BA) and Urban Policy (MA) in 2013. After moving to Istanbul the same year, he continued his studies and completed a second MA in Argumentation Theories (Münazara) at Alliance of Civilization Institute (Ibn Haldun University) in 2018. His researches focus on Political Theory, French Foreign Affairs and French Immigration Policy. Beside French, he speaks fluently English, Turkish and Arabic. Currently, he works as Research Assistant at the European Studies Department of SETA Foundation.

Syed Furrukh Zad Ali Shah is Assistant Professor at Faculty of Contemporary Studies, National Defence University Islamabad Pakistan. He received PhD as the German Academic Exchange Service (DAAD) doctoral candidate from the University of Erfurt Germany in 2016 on cultural politics of Islamophobia in Western Europe, which is titled 'Spaces of Engagement: Relocating European Islamophobia in Muslim Diaspora Enclaves'. He holds a MPhil in International Relations (2004) from Quaid-i-Azam University, researching on 'Genocide: How to Reckon with Past Wrongs'. As Assistant Professor of International Relations, he taught at National University of Modern Languages & Sciences, Quaid-i-Azam University, and Fatima Jinnah University in Pakistan (1996–2011) and at University of Erfurt, Germany (2012–2016). His research interests are focused on Muslims in the West, Islamophobia Politics and Political Islam.

Farid Hafez is currently Senior Researcher at the University of Salzburg, Department of Political Science and Sociology. He is also Senior Researcher at Georgetown University's 'The Bridge Initiative'. In 2017, he was Fulbright Visiting Professor at University of California, Berkeley and in 2014, he was Visiting Scholar at Columbia University, New York. Since 2010 he has been the Editor of the *Islamophobia Studies Yearbook*, and since 2016 the Co-editor of the *European Islamophobia Report*. He serves as an adviser and reviewer for a number of boards and journals. He has received the Bruno Kreisky Award for the political book of the year for his anthology *Islamophobie in Österreich* (Studienverlag, 2009) co-edited with John Bunzl. Currently, his research focuses on Muslim youth movements in Europe. He earned his PhD in Political Science from the University of Vienna. Hafez has more than 80 publications and regularly publishes in leading journals and publishing houses.

Derya Iner is Senior Lecturer and Research Coordinator at the Centre for Islamic Studies, Charles Sturt University, teaching and researching subjects on contemporary issues related to Islam, Islamic cultures and Muslims. She completed her PhD in Cultural Studies and Gender Studies in Wisconsin-Madison (USA). Her research focus on Islamophobia, especially women and children's experience with Islamophobia, Western Muslim Youth and Religious identity, and early twentieth-century Ottoman intellectual history. She is the chief investigator and editor of the Islamophobia in Australia 2014–2016 report, whose second issue is in progress.

May Kosba is a doctoral student in the Cultural and Historical Studies of Religion at the Graduate Theological Union, Berkeley, CA, from which she holds an MA in Islamic Studies at the Centre for Islamic Studies.

Jemal Muhamed is a PhD candidate in Political Science and International Relations at Istanbul Sabahattin Zaim University. He earned his undergraduate degree in Political Science and International Relations in 2013 from Dire-Dawa University in Ethiopia. After working as a graduate assistant at Samara University for two years, Muhamed joined Addis Ababa University, where he obtained his master's degree in Peace and Security Studies in 2017. Since then, he has served as an instructor in the department of Civics and Ethical Studies at Samara University in Ethiopia where he offered various courses for undergraduate programs in International Relations, International Organizations and Law, Peace and Conflict, Research Methods, Federalism and Local Government, Politics of Development, and Civics and Ethics. While completing his PhD, he is also an Associate Researcher at the Centre for Islam and Global Affairs at Istanbul Sabahattin Zaim University. His research interests include peace and security, conflict management, and democratization and transnational politics in the North-East (Horn) of Africa in broader contexts of the Middle East and international politics.

Katy Nebhan is a historian with a particular interest in Australian masculinities and the development of minority communities within a distinctive Australian culture. She has worked on heritage preservation in New South Wales and has written on the Afghan cameleers, Australian Muslim history and popular culture. She is currently working on a research project at Centre for Islamic Studies and Civilisation, Charles Sturt University.

Mohamed Nawab Osman is the Coordinator of the Malaysia Program at RSIS. He also coordinates RSIS' Seminar Series on Muslim Societies in Asia. His research interests include the domestic and international politics of Southeast and South Asian countries, transnational Islamic political movements and Islamophobia Studies. He has written various papers, books and journal articles relating to his research interests. He is the author of *Hizbut Tahrir Indonesia: Identity, Ideology and Religo-Political Mobilisation* (Routledge, 2018) and *Islam and Peace-Building the Asia-Pacific* (World Scientific, 2017). Some of his articles have been featured in prominent journals such as

Contemporary Islam, Journal of Muslim Minority Affairs, Islamophobia Studies, Sociology of Islam, Southeast Asia Research, South Asia and *Contemporary Southeast Asia.*

Müşerref Yardım graduated from the Eastern Languages Department at the Liège University (Belgium) and has an MA in Islamic Civilization from Sorbonne University (France). After completing her PhD in the field of Sociology of Religion at Strasbourg University (France) in 2010, she worked for three years at the Institut Européen des Etudes Religieuses et Scientifiques in Brussels. Since 2014 she has been working as an Assistant Professor in the Sociology Department of Necmettin Erbakan University, Faculty of Social Sciences and Humanities. Her specialisms include Islamophobia, Colonialism, Multiculturalism, Racism, Discrimination, Othering and Hate Speech within European Media.

Acknowledgements

We would like to express our sincere gratitude to all scholars who contributed to this book, and Hacı Mehmet Boyraz, Zeliha Eliaçık and Şeyda Karaoğlu for their valuable assistance throughout the publication process of this book.

Introduction

Enes Bayraklı and Farid Hafez

In the last decade, many studies explored Islamophobia in Western societies, where Muslims constitute the minority. Muslim societies, however, have been nearly neglected as hotspots of Islamophobia. One of the reasons for this is the obvious fact that Muslims make up the majority in most of these countries. But can Islamophobia be exclusively explained based on a majority–minority relation?

This book shows how anti-Muslim racism plays a significant role in predominantly Muslim societies and participates in Muslim countries' public policy, state ideology, elite/masse relations and media orientation. Therefore, Islamophobia does not only define the relationship between majorities and minorities (as it can be observed in Western societies), but more specifically, one between the powerful versus the powerless. While this relationship is often manifested by antagonizing Westernized Muslim elites versus conservative Muslim masses, Islamophobia in the form of epistemic racism is as much existent within Islamic discourses that are based on a Eurocentric outlook of the world.

Therefore, it can be argued that Islamophobia in the Muslim world and Islamophobia in the West stem from similar ideological and epistemological backgrounds. This can be seen from the similarity between the Islamophobic discourse and debates of Muslim societies with those of Western societies. Nevertheless, there are differences based on the historical, social, demographical and political contexts of the respective societies as well.

Rich in case studies covering different Muslim majority countries, this book constitutes an unprecedented attempt to make sense of Islamaphobia and a must read for anyone interested in contemporary Muslim societies. It is a must read for anyone interested in contemporary Muslim societies.

This book presents a critical perspective on an underexposed topic whose importance is related to larger issues of international relations, emphasizing the crucial role played by colonial power up to the present day.

In this study, Islamophobia is defined as anti-Muslim racism. It is about a dominant group of people aspiring to seize, stabilize and widen their power by means of defining a scapegoat – real or invented – and excluding this scapegoat from the resources, rights and definition of a constructed 'we'. Islamophobia operates by constructing a static 'Muslim' identity, which is attributed in negative terms and is generalized for a whole group of Muslims, often placed in opposition to ruling governments. In Muslim countries, Islamophobia can especially be understood as a way of regulating and disciplining Muslim subjects who are perceived as a threat to the dominant groups in power, thus framing Islamophobia as political. Islamophobia, as a form of racialized governmentality, aims at undermining a power-critical Muslim identity that especially questions the assumptions of a Western epistemological hegemony that is shared by Muslim elites.

In the first chapter entitled 'Making sense of Islamophobia in Muslim societies', Enes Bayraklı from the Turkish German University, Farid Hafez from Salzburg University and Georgetown University and Léonard Faytre from Ibn Haldun University discuss different approaches that allow us to better understand Islamophobia in Muslim majority societies. They argue that anti-Muslim racism does not only result from a majority–minority relation, but from a power relation between powerful and powerless groups as well. By focusing on the ideological and political ruptures between Westernized secular Muslim elites and conservative Muslim masses, the authors explain how Muslims can actually be Islamophobes. They suggest to look at Islamophobia through the lenses of world-systems theory, epistemic racism and secularism. They draw on the concepts of self-Orientalization and self-Westernization to explain how some segments of Muslim societies approach their identity, their tradition and their own world-view through an alien outlook, namely Western Orientalism. The authors underline this process in order to explain the possibility of Muslim self-hatred. The latter is not only rooted in colonization, but more generally in the encounter with the powerful modern secular West at the turn of the nineteenth century. As a result, Islamophobia is conceived here as a form of racialized governmentality that aims to undermine a distinct Muslim identity.

The second chapter entitled 'Islamophobia in Muslim majority states: 'religion-building' and foreign policy' written by Hatem Bazian from the University of California, Berkeley advances debate drawing on Talal Asad's critical reflections on secularism. Hatem Bazian starts his chapter by proposing a distinct and historically focused notion of Islamophobia in Muslim majority societies. He locates Islamophobia primarily as a 'process emerging out and shaped by the colonial-Eurocentric hegemonic discourses dating to late 18th century', which also emphasizes the role of internalization by post-colonial elites.

In the third chapter entitled 'Islamophobia in the contemporary Albanian public discourse', Rezart Beka from Georgetown University explores the ways Islamophobia is manifested in the post-communist Albanian public discourse. The chapter traces the extent to which Albanian public intellectuals have utilized global Islamophobic paradigms, like Huntington's Clash of Civilizations, the idea of 'Islamofascism' or the narrative of a 'European Judeo-Christian identity' to apply them to the Albanian context.

In the fourth chapter titled 'Post-coloniality, Islamization and secular elites: tracing Islamophobia in Pakistan', Syed Furrukh Zad Ali Shah from the National Defence University, Islamabad identifies how secular elites, influenced by the Western episteme of secular modernity, carry Islamophobic prejudices towards

Islam in the Pakistani context, apart from its civic critique. The chapter is a valuable contribution to the book since, according to the author, Islam in Pakistan has frequently and fervently been employed by the state establishment to develop the ideological foundations of the post-colonial polity.

In the fourth chapter, Ali Aslan from Ibn Haldun University, with his contribution titled 'The politics of Islamophobia in Turkey' argues that Islamophobia was central to the construction and reproduction of a modern nation-state in Turkey. The author contends that the politics of Islamophobia was specifically exploited for that goal, constructing Islam and Muslims as the enemy of the newly established secular regime and keeping religion and the religious outside of the state. According to Aslan, Islamophobia first served to replace the Ottoman Empire with the secular–nationalist Turkish Republic and was later deployed to produce a secular–nationalist reality. However, this second phase produced an autocratic and alienated political order, which was opposed by the democratic bloc that included the religious–conservative masses and the notables in the aftermath of the 1940s. As a result of this, this century-long political struggle ended with the victory of the democratic forces and the dismantlement of the Kemalist bureaucratic tutelage in Turkey in the 2000s.

The sixth chapter, 'Islamophobia in satirical magazines: a comparative case study of *Penguen* in Turkey and *Charlie Hebdo* in France', written by Müşerref Yardım from Necmettin Erbakan University and Amina Easat-Daas from Leeds University, critically analyses and compares the nature of Islamophobic cartoons from a Turkish magazine, *Penguen*, and a French magazine, *Charlie Hebdo*. This chapter highlights the commonalities and the differences between Islamophobia in Western and Muslim societies through the comparison of two cases.

May Kosba from the Graduate Theological Union in Berkeley contributes to the work with the seventh chapter titled 'Paradoxical Islamophobia and post-colonial cultural nationalism in post-revolutionary Egypt'. The chapter debates that, in the years following the aftermath of Egypt's 2011 revolution, the country has witnessed a rise in the demonization of al-Ikhwan or the Muslim Brotherhood. Kosba asserts that the current Egyptian government and its allies have generated a fear of Islamists in the media and in religious institutions, particularly a fear of the Muslim Brotherhood, which was the main force behind the first freely elected s in the history of modern Egypt. She also argues that this fear-mongering narrative has often resulted in Islamophobic language, policies and actions, familiar to those in the West and that have contributed to the rise of Islamophobia in the form of a widespread anti-Ikhwan sentiment.

Deina Abdelkader from Harvard University, in the eighth chapter titled 'Old wine in new bottles: secularism and Islamophobia in Egypt', presents the struggle between the secular and religious divide in Egypt, which culminated in the creation of the Muslim Brotherhood in 1928. The roots of Western liberal democracy are also discussed in this chapter in juxtaposition to similar roots of the principle of 'the Common Good'. The last part of the chapter focuses on tying the historical and ideological roots to what has transpired since the Egyptian revolution of 2011.

In the ninth chapter entitled 'Internalized Islamophobia: the making of Islam in the Egyptian media', Sahar El Zahed from the University of California investigates and elaborates on the ways in which various meanings of Orientalism inform the making of Islam and Muslims among the secularized intelligentsia and policy-makers in Egypt. Through an analysis of segments from five leading Egyptian TV programmes and a presidential speech, El Zahed explores the ways in which such programs and speeches engage in so-called 'Self-Orientalism'.

The following chapter, titled 'The confluence of race and religion in understanding Islamophobia in Malaysia' and written by Mohamed Nawab Osman from the S. Rajaratnam School of International Studies, discusses Islamophobia in the context of Malaysia by examining the historical and contemporary structures of power that enabled the rise of Islamophobia, the factors that rendered Islamophobia increasingly normalized, as well as the manifestations of Islamophobia in Malaysia. The chapter proposes that Islamophobia in the Malaysian context needs to be understood from the lens of racism since previously held cultural and racial biases against the Malay–Muslim majority populace in Malaysia have now translated into bias against the Islamic faith.

In his chapter 'Securitization of Islam in contemporary Ethiopia', Jemal Muhamed from Sabahattin Zaim University focuses on Islamophobia in Ethiopia. He argues that Islam has been securitized in Ethiopia through the implementation of legislative changes and institutional practices towards Ethiopian Muslims that affect the latter in different ways.

In the last chapter entitled 'Islamophobia from within: a case study on Australian Muslim women', Derya Iner and Katy Nebhan from Charles Sturt University explore the internal Islamophobia within the Muslim community in Sydney and thereby unpack the intersections between internal and external Islamophobia. The chapter gives voice to those Australian Muslim women who are struggling with Islamophobia from Muslims within a larger context of a minority status.

We hope this book will be a reference study to gain an insight into the various aspects of Islamophobia in Muslim majority contexts and will encourage further studies and debate in this area.

Istanbul and Salzburg, August 2018

1 Making sense of Islamophobia in Muslim societies

Enes Bayraklı, Farid Hafez and Léonard Faytre

Introduction

The vast literature in the emerging field of Islamophobia Studies has been focusing on Islamophobia in what many people refer to as the 'West' in a geographic way of understanding. Or at least, Islamophobia was analysed in terms of Western political forces, which represent powers that are located there such as US foreign policy, although its scope reaches countries such as Iraq and Afghanistan. This book is a first attempt to shift the discussion to a different context. It is not meant to redefine Islamophobia as such, but rather to look at how Islamophobia plays a role in a context where Muslims are not the minority in a society, but constitute the majority of a society. Muslims are in the minority status in many 'Western' countries, where this goes hand in hand with less economic and political power. Even in countries with a large Muslim population, however, Islamophobia can play a significant role.

In this chapter, we try to disclose the main dynamics that make sense of Islamophobia in predominantly Muslim societies. By 'Muslim societies', we refer to societies with a Muslim majority population. First, we suggest framing the notion of the 'West' not as a territorial category, but as one of power. With the global hegemony of the United States as the super power on the globe, Islamophobia can be understood as a continuation of an already existing global structure of racialization where 'culture' and 'religion' have replaced 'biology' (Mbembe, 2014, p. 7) The whole world is home to Islamophobia, especially in the form of epistemic racism. The latter, which is seen as one of the most hidden forms of racism, is defined by Ramón Grosfoguel as a tradition in which 'the "West" is considered to be the only legitimate tradition of thought able to produce knowledge and the only one with access to "universality", "rationality", and "truth"' (Grosfoguel, 2010, p. 29).

This does not mean, on the other hand, that Islamophobia is expressed in the same form in every context. Obviously, in the political context of a kingdom or an autocratic state, Islamophobia may function differently but, in essence, the phenomenon is connected to the global political context that is very much structured by the post-colonial order and related to contemporary US hegemony in the world. Second, since many of the political elites in Muslim societies have been educated in the centres, some even in the higher learning institutions, of the global North, many among these Westernized elites think along the same patterns as 'white men'. This is true for formerly colonized countries such as Egypt, Pakistan or Algeria, as well as self-Westernized countries such as Turkey and Iran before the revolution. Therefore, the regulation of Islam in many Muslim countries has become a way of regulating an identity that was regarded as a threat to the Western-like secular nation-state. Third, this reflects a notion of Islamophobia that was suggested by Salman Sayyid in his writings. According to Sayyid, Islamophobia is about making it impossible for a Muslim political identity to exist. For him, the challenge of being Muslim today is that there is no epistemological or political space for its identity (Sayyid, 2014, p. 8). Accordingly, the inclusion of Islam in Western epistemology as a concept would destabilize the colonial order. Sayyid wants to introduce a post-positivist, post-Orientalist and decolonial perspective to create exactly this space. Christian political identity, such as Angela Merkel's Christian Democratic Party, may be regarded as part and parcel of our current political order, whereas this is not the case on behalf of Islamic political identities. This aspect is strongly connected to the fourth aspect of Islamophobia, which is self-Orientalization, meaning non-Westerners' appropriation of a Western understanding of the world. One could here intervene to argue that this framing may support a non-critical support of political Islam. This is not the case since both forms of Islamophobia – conceived as a form of epistemic racism and self-Orientalization – can be found among those actors propagating an ideology of political Islam or Muslim theologians who reproduce Western dominance by attempting to imitate it and hence become nothing more than a reflection of Western patterns of thought.

While epistemic disobedience (Mignolo, 2009) becomes a necessity to relocate the subaltern Muslim subject in the world, this also invited reductive –what some called nativist or fundamentalist (Ali, 2002, p. 126) – perspectives to counter the influence of colonialism and fight it back. We argue that the problem at hand is more complex. Since racism, such as, in our case, anti-Muslim racism, is not about an intentional act but is structural and works unconsciously, it can also be part of Islamist discourses who often mirror the essentialist and reductionist identity politics of their Western counterparts.

World-systems theory, epistemic Islamophobia and secularism

Islamophobia is another form of epistemic racism, since Islam is excluded and denigrated and perceived as antithetic to the modern secular tradition by the dominant West (Grosfoguel, 2010, p. 29). In his reflection on the *Formations of the Secular* (2003), Talal Asad demonstrates how Muslims in Europe are both present and absent from the secular Europe. Present on one side, because of Muslim immigration to the Old Continent and their subsequent place in the European public life (work, education, media etc.). Absent on the other, because Muslims are perceived as carrying values that contradict those of the European sacrosanct principle, namely the subordination of the divine authority by the worldly power (i.e. secularism). In this regard, 'Muslims may be *in* Europe but are not *of* it' (Asad, 2003, p. 164). We argue that this observation does not only speak to Muslims in Europe, but to those in many Muslim majority societies as well.

In *Local Histories/global Designs* (2000), decolonialist author Mignolo helps us understand the roots of epistemic Islamophobia in Muslim societies through his reflection on the notion of coloniality. By drawing on Quijano's notion of 'coloniality of power' (Quijano, 2000) that assumes a hierarchical structure of the whole world between the dominating-made product (from the white Western man) and the dominated-made product (from any non-white Western man) in every social sphere (ontology, epistemology, language, sign, economy, politics, etc.), Mignolo introduces the concept of 'world views in collision'. In fact, Mignolo profoundly demonstrates how the encounter between European local cultures and non-European worlds at the beginning of the sixteenth century did not only lead to the 'transition from one culture to another' (that is Malinowski's concept of 'acculturation') or to the complex interbreeding of cultures (that is Ortiz's concept of 'transculturation') but rather to coloniality of power, which 'presupposes the colonial difference as its condition of possibility and as the legitimacy for the subalternization of knowledges and the subjugation of people' (Mignolo, 2000, p. 16).

Mignolo describes this Europeanization of the world as an offensive process that colonizes any sphere of the 'being' and that deeply reshapes the colonized's approach to the world, namely his understanding of ontology (definition of human being and of its relation to the inner and supra-worlds), of psychology (subconsciousness, self-representation), of linguistics (discourse, use of certain concepts), of epistemology (definition of knowledge, divine and secular knowledge), to politics (state, nation, secularism), of economy (capitalism, industry, centre–periphery) etc. At the end of this destructive process, the colonized is not allowed to 'be' outside the Europeanized world. Put differently, Mignolo draws an intrinsic link between Europeanism (i.e. Western colonial design of the world), Orientalism (i.e. Western approach to the non-Western world), and self-Orientalism (i.e. the adoption of an Orientalist approach by non-Westerners/natives/indigenous).

Another decolonial author, Ramón Grosfoguel, argues that Islamophobia takes root in Western imperialism at the global scale, leading to 'self-valorisation' of Western epistemological tradition and rising it up to the rank of 'universality', 'neutrality', 'rationality' and 'philosophy'. This is a global phenomenon. Starting from the fifteenth century (the destruction of Al-Andalus and the conquest of the American continent) onwards, the 'West' claimed intellectual superiority over other civilizations following its growing political domination (slavery, colonization, Westernization, etc.). One of the results of this long global process was the creation of the 'world-system' we all live in, which is yet again designed and dominated by the Western framework and world-view. For Grosfoguel, we all live in a world-system characterized as the 'modern colonial Westernized Christian-centric capitalist patriarchal world-system' (Grosfoguel, 2012).

In this definition, globalization does not only involve 'international division of labour and a global inter-state system' but also

> as constitutive of the capitalist accumulation at a world-scale, a global racial/ethnic hierarchy (Western versus non-Western peoples), a global patriarchal hierarchy (global gender system and a global sexual system), a global religious hierarchy, a global linguistic hierarchy, a global epistemic hierarchy, etc.
>
> (Grosfoguel, 2006)

This epistemic racism/sexism is the underlying discourse (in the Foucauldian sense) of the world we live in. In this context, the Islamic civilization's knowledge, values and way of life are automatically dismissed as 'particularistic', 'provincialist', 'subjective', 'undemocratic', 'irrational' and 'non-universal'. From this perspective, the Westernized political, cultural, etc. elites in Muslim majority countries can either be regarded as part and parcel or as operating within the epistemological framework of a racial structure. Indeed, post-colonial political elites work within the frame of the nation-state, a system that goes back to the Westphalian concept of sovereignty (seventeenth century). Again, the broad context in which elites are involved represents itself in the European local experience that became hegemonic on a global scale. This intellectual 'dependency' or 'captive mind' (Alatas, 2005) is particularly obvious for those cultural, political and other elites who were educated outside of their native homelands in Western universities. With this hegemony of knowledge production in the centres of the global North, a non-Muslim perspective on Islam has become the starting point for many Muslim thinkers and policy-makers, as will be later discussed in this chapter.

Centre–periphery relations and the birth of Westernized elites in Muslim societies

In what is often imagined as the 'Muslim world' (on the evolution of this term, see Aydin, 2017), the collision of world-views during the modernization and Westernization process (Mignolo, 2012) led to the decreasing role of Islamic normative perspectives in favour of the modern nation-state world-view, with more and less conflicts, resistance, and disturbance according to each country. Hallaq argues that,

> beginning in the nineteenth century and at the hands of colonialist Europe, the socio-economic and political system regulated by the Sharīʿa was structurally dismantled, which is to say that the Sharīʿa itself was eviscerated, reduced to providing no more than the raw materials for the legislation of personal status by the modern state. Even in this relatively limited sphere, the Sharīʿa lost its autonomy and social agency in favour of the modern state.
>
> (Hallaq, 2013)

As a result, the establishment of European domination over other ontologies, epistemologies and ways of life (materialized today by globalization) took place in a geographic space where 'the Islamic normative structure [is used to] serve both as a religion and as a way of life for its adherents' (Hussain, 1984). This ontological contradiction between Western modernization and Islam is still structuring most of the political conflicts in the region.

How did the anti-Islamic tradition of Westernization manage to prevail in predominantly Muslim societies? The first answer is to point out the role of colonization in the destruction of Islamic normative structures and the shift to the European nation-state model through the establishment of modern administration, military and education by force. Yet Westernization took place in non-colonized countries such as Turkey, Iran and – to a lesser extent – Afghanistan as well. Therefore, besides colonization, one should underline the decisive role played by secularized Muslim elites in the rise of the European modern nation-state model as both a practice (establishment of modern institutions, bureaucracy or schools for example) and an ideology (modernization as civilizational path, discourse and world-view). Dahl defines a 'ruling elite' as 'a group of people who to some degree exercise power or influence over other actors in the system' (Dahl, 1958) while Hussain adds that, according to elite theory, it is those who concentrate political power and 'who guide the destiny of their country' (Hussain, 1984).

The neo-Marxist centre–periphery perspective defines secularized and Westernized Muslim elites as intermediaries between European dominant powers and Muslim dominated peoples. Indeed, in the centre–periphery theory, while

> the metropolis expropriates economic surplus from its satellites and appropriates it for its own development, thereby creating the polarization of the capitalist system into metropolitan centre and peripheral satellites, [...] the existence of the third category [here Muslim countries' elites] means precisely that the upper stratum is not faced with the unified opposition of all the others because the middle stratum is both exploited and exploiter.
>
> (Hussain, 1984)

The centre–periphery perspective offers a useful framework to understand economic relations between dominant and dominated countries worldwide. Completed by post-colonial considerations on European imperialism, the centre–periphery perspective draws a general outlook in which predominant Western countries directly or indirectly shape Muslim countries through the complex mediation of secularized and Westernized Muslim upper-class elites. It is possible to categorize the constitution of such elites in history through two main dynamics:

a   *Colonization*: Elites first suffered capitalization of the indigenous economy, as well as Westernization of values through the occupation of their country by a foreign power. Then, they either fought colonial power by reclaiming

European Enlightenment values (Algeria, Tunisia, Egypt, Senegal) or worked with it to remain at the head of the country (Malaysia, Iraq, Jordan).

b   *Self-Westernization*: Domestic elites got engaged in the capitalization of the economy and Westernization of values without being subjected to any foreign colonization in the long run because they believed it to be in the best interest of their countries and they thought it impossible to resist the advance of Western powers without modernizing and Westernizing their societies (Turkey, Iran, Afghanistan).

Although the process of Westernization in each of these countries from the end of the eighteenth century until today is complex and differs in every case, almost all the secularized elites of these countries engaged in a radical reconsideration of the Islamic tradition/world-view/way of life that they consequently considered to be an obstacle to the establishment of a modern state, the only path to civilization.

The Malaysian sociologist Syed Farid Alatas shows how Westernization (or modernization) constitutes an ideological dynamic of change, an 'attitude or mentality that subordinates the traditional to the modern' (Alatas, 2005). Even though Muslim elites may have supported modernization in the last two centuries in order to better protect indigenous regimes (military, administrative and educational modernizations to balance European technological advance in Qajar and Ottoman states), to reclaim independence (resistance movements in Algeria, Senegal, Tunis, Egypt) or for purely pragmatic interests (exploitation of rubber in Malaysia, elites of the brand new states of Kuwait, Iraq, Jordan, etc.), their engagement in reform has never gone without ideological motives, a burden of civilizational rehab put by Muslim elites on their respective societies.

In other terms, the use of European modern state-based instruments to reform political, economic and military apparatuses also involved a set of moral principles that came with modernity (Hallaq, 2013.) For instance, an assertive secularism against an ancient regime theocracy (Young Turks, Kemalism, Reza Shah Iran), nationalism against the Islam-based Ummah (pan-Arabism, race-based nationalist movements), modern military rule against the Ulema clergy (Pakistan and Algerian armies), communist people's sacralization against divine sacralization (Afghan communist People's Democratic Party of Afghanistan (PDPA) party, Iraqi and Syrian Baath parties) being concomitantly carried on – often in paradoxical ways entangled with references to Islam – in most Muslim countries. Therefore, after having been the first subjects of European conquests and/or domination, Muslim elites became the main agents of the diffusion of European standards over Muslim societies. Put differently, the Muslim elites were in an ambivalent position as both 'exploited' (by European countries) and 'exploiter' (of Muslim masses). This position led to the violent opposition between secular Muslim elites and conservative Muslim masses. In his article 'Centre–Periphery Relations: A Key to Turkish Politics?', Şerif Mardin (1973) interprets this opposition as continuity with the traditional Ottoman cleavage between urban orthodox dwellers (the centres of power) and rural heterodox nomads (the periphery). According to Mardin, the traditional urban–elite/rural–masses opposition has been replaced by one of the modern secular–elite/conservative–masse: 'In this newfound unity [the Kemalist Turkish modern state], the periphery was challenged by a new and intellectually more uncompromising type of bureaucrat' (Mardin, 1973, p. 179).

Education and the military constituted two major institutions in the birth and development of Westernized elites in Muslim countries. The historian Benjamin Fortna (2002) demonstrated how the spread of European education in the Ottoman Empire in the middle of the nineteenth century – through either European and US missionary schools or Westernized domestic schools (*mekteb*) – led to the wide diffusion of materialism and positivism paradigms among Muslim elites. This ontological shifting from divine authority (metaphysics) to mundane priorities (physics) goes back to 'a new psychology that emerged in Europe in early modernity' (Asad, 2014) and thus directly challenged the civilizational role of Islam as a tradition that structures society upon spiritual and non-material principles. Niyazi Berkes (1964) gives an account of the nineteenth-century Westernized military, medicine and engineering schools. He describes Ottoman students as progressively disconnected from traditional paradigms and values, permissive to European ideas of anti-clericalism, scientism and distrust of masses. Berna Kılınç (2005) notes that

> it was in this period that a new system of schools for the education of bureaucrats was introduced, which led to the eventual eclipse of the traditional religious school system (*medrese*) along with the diminution of the political influence of the learned clergy (*ulema*).

Sarfraz Husain Ansari (2011) also underlines the impact of the elite's education upon the modernist and anti-clerical vision of Pakistan's first statesmen (Muhammad Ali Jinnah, Liaquat Ali Khan, but also Ayub Khan who studied at Sandhurst Military Academy in the UK). Similarly, Albert Hourani (1983) links the French and military education of North African elites at the end of the nineteenth century to their liberal and modern stance (for instance, the Egyptian Ismail Pasha who ascended to the throne in 1863 or Khayr al-Din who became the Grand Vizier of the Beylik of Tunis (1873–1877)).

Since secularist and anti-traditionalist reforms were widely unpopular among Muslim masses, the use of political violence by ruling elites became the main instrument of holding grip on political power at the turn of the twentieth century and onwards, materialized for example by the Kemalist regime in Turkey (1923–1950), the Shah regime in Iran (1923–1946), the communist rule in Afghanistan (1978–1989), the military rule in Algeria, Tunisia, Pakistan and Egypt etc. This authoritarian turn of Westernized Muslim elites emphasized the polarization between the secular military bureaucratic ruling class and the Islamist conservative masses, resulting in an unresolvable dispute over fundamental values in those countries (secular versus religious, people's authority versus elites authority). This was an unprecedented division in Muslim societies since Islam constituted 'the medium of communication between the elite and the mass cultures' until the beginning of the twentieth century (Kadıoğlu, 1998).

As a result, the birth and growth of Westernized elites encountered many contestations not only from the masses but also – and foremost – from a counter elite that promoted the Islamic tradition. Those trends, commonly called 'Islamism' or 'political Islam', contest the full imitation of the European modern state and of its resulting paradigms. According to the country, the counter elite is composed of Muslim clerics (*Ulema*), young revolutionaries and conservative entrepreneurs or intellectuals (Weiner and Banuazizi, 1994). They are reclaiming the right to define the collective 'we' and to rule the country. Yet, while these movements claim a kind of restoration of the *ancien régime* – or at least greater acceptance of Islam in the public and political space – they are all acting within the framework of the modern state and politics (see the Islamic Republic of Iran, Adalet ve Kalkınma Partisi-Justice and Development (AK) Party's rule in Turkey, Ennahdha Party in Tunisia, Muhammed Morsi's Presidency in Egypt etc.). For this reason, both Talal Asad and Wael Hallaq interrogate the capacity of Islamic political movements to 'restore' or 'recover' the Islamic tradition as a complete world-view against the Western nation-state model. (Asad, 2014; Hallaq, 2013) In any case, conservative counter-elites contribute to the legitimization of the very existence of Muslim conservatists in the society and to their reinclusion into the collective discourse and political arena, interrogating and destabilizing the dominant global structure.

Self-Orientalization

According to Bezci and Çiftçi (2012), the notion of self-Orientalism refers to the adoption of a Western Orientalist approach by non-Western indigenous people. Accordingly, self-Orientalism reflects the continuation of colonialism in non-Western countries. It is the reason why Georgiev (2012) discusses 'self-orientalization' and not 'self-Orientalism', pointing out an ongoing process that keeps shaping non-Western countries up to this day.

Discussing the psychological implications of colonialism upon the colonized, Franz Fanon has already put an emphasis on what racism does with its victim and explored how colonial subjects came to identify with their oppressors (see his *Black Skin, White Masks* 2008([1952])). Hamid Dabashi (2011) draws on Fanon's insights and departs from where Fanon ended his work, analysing the role of native informers in the imperial project of the United States and Europe in his *Brown Skin, White Masks*. Dabashi especially looks at those intellectuals who migrated to the West and were often used by the imperial powers to misrepresent their home countries. While Dabashi reveals the important strategic role of native informants inside the 'empire', one cannot dismiss the important role of those persons outside the empire who legitimize Western hegemony in Muslim societies as Muslims. One can claim here that there is an intrinsic link between the legitimizing of Western hegemony and Islamophobic discourse.

In other terms, the promotion of the Western way of life in Muslim societies by Westernized elites goes in parallel with hate attacks on Islam, which is conceived as an ontological threat. Yassir Morsi shows through three case studies presented in his *Radical Skin, Moderate Masks* – also drawing on Fanon's epic work – the complexity of navigating through the contemporary world that is shaped by the norms of the white man as a Muslim (Morsi, 2017).

In fact, many of the most vocal Islamophobes within the global North have been Muslims who regularly draw on their insider perspective to further support Islamophobic discourses. This is also true when it comes to Muslim countries. For decades, Muslim elite supporters of authoritarian governments continually argued to Western leaders that free elections would bring Islamists to power. They portrayed themselves as defenders of secular regimes. Paradoxically, this rhetoric legitimizes extreme political violence against the Islamic conservative opposition such as the massacre of Muhammad Morsi's supporters in Egypt in the summer of 2013. At that time, domestic elites such as the Egypt's former Mufti, Sheikh Ali Gomaa, called for the murder of the supporters of the first freely elected president of Egypt, depicted as 'heretics and traitors' and 'dogs of hellfire', (Osman, 2013; Asad, 2014) thus using a rather 'religious language'. Imogen Lambert (2017) underlines the paradox between the Western liberal approach to secularism and its authoritarian implementation in Muslim countries. By discussing the notion of 'liberal Islamophobia', the author first shows how European liberals/leftists are condemning racism in the West (including anti-Muslim racism) while supporting authoritarian Islamophobic regimes in the Middle East. She then demonstrates that this ambivalent position corresponds to the hate of Islam among liberal intellectuals in Muslim countries:

> Of course, Egyptian liberals are not alone in their hostility to social and political groups with connections, however remote, to Islam. The Syrian and Lebanese secular left are guilty of much of the same. They similarly opposed the Muslim Brotherhood, were unapologetic about their support for the 2013 coup, and slandered the Rabaa martyrs. While some claim to support the Syrian revolution, for example, they continually disown Islamist factions such as Ahrar Al-Sham, Jaysh Al-Islam, and other mainstream 'Muslim groups' in the Free Syrian Army (FSA) for no clear reason other than their Islamic orientation.
>
> (Lambert, 2017)

Yet, while Muslim Islamophobes operating in the West have been discussed widely, there is little research on Muslim Islamophobia in Muslim majority countries. One can argue here that this form of racism takes its roots from the 'double-consciousness' concept that is developed by W. E. B. Du Bois in his *The Souls of Black Folk* (1903):

> It is a peculiar sensation, this double-consciousness, this sense of always looking at one's self through the eyes of others, of measuring one's soul by

the tape of a world that looks on in amused contempt and pity. One ever feels his two-ness, – an American, a Negro; two souls, two thoughts, two unreconciled strivings; two warring ideals in one dark body, whose dogged strength alone keeps it from being torn asunder. The history of the American Negro is the history of this strife – this longing to attain self-conscious manhood, to merge his double self into a better and truer self. In this merging he wishes neither of the older selves to be lost. He does not wish to Africanize America, for America has too much to teach the world and Africa. He wouldn't bleach his Negro blood in a flood of white Americanism, for he knows that Negro blood has a message for the world. He simply wishes to make it possible for a man to be both a Negro and an American without being cursed and spit upon by his fellows, without having the doors of opportunity closed roughly in his face.

In other terms, the epistemic racism that comes with Western hegemony also presents an irreconcilableness between being Muslim and being in the globalized Western world today. This double-consciousness still plagues the Muslim subject as any other subaltern subject, as it is constantly questioning its identity, whether it belongs to a traditional world-view or to a globalized Western one. The Muslim subaltern subject is continuously confronted with the question of what is the place of the representative of a passive, backward, uncivilized and primitive, or more specifically undemocratic, unmodern, radical and extremist religion?

Facing this identity crisis between alien Western modernism and traditional Islam, elites of many Muslim countries attempted to develop alternative senses of belonging at the turn of the twentieth century. In his study on the discourse of the Aryan race in Iran (2011), Reza Zia-Ebrahimi shows that domestic elites constructed their nationalist discourse upon the Aryan origin myth. Zia-Ebrahimi explains that one reason for the persistence of this narrative lies in the trauma of the encounter with Europe and in the strategies designed to manage it. In the same way, Egyptian secular elites stressed on the Pharaonic heritage and on Pan-Arabic aspirations (Asad, 2014), Turkish Kemalists presented the pre-Islamic Hittite and Sumerians as ancestors of Turks, (White, 2013) while Tunisian elites underlined the non-Muslim legacy of the Phoenician civilization (Baram, 1990).

Self-Orientalism and double-consciousness are such powerful dynamisms that they also impacted leading Muslim figures. Mehmet Akif Kireçci (2007) has shown in his PhD thesis that nineteenth-century Muslim scholars such as Al-Tahtawi, Taha Husayn and Ziya Gökalp adopted the paradigm of modernity in their understanding of Islam. According to Kireçci, these supporters of 'Islamic Renaissance' (*Nahda*) constitute examples of self-Orientalism among the Islamic clergy. Yet, such intellectual imbrications are self-contradicting for Grosfoguel, since he conceives 'self-Orientalism' (and the related notions of modernity, civilization, secularism, etc.) as the epistemic roots of Islamophobia in Muslim societies (2010). Likewise, in his article on the historical background of Islamophobia in Turkey, Mencet (2018) identifies self-Orientalism as both the result of

Western imperialism and the main cause of contemporary Islamophobia. He argues that self-Orientalism is still widespread in many spheres of the Turkish society such as literature, press, arts and bureaucracy. Consequently, one can observe the open and constant expression of Islamophobia in this predominantly Muslim country.

Governing Islam in Muslim countries

From the perspective of Muslim societies, the encounter with colonial powers has been accompanied by 'cultural imperialism' (Laouri, 1976, p. 100). This shaped the way Muslim societies entered into modernity and how the latter construed their modern nation-states. (Akhbari *et al.*, 2017) In the edited volume *Colonial and Post-Colonial Governance of Islam: Continuities and Ruptures*, (Maussen, Bader and Moors, 2011) the authors trace current post-colonialist state policies towards Islam back to their colonialist experience and public policy of Islam in use during this period. The authors map different configurations of opportunities for Muslim life and distinguish between different modes in the governance of Islam:

> First, there is the regulation of religious education and religious authority [...]. Second, there are institutional arrangements and practices that aim to regulate property and facilities [...]. Third, authorities in colonial and post-colonial contexts contribute to arranging the relations between Islam, law and social life. This includes the recognition and/or codification of Islamic law and the balancing of religiously based legal claims with systems of customary law (adat) [...]. Fourth, there are attempts to create, recognise and possibly institutionalise organisational platforms to speak for Islam and Muslim populations, for example, in the form of Muslim councils.
>
> (Maussen, Bader and Moors, 2011, p. 18)

All of these three dimensions reveal the central aspect of power relations and suggest considering state agencies as actors that discipline their Muslim societies, from education (defining what the true Islam is from a bottom-up perspective) to economic power (property issues, especially of the classical foundations that were monopolized by state bureaucracy), legal power (reducing the role of Islamic law in social life), institutionalizing the representation of Islam (who then define what the true Islam is from a top-down perspective). This does not mean that there is a linear development in the governance of Islam, as various articles in this book, as well as other studies, reveal (Feuer, 2018) There are differences in the configuration of different factors such as regime ideology, political opposition and the religious institutional endowment.

Often, the role of Islam and Muslims in politics in Muslim majority countries is reduced to an ideological struggle. However, rather than a struggle between the secular and the religious, as some portray it, we argue that this is a struggle over the Western notion of secularism itself. Hakan Yavuz has revealed in his work *Cleansing Islam from the Public Sphere* (2000) that Kemalists' conception of '*laïcism* is not only a separation between religion and society', but more a 'regulation of social life, education, family, economy, law, daily code of conduct, and dress-code in accordance with the needs of everyday life and the Kemalist principles'. As a result of this ideology, the Kemalist state attempted to shape a secular–national–Islam whose religiosity was confined at home and deprived of any exterior expression and political role (Haken Yavuz, 2000). For years, the Kemalist state used institutional tools in order to enforce this Islam policy through institutions such as the Diyanet (Directorate of Religious Affairs), Imam Hatip schools training young Muslim future imams, religious instruction in schools, etc. Similarly, today, European governments try to regulate Islam and Muslims by institutionalizing the Islamic religion (Bayraklı, Faytre and Hafez, 2018).

Similarities and differences between Western Islamophobia and homegrown Islamophobia in Muslim countries

If we recognize Islamophobia to be 'about a dominant group of people aiming at seizing, stabilizing and widening their power by means of defining a scapegoat – real or invented – and excluding this scapegoat from the resources/rights/ definition of a constructed "we" ', (Bayraklı and Hafez, 2015) we then find many similarities between Islamophobia in the West and in Muslim countries. Indeed, in both contexts, Islamophobic discourses depict Muslims and their culture as a threat to the modern secular way of life. Thus, many common anti-Muslim discourses or/and policies can be found in both contexts.

For instance, fear-mongering about 'creeping Sharia' perceived as a judiciary threat ('Alcohol will be banned, and men and women will be separated in public transport'); the manifestation of Muslim symbols in the public sphere such as mosques, minarets, headscarves, burkinis, women beaches (headscarf ban appeared first in Turkey and Tunisia before Europe); employment discrimination against conservative Muslims; Halal slaughter of animals that is depicted as cruel and barbaric; and, finally, the very presence of conservative Muslims in the country ('Turkey will become Iran', 'Egypt will become a theocracy', 'Europe is invaded and will be soon Eurabia') can be observed both in the global North and in Muslim societies.

In sum, Islamophobia works in both Western and Muslim countries as a discriminatory practice against what is perceived as 'civilizational backwardness' that legitimizes, if necessary, the use of violence, as can be seen with deadly military crackdowns of free elections. This dynamic is intensified and strengthened by the constant humiliation of Muslims and Muslim life style in the media and social media in Muslim countries.

Moreover, in both Western and Muslim countries, Islamophobia arises when conservative Muslims become more visible in different aspects of social life such as in education, employment and politics, thus challenging the establishment either through civic movements or political parties. In this case, both Western and Muslim Islamophobes often argue that they are only fighting political Islam – or Islamism – and not Muslims as individuals or Islam as a religion. Muslim elites especially even build on Islamic discourses to legitimize themselves and to present themselves as part of their nations rather than aliens.

Despite these similarities, Islamophobia also presents different configurations according to whether it operates in Western or in Muslim countries. In the West, Islamophobia targets a minority Muslim community based either on their ethnic origin (racialized discourse against real or perceived Arab-origin, Pakistan-origin, etc.) or on their religion (anti-Islam discourse). Therefore, Islamophobia is there indirectly linked to immigration, the multicultural issue and the perception of the 'incomer-other' that is not even respected as part and parcel of the society in the fourth generation after their first immigration. At the same time, both in Muslim and non-Muslim majority countries, both figures of the backward and violent Muslim subject operate as the enemy within.

In Muslim societies, however, conservative Muslims constitute the dominant social group in term of demography, historical heritage and sense of belonging. There, elite-led Islamophobia is the result of a secularist and Westernized project that aims to replace the *ancien régime* by the establishment of a Western-like modern nation-state. The complexity of Islamophobia in Muslim countries lies in the conjuncture that Muslims, who draw on Islam as a legitimate source for their world-view, are subject to Islamophobia by other Muslims – and not by Christian-secularized Westerners. Perceived as an antagonistic way of life, the Islamic tradition poses a 'real threat' to the political project of the secular elites in minority, who have systematically prevented large parts of their societies from holding power. As it was already mentioned, these elites have not managed until now to implement their secular-Westernized agenda upon conservative Muslim societies without the use of violence, be it in authoritarian democracies, de facto military rule or kingdoms. This tough struggle of power between two distinct visions of the society explains why the expression of Islamophobia in Muslim countries is much more brutal and coercive than in the West, as demonstrated by constant military coups and massacres in Muslim societies.

Conclusion

In this introduction, we suggested various angles from which one can analyse Islamophobia in Muslim majority countries. By proposing the lenses of world-systems theory, epistemic racism and secularism, we argue for an understanding of Islamophobia from a global perspective, while not ignoring its local materialization, as exemplified by the following case studies in this book. Hence, our suggestion is to translate centre–periphery relations into a local context and to critically look at the Westernization and self-Orientalization of the elites of Muslim societies. While there are certainly similarities and differences between Islamophobia in the global North and in the global South, Islamophobia in Muslim majority countries can also be legitimized by a discourse that is based on Islamicate references. This theoretical chapter is an attempt to evoke more discussion on a neglected area of research, which we feel is time to address.

As disclosed above, the ontological opposition between the Western secular way of life and the Islamic world-view following the European encounter at the turn of the nineteenth century has annihilated the consensus over Islam-based fundamental values and paved the way for conflicts over power between growing Westernized secular elites and Islamic conservatives clergy/masses. While the introduction aimed to explain the roots and the main implications of this conflict from a theoretical stand, the following case studies provide concrete illustrations of the expression of Islamophobia in Muslim societies.

In other words, Islamophobic policies, measures and techniques are used by Westernized secular Muslim elites in order to regulate and discipline conservative Muslim subjects who are perceived as a threat to the state's secular ideology. They clarify the construction of a static 'Muslim' identity, which is attributed in negative terms and is generalized for a whole group of Muslims, often placed in opposition to ruling governments. They expose with examples the racialized governmentality that aims at undermining a power-critical Muslim identity that especially questions the assumptions of Western epistemological hegemony that is shared by Muslim elites. In sum, they dissect, through multidisciplinary approaches, the socio-political aspects of Islamophobia that are taking place in Muslim societies.

Bibliography

Akhbari, R., Saffari, S., Abdolmaleki, K., and Hamdon, E. (Eds) (2017). *Unsettling Colonial Modernity in Islamicate Contexts*, Cambridge Scholars Publishing, Newcastle.

Al-Alatas, S. F. (2005). 'Islam and Modernization', in Nathan, K. S. and Kamali, H. S. (Eds), *Islam in the Southeast Asia*, Singapore, ISEAS–Yusof Ishak Institute.

Ali, T. (2002). *The Clash of Fundamentalisms: Crusades, Jihads and Modernity*, Verso, London/New York.

Ansari, H. S. (2011). 'Forced Modernization and Public Policy: A Case Study of Ayub Khan Era (1958–69)', *Journal of Political Studies*, Vol. 18, No. 1.

Asad, T. (2003). *Formations of the Secular, Christianity, Islam, Modernity*, Stanford University Press, Stanford.

Asad, T. (2014). 'Thinking about Tradition, Religion, and Politics in Egypt Today', *Critical Inquiry*, University of Chicago, https://criticalinquiry.uchicago.edu/thinking_about_tradition_religion_and_politics_in_egypt_today/, date of access: 8 December 2018.

Aydin, C. (2017). *The Idea of the Muslim World. A global Intellectual History*, Harvard University Press, Harvard.

Baram, A. (1990). 'Territorial Nationalism in the Middle East', *Middle Eastern Studies*, Vol. 26, No. 4.

Bayraklı, E. and Hafez, F. (2016). 'Introduction', in Bayraklı, E. and Hafez, F. (Eds), *European Islamophobia Report*, Istanbul, SETA.

Bayraklı, E., Faytre, L. and Hafez, F. (2018). 'Engineering a European Islam: An Analysis of Attempts to Domesticate European Muslims in Austria, France, and Germany', *Insight Turkey*, Vol. 20, No. 3, Summer.

Berkes, N. (1964). *The Development of Secularism in Turkey*, McGill University Press, Montreal.

Bezci, B. and Çiftçi, Y. (2012). 'Self Oryantalizm: İçimizdeki modernite ve/veya içselleştirdiğimiz modernle°me', *Akademik İncelemeler Dergisi* (Journal of Academic Inquiries), Vol. 7, No. 1.

Dabashi, H. (2011). *Brown Skin, White Masks*, Pluto Press, London.

Dahl, R. A. (1958). 'A Critique of the Ruling Elite', *The American Political Science Review* Vol. 52, No. 2.

Du Bois, W. E. B. (1903). *The Souls of Black Folk*, A.C. McClurg, Chicago.

Fanon, F. (2008 [1952]). *Black Skin, White Masks*, Pluto Press, London.

Feuer, S. J. (2018). *Regulating Islam. Religion and the State in Contemporary Morocco and Tunisia*, Cambridge University Press, Cambridge.

Fortna B. (2002). *Imperial Classroom, Islam, the State, and Education in the Late Ottoman Empire*, Oxford University Press, Oxford/New York.

Georgiev, P. K. (2012). *Self-Orientalization in South East Europe*, Springer, Berlin.

Grosfoguel, R. (2006). 'World-Systems Analysis in the Context of Transmodernity, Border Thinking, and Global Coloniality'. *Review*, Vol. 19, No. 2.

Grosfoguel, R. (2010). 'Epistemic Islamophobia and Colonial Social Sciences', *Human Architecture: Journal of Sociology of Self-Knowledge*, Vol. 13, No. 2, Fall.

Grosfoguel, R. (2012). 'The Multiple Faces of Islamophobia', *Islamophobia Studies Journal*, Vol. 1, No. 1, Spring 2012, https://irdproject.com/the-multiple-faces-of-islamophobia/, date of access: 8 December 2018.

Hakan Yavuz, M. (2000). 'Cleansing Islam from the Public Sphere', *Journal of International Affairs*, Vol. 54, No. 1.

Hallaq, W. B. (2013). *The Impossible State: Islam, Politics, and Modernity's Moral Predicament*, Columbia University Press, New York.

Hourani A. (1983). *Arabic Thought in the Liberal Age, 1798–1939*, Cambridge University Press, Cambridge.

Hussain A. (1984). *Political Perspectives on the Muslim World*, Macmillan, London.

Kadıoğlu, A. (1998). 'Republican Epistemology and Islamic Discourses in Turkey in the 1990s', *The Muslim World*, Vol. 88, No. 1.

Kılınç B., (2005). 'Ottoman Sciences Studies – A Review', in Irzık, G. and Güzeldere, G. (Eds), *Turkish Studies in the History and Philosophy of Sciences*, Berlin, Springer.

Kireçci, M. A. (2007). 'Decline Discourse and Self-Orientalization in the Writings of Al-Tahtawi, Taha Husayn and Ziya Gökalp: A Comparative Study of Modernization in Egypt and Turkey' *Dissertations available from ProQuest*. AAI3260932.

Lambert, I. (2017). 'The Case of Liberal Islamophobia', *Muftah.org*, 15 September 2017, https://muftah.org/case-liberal-islamophobia/#.W0XA89UzaUk, date of access 11 October 2018.

Laouri, A. (1976). *The Crisis of the Arab Intellectuals*, University of California Press, Berkeley.

Mardin, Ş. (1973). 'Centre-Periphery Relations: A Key to Turkish Politics?', *Daedalus*, Vol. 102, No. 1.

Maussen, M., Bader, V. and Moors, A. (2011). Introduction, in Maussen, M., Bader, V. and Moors, A. (Eds), *Colonial and Post-Colonial Governance of Islam: Continuities and Ruptures*. Amsterdam University Press, Amsterdam.

Mbembe, A. (2017). *Critique of Black Reason*, Duke University Press, Durham/London.

Mencet, S. M. (2018). 'Tarihsel Arka Planıyla Türkiye'de İslamofobi', *Muhafazakar Düşünce*, Avrupa'da aşırı sağ ve islamofobi, yıl 14, Sayı 53, Ocak-Nisan, Ankara.

Mignolo, W. D. (2009). 'Epistemic Disobedience, Independent Thought and Decolonial Freedom', *Theory, Culture and Society*, Vol. 26, No. 7–8.

Mignolo, W. D. (2012 [2000]). 'Introduction: On Gnosis and the Imaginary of the Modern/Colonial World System', in *Local Histories/Global Designs, Coloniality, Subaltern Knowledges, and Border Thinking*, Princeton, Princeton University Press.

Morsi, Y. (2017). *Radical Skin, White Masks. De-Radicalizing the Muslim and Racism in Post-Racial Societies*, Rowman & Littlefield, London/New York.

Osman, A. (2013). 'Religion and Politics in Post-coup Egypt', *openDemocracy*, 28 November 2013, www.opendemocracy.net/north-africa-west-asia/amr-osman/religion-and-politics-in-post-coup-egypt, date of access: 8 December 2018.

Quijano, A. (2000). 'Coloniality of Power, Eurocentrism, and Latin America', *Nepentla: Views From the South*, Vol. 1, No. 3.

Sayyid, S. (2014). *Recalling the Caliphate. Decolonization and World Order*, C. Hurst & Co. Publishers, London.

Weiner, M. and Banuazizi, A. (1994). *The Politics of Social Transformation in Afghanistan, Iran, and Pakistan*, Syracuse University Press, New York.

White, J. (2013). *Muslim Nationalism and the New Turks*, Princeton University Press, Princeton.

Zia-Ebrahimi, R. (2011). 'Self-Orientalization and Dislocation: The Uses and Abuses of the "Aryan" Discourse in Iran', *Iranian Studies*, Vol. 44, No. 4.

2 'Religion-building' and foreign policy

Hatem Bazian

Introduction

At the outset of this chapter, we must take account that Islamophobia in Muslim majority states requires a different definition that can address the specificity of the phenomena and the set of factors that are at play in this context. The definition must take account of the basic fact that Islam is deeply rooted in these Muslim majority states and the contentions revolve around its role in modern nation-states, in mostly post-colonial settings that attempt to form a secular polity in religiously committed communities. As such, the writing approach to Islamophobia in Muslim majority states is far more complex and daunting because it calls for deciphering legitimate contestations arising from different philosophical, theological, legal and historical interpretations of the textual sources versus problematizing Islam, as Islam, in society by a utilitarian use of these existing differences to drive towards maintaining or claiming power as well as giving support for external interventions. The idea of who speaks for Islam (Esposito and Mogahed, 2008) and what type of Islam is entangled with the modern mostly secular nation-state projects complicates the task at hand. Islam, in post-colonial secular nation-state projects, is both central and peripheral to the genesis of each state.[1] Accounting for differences within the vast and complex Islamic tradition and history while separating it from those elements that are being monetized or problematized in a modern post-colonial nation-state setting will be the primary source of confusion and I admit might bring about possible weakness in some of my own analysis. Admitting to this possibility at the outset is an invite for the reader to engage in this work and offer alternatives that might bring a better understanding of what is underway in Muslim majority states.

Another note of caution, the scope of this work takes a selective and limited sample from a number of countries and is not intended nor is it possible to cover details of all or even some Muslim majority states around the globe in a single chapter. If critics point to this fact as a sign of weakness, then I concur that it is the case and invite scholars and researches to undertake a detailed and a single country approach in future investigation to remedy the wide gap in this initial work. The task at hand is to theorize the notion of Islamophobia in Muslim majority states, which I admit is not a simple and straightforward endeavour. The approach to this theorization must begin with a definition[2] of Islamophobia in Muslim majority states that can point to the nature of the phenomena.

Accordingly, I define Islamophobia in Muslim majority countries as:

> a political, social, economic, military, cultural and religious process emerging out and shaped by the colonial-Eurocentric hegemonic discourses dating to late eighteenth century, constituted and internalized through an imitative project by post-colonial elites that posited itself or was designated by Western powers as the custodian for the modern, secular, nationalist and progressive Muslim nation-state projects.

The definition addresses the historical background that bears on the forging of modern nation-state project, which was cantered on replicating the European state formation experience that witnessed a break away from the Church, the actual centre of power in the pre-modern Europe.

At the core, Islamophobia in Muslim majority nation-states emerges out of a nineteenth and early twentieth-century developments that witnessed shifts among Muslim elites away from Islam, as an epistemological foundation for the society, and into embracing a particular anti-Islamic modernity and secularity (Hourani 1983, pp. 67–193; Kurzman 2002; Asad, 2003, pp. 205–256). Losses by the Ottomans on the battlefield and shrinking territories and fragmentation resulted in an evaluation of the causalities for this rapid deterioration of position visa via European powers. Among many possible options, barrowing and adopting European scientific know-how and military technology was the chosen response by the Ottomans, which was considered the best choice without undermining the Islamic foundations of the society. Initially, the effort called for bringing German and French advisers to help train the Ottoman army in adopting new military technologies and methods. However, in a short period the effort went further to transform the Ottoman educational system and adoption of the European methods, for the military in the beginning but became invasive to cover every aspect of the bureaucracy. Precisely in late nineteenth century, Muslim elites shifted into secular Eurocentric epistemology, which contributed to the development of an antagonistic world-view towards Islam (Provence, 2017, pp. 6–48).[3] Islamophobia in its early formation emerges out of this adoption and abandonment of Islam's ontological and epistemological foundations. This should not mean that the specific societal problems did not exist, they did and still do today but the theorization of the causalities was a faulty one and the sought after remedies made the problem more acute.

A second aspect to approaching Islamophobia in Muslim majority nation-states must also begin with the colonial project that problematized the 'native' populations and their relationship to Islam, as a source ontological and epistemological meaning. The colonial and Orientalist project posited that Muslims are violent, terrorist, barbaric, uncivilized, backward, despotic, oppressive towards women, irrational, and a death culture celebrating destruction while suffering deficiency in human rights, innovation, progress, love, mercy and imagination. At the core, colonialism was not a mere mechanism for control and domination of territory and resources; rather it was a project centred on developing an internalized sense of inferiority in the colonized population and constituting the supremacy of Eurocentric epistemology (Grosfoguel and Mielants, 2006). Thus, colonialism forged the inferiority of the colonized and the superiority (racial, political, economic, social and religious) of the colonizer in all fields.[4] I will get to this point in more detail later on but also the Muslim world is impacted by a more complex set of imprints that bear on its contemporary entanglement with the modern world.

Not to imply that colonialism is the only factor at play, on the contrary the Muslim world has many imprints that bear on its collective discourses and impact the relationship to Islam, as the primary field of contemporary contestations in modern post-colonial nation-state. The list of imprints that have a bearing on the collective world-view of the Muslim world include the Crusades; the Inquisition; the expulsion from Spain in 1492; colonization; nineteenth- and early twentieth-century Islamic reforms and push towards modernization of the military; nationalism and drive towards modernity in politics, economics, education and social structures; the Orientalist decline thesis and 'theories' and projects set up to supposedly reverse it; the anti-communist and anti-nationalist Cold War and post-Cold War discourses; discovery of Oil, globalization, privatization and technology; regional conflicts in Sub-Sahara Africa, Yemen, Somalia, India–Pakistan–Bangladesh and the post-colonial divisions; the invasions of Afghanistan and Iraq, the open-ended war on terrorism; the Clash of Civilization arguments; the Israeli–Palestinian conflict; the Arab Spring; and last but not least the Muslim sectarian divide. Approaching Muslim majority societies and modern post-colonial nation-state must take account of the historical specificity and its impact on the contemporary and unfolding events in each setting. Thus, Islamophobia in Muslim majority nation-states has distinctive features that the genesis of which must be understood while keeping in mind the above listed imprints because they impact the contemporary developments in a complex way. The list of imprints is not intended to be exhaustive nor will this chapter be able to tackle any single one of them in detail but are included to offer an illustration to the complex nature of theorizing and understanding the genesis of Islamophobia in Muslim majority states in a post-colonial world order bereft with conflicts and contradiction.

Islamophobia in Muslim majority states: history and context

My interest in the role of Islam in Muslim majority states has been a scholarly and intellectual concern for over 30 years and is not only an outcome of recent events. Admittedly, the intensified focus on Islam post 9/11, the Israeli propaganda machine use of Islamophobia as a communication strategy to demonize the Palestinians (Bazian, 2015, pp. 1057–1065) and the events that led to the Arab Spring and post-Arab Spring (Bazian, 2014) brought the urgent need to examine the demonization of Islam in Muslim majority states discourses. I would like to situate the examination of Islamophobia by discussing three different examples that shaped my view of the serious existence of an Islamophobic problem in Muslim majority state settings. Each one serves to contextualize the problem before embarking on addressing the causes behind it.

In the first case, I was alarmed by the visit and official welcome by Al-Azhar to Marine Le Pen, the leader of the extreme right French National Front party, which marked a level of recognition and linking between domestic Muslim world contestations and the global Islamophobia industry. Why would such a visit occur and why would Al-Azhar welcome a well-known and established Islamophobe? The French National Front Party and Marine Le Pen are not your casual French visitors, as she represents a very vicious and racist segment of the far-right forces in Europe and is very much a leading voice in anti-Muslim and anti-immigrant discourses. At the time of the visit, Le Pen was unleashing an avalanche of xenophobic and Islamophobic attacks on disenfranchized Muslim and sub-Saharan African immigrants in France. The visit and welcome, I maintain, inscribed creditability in Marine Le Pen, a party leader that has neo-Nazi origins and advocates racist and white supremacist policies in France. Al-Azhar gave the reasons for the meeting as 'openness to positive dialogue with all currents and intellectual trends and in order to promote Muslim interests across the world' (Taylor, 2015).

For her part, Ms Le Pen wrote a Twitter post about the visit: 'Meeting in Cairo with the highest Sunni authority: strong agreement on the fight against extremism'. Al-Azhar's own press release said the meeting was 'to discuss matters related to erroneous ideas and concepts about Islam and extremist ideologies and racism that some Muslims in Europe are suffering from'. Furthermore, Al-Azhar's statement indicated that Tayeb warned Le Pen about her 'hostile opinions' of Islam, which in his view must be 'reviewed and corrected', and that the Sunni institution had 'serious problems' with the National Front's positions on this matter (Egyptian Streets, 2015).

It was clear that Al-Azhar and Le Pen issued divergent statements afterwards and were in damage control mode as responses to the meeting in France took a very negative tone among Muslim and civil society representatives. National Front leaders and supporters were very critical of Le Pen's visit and condemned the meeting. Likewise, the Arab press was very critical of the meeting and took issue with the welcome extended to a major Islamophobic figure. Welcoming Le Pen to Al-Azhar points to the shifts that were under way in Egypt which inserted the historical seat of Sunni scholarship into the domestic French debates pertaining to French Muslim communities and their status, which are heavily Islamophobic in nature. Certainly, the National Front and its leader have been contesting the role and place of Muslims and sub-Saharan Africans in French society while seeking greater restrictions on immigrants. Le Pen was seeking a Muslim cover for her then presidential campaign and an attempt to rehabilitate her deeply xenophobic image in an appeal to the right-of-centre and possibly independent voters. Visiting Al-Azhar was hoped to accomplish this goal and help insert the institution once more into the debate concerning the status of French Muslims. In 2003, Al-Azhar defended the French veil ban and issued an opinion that sanctioned the proposed law, which won wide approval. The important fatwa was issued by then Al-Azhar Sheikh Mohammed Sayyed Tantawi, who delivered the opinion during a visit to Egypt by then French Minister of the Interior Nicolas Sarkozy (Eltahawy, 2009).

Sarkozy was running for the presidency at the time and Islamophobia and anti-immigrant policies were an important building block in his campaign. Al-Azhar extended a Muslim cover and granted Sarkozy much-needed breathing room to shift more to the right and monetize Islamophobia and anti-immigrants sentiments into votes at the ballot box. Le Pen was following in Sarkozy's footsteps, but this time the debate is much deeper, and problematizing the Muslim subject in France has become a mainstay of French politics and likewise in Egypt, which certainly predates the events of the Arab Spring.

Not to imply that Egypt or Marine Le Pen are the only ones being welcomed in parts of the Muslim world, on the contrary others are being met with open arms. 'Will Dubai's good times last?' was the 31 December 2015, *Asia Times* article by non-other than Daniel Pipes, who confided that 'I recently visited the United Arab Emirates to seek answers' (Pipes, 2015) to the question. Another visit was announced and planned for 4–11 November 2017, (Pipes, 2017b) and promoted with the following opening line, 'I am pleased to inform you that a few spots remain for the trip to Dubai and Abu Dhabi on Nov. 4–11, 2017. I hope you will join me' (Pipes, 2017a). In promoting the programme and visit, Pipes indicated that: 'In preparation for this trip, I spent a month in the UAE in 2015–2016; you can see my two articles reflecting on the country here and here' (Pipes, 2017a). The relations and links between Western Islamophobes and elites in part of the Muslim world is a development that raises serious concerns of legitimizing and providing a stage for some of the most pernicious anti-Muslim voices in the West.

In the second case, the front runner in the 2014, Tunisian presidential elections Beji Cassid Essebsi cast himself, starting with the formation of the new party Nidaa Tounes, as the rescuer of the country from a supposed Islamist party. Because, in Essebsi's view, 'the Islamists don't have experience being in power. They are incompetent and have been in favour of radical Islamist movements' (Weymouth, 2013). In another interview with France24 Mr Beji pushed further on this framing declaring, 'Islamism is a political movement that instrumentalizes the religion to get to power, which has nothing to do with religion. Islam here in Tunisia is a religion of openness, of tolerance' (France 24, 2014).

Essebsi's strategy was centred, on the one hand, on casting the Islamist as 'incompetent' and unable to effectively rule thus should not be allowed to govern. On the other hand, Essebsi makes sure to problematize political Islam while offering himself and Nidaa Tounes as the custodian of the Tunisian national project with the expertise and know-how to rebuild the collapsed state. The interview in France is very important because it engages a French political elite that is highly Islamophobic and problematizing Islam further fits into domestic programmes directed at otherizing Muslims in France.[5] In this context, Islamophobia in France is given an Arab and Muslim leadership cover if not an alliance on policy levels, which was similar to the Le Pen's visit to Egypt.

For outside observers, the Tunisian presidential election was framed as a competition between a secular candidate, Nidaa Tounes's founder Beji Cassid Essebsi, versus a human rights activist Moncef Marzouki, who was defamed of being close to Ennahda, thus soft on Islamist. Here, Islam or an Islamic party is a threat that must be countered while closeness and appeal to the ex-colonial motherland is celebrated and welcomed to rescue the country. At the time, the vote was the second round pitting the two top vote getters in an attempt to elect a new president for a 5-year term. Since the 2011 revolution Tunisia has been in a state of turmoil and an unsettled political and security situation that witnessed assassinations and an emergent militant insurgency. The Ennahda Party won the immediate elections after the revolution but was unable to govern effectively while being beset with a deepening economic crisis and a most fractured political landscape that provided an opening to the old guard to come back into centre stage through Nidaa Tounes and an effort to contest the elections.

The second round of presidential elections took place after Nidaa Tounes came first in the 26 October 2014 parliamentary elections winning 85 seats with Ennahda coming in second place with 69 of the 217-seat Parliament.[6] Parliamentary results and the first round of the presidential vote point to a shift away from the revolutionary coalition and a return to Ben Ali's old guards under the new rubric of Nidaa Tounes, but why was it necessary to appeal to Islamophobic themes considering the post-Arab Spring development?

Indeed, the framing of the elections took a reductionist approach by constructing a secular–religious binary in the then upcoming vote while glossing over critical developments in the country since the 2011 peaceful revolution. The old guard that has ruled the country since independence has come back into the driver's seat through the careful use of Islamophobic themes and framing Islamic parties as a threat that can be trusted. The cast of old guard characters offered themselves as the champions of a post-revolutionary Tunisia through the deployment of Islamophobic themes.

Consequently, the 2014 Tunisian elections needed to be placed in the larger regional context whereby the old bureaucratic faces, military and security apparatus, neoliberal economic elites and authoritarian-minded politicians were back in the driver's seat by utilizing Islamophobic tropes. In addition, the ever-present machination with ex-colonial and Western powers was needed in order to project creditability and assurance to keep the ship moving in the 'right' post-colonial, 'modern and progressive' direction. When it comes to Tunis and political developments in the Arab world, reality is indeed the theatre of the absurd since Essebsi and the ancient regime guards are accusing others of being incompetent in running the economy and the country! Mind you this charge is coming from a group that was in a position to drive the country into the ground, practiced torture regularly and imprisoned anyone that dared to challenge its dictatorial rule for more than 30 years. Fear of Islam and monetizing into votes at the ballot box made it possible to reconstitute the old order but under a new garb and aided by support from an Islamophobic ex-colonial power.

What is significant is that the use of Islamophobia and constructing a fear of the Islamic party was used to obfuscate and remove critical analysis of what has been under way for a long time. Certainly, the split in Tunisia's society is more a North–South one than secular–religious one. Also, it is a split between an elite that relegated to itself the right to construct the state in its own distorted post-colonial image and narrow interests while preventing all others from having a say about it. Those who took power briefly after the 2011 revolution were ill prepared to deal with the multitude of economic, political, social and religious problems inherited from a most corrupt regime. However, a problem 50 years in the making can't be undone in a few months by new political actors, Muslim or otherwise. From one perspective, we can say that the post-revolution government was unable to find a solution to the problems they inherited, which is a correct assessment of the factual record but the reasons for it are located in the structures inherited over generations since independence and constant external intervention; rather than in Islam or being an Islamic party. One can fault Ennahda for using their Islamic identity to frame a type of moral politics but this is not unique to Tunis or Muslim societies considering the role religion plays across the world.

The ousting of Ben Ali and his regime was a step in a long process intended to bring about the birth of a real modern state where the rule of law is foundational and citizens are accorded their rights fully. Furthermore, the transition away from authoritarian rule is not a function of one election or vote but about building democratic state institutions that can protect and nurture a vibrant civil society that can resist the ever-present tendency for dictatorship. Tunisia's state project is a work in progress and has numerous challenges at hand with the constant risk of sliding back into a despotic form of government. As it stands today, Essebsi is really starting to use the same type of language and approach that created the despotic regime in Tunisia in the first place and problematizing the opposition through the careful use of Islamophobic discourses and utilization of fear of Islam's role in society.

By problematizing and otherizing the democratically inclined Islamists, Essebsi opted to ride the wave of Islamophobia and monetize it into votes at the ballot box. In this way, the elections are focused on the supposed threat of the Islamists rather than offering an agenda on how the economic and political issues will be solved. The elites around Essebsi offer neoliberal economics, foreign investments, further privatization and possible loans or investment from the Gulf States, which was also similar to what Ennahda offered upon coming to power after the 2011 revolution. In economic terms, Tunisia (King, 2003) was facing a monumental challenge with unemployment hovering around 30 per cent, skyrocketing inflation, collapsed infrastructure and an elite that stashed billions outside the country, mainly in France.

Adding to this economic and political mix was a pernicious insurgency fuelled by external support from the Gulf States that opted to frustrate and roll back any and all inspired movements for change in the region. The complexity of the internal situation was furthered by the intervention of regional and global actors wanting a 'new' order that is more inline with their own economic and political plans than anything independent or unique in Tunisia and other Arab Spring countries. Gulf States strategy included funnelling money into elections, supporting violent groups and calling for even more draconian approaches to Islamic parties with the intent of terrifying the populace back into submission and accepting the ancient despotic guards. This is clearly evidenced in Egypt, Lybia and Syria, however Tunisia also experienced this and it continues to influence the current political climate.

Tunisian parliamentary and presidential elections were marketed as a fight between the secular-minded Essebsi and Islamist-supported Marzouki. However, a more accurate assessment would be to think of the population being forced into a binary so as to keep it away from asking more critical questions about the background and the real ability of the old despotic but new 'democratic' leadership. How would the old guard fix what they themselves broke, stole and bankrupted at least for the past 30 years? Using Islam as the bogeyman was an easy and well-tested strategy and has been deployed successfully in Europe; today it is in vogue in Tunisia, Egypt, Libya, Turkey, Pakistan, Bangladesh and other Muslim majority states. Islamophobia was monetized into votes at the ballot box in Tunisia and the results led to further demonization of Muslims at home and abroad.

In the third case, a 11 March 2018 editorial by Mr Salah Muntasir in *Al-Ahram*, a major Egyptian daily newspaper, addressed a suggestion to Mohamed Salah, Liverpool's leading striker of Egyptian origin, to change his appearance or get a 'new look'. On the face of it, the editorial could have been mistaken for the fashion section or celebrity news and development, which was not the case since this was a piece published as regular political column and not in the sport or entertainment pages. The critical part of the editorial on Mohamed Salah recommended:

> his need for a 'new look' so as to change his appearance in front of his fans. It is imperative for his to shave his thick beard that does not match his age and stardom, which [if not done] would place him, at least from appearance, in the same basket with the extremist fundamentalist if not even placing him with the terrorist or at least those who are sympathetic with them. After this, [Muhammad] has to totally re-examine his bushy hair style that appears untidy and puffed-up as if the barber did not know his way into it for years.
>
> (Muntasir, 2018a)

This editorial was met with some push back from other columnists on the neutrality of the beard and that the specific look that Muntasir criticized can be a fashion statement rather than religious in nature (Ghazali, 2018). Not content with leaving the issue and the debate, Muntasir wrote a follow-up column titled 'Mohamed Salah and His Hair' (Muntasir, 2018b), which made a far more explicit link between the beard and terrorism. In a 14 March 2018 editorial responding to critics, Muntasir lists six reasons for his position on Salah's hair and beard, but the most critical were items 4 and 5:

4. The truth that no one can deny is that Egypt is facing ferocious war against terrorism that [saw] hundreds of martyrs fall from the sons of military forces and police while defending the Egyptians, whom safety and security are targeted by terrorism. Therefore, we are in an extraordinary period that requires the Egyptian person expresses his opposition to terrorism.

5. If it is correct that not every bearded person is a terrorist, then it is clear that every terrorist possess a beard. Therefore, there is the opinion that pleads with Mohamed Salah, the 100% young patriotic person he is, that he does not put himself in any type of doubt, which we don't want for him and he does not wanted certainly for himself.

(Ibid.)

The debate concerning Mohamed Salah's hair and beard is paradigmatic of the pernicious nature of Islamophobia in Muslim majority states and Egypt representing an extreme case in this point, but it is by no means isolated from the general trend. I focused on the debate about the beard and hair of a man, Mohamed Salah, because the norm has been a constant pre-occupation with Muslim women, and with the wearing of the hijab and niqab (Wiles, 2007, p. 699), which has been a main stay of Orientalist writings and of contemporary Islamophobes across the world. Muslim men's hair and beards represent the re-emergence of a specific type of Islamophobic discourse that had an earlier manifestation during the 1920s and 1930s, when Muslim majority states, including Turkey, Iran and Egypt to name a few, embraced a set of secular reforms that sought to disconnect society from the traditional and religious legacies of the past and embrace secular modernity. The contestation of men's and women's dress in Muslim majority nation-states has been a mainstay of the secular and modern nation-state project and the re-emergence in the current period is a continuation of this phenomena.

The above three examples are not exhaustive of what is underway in Muslim majority nation-states and each example was selected to point to a particular development and not necessarily to isolate it in a given country or in the nation-states mentioned above. Certainly, the post-Arab Spring focused attention on the role of religion in modern Muslim nation-states but this has been the case since the colonial era. Critically, examining the epistemological trajectory of this contestation should occupy the better part of our efforts, which will be addressed in the following pages.

From Cold War embrace to 'religion-building'

Islamophobic elites in Muslim majority nation-states have adopted almost all of the countering violent extremism policies developed in the US and Europe, which are built on extensive Orientalist and stereotypical imaginary and the targeting of the Muslim subject as a unique violent specimen different than all other human groups. One can even ask the question whether Muslims are granted a human status or if sub-humanness is the only default status. Immediately after the events of 9/11, strategies were put to work to bring about the transformation of the Muslim world anew, which was articulated by Cheryl Benard, in *Civil Democratic Islam*, using the following framing: 'It is no easy matter to transform a major world religion. If "nation-building" is a daunting task, "religion-building" is immeasurably more daunting and complex' (Benard, 2003, p. 3). While the report might seem to be a little dated, nevertheless the main arguments advanced by it are still at work today. Rand's 'religion-building' project is still underway and called for stoking intra-Muslim conflicts so as to bring about an Islam that is compatible with the modern world, meaning the Western version of it. According to Benard, the problem in the Muslim world is that

> Islam's current crisis has two main components: a failure to thrive and a loss of connection to the global mainstream. The Islamic world has been marked by a long period of backwardness and comparative powerlessness; many different solutions, such as nationalism, pan-Arabism, Arab socialism, and Islamic revolution, have been attempted without success, and this has led to frustration and anger. At the same time, the Islamic world has fallen out of step with contemporary global culture, an uncomfortable situation for both sides.
>
> (Ibid.)

The definition of the problem is over-generalized, encompassing 1.2–1.4 billion people and almost 55 Muslim majority nation-states. Transforming the problem from the end of the Afghan–Russian war into a crisis engulfing the totality of the Muslim world is a very poor attempt at theorization.

Remedying this defined crisis, for Benard and those involved in this project, involves navigating, fomenting and managing conflicts between fundamentalists, traditionalists, modernists and secularists. In *Civil Democratic Islam*, Benard admits

> these groups hold distinctly different positions on essential issues that have become contentious in the Islamic world today, including political and individual freedom, education, the status of women, criminal justice, the legitimacy of reform and change, and attitudes toward the West.
>
> (Ibid.)

The groups closest to the West are the 'modernists and secularists' but each group faces limitations on its ability to capture ground in the Muslim world. Salient in Benard's framing is the notion that Islam is the problem and the various clusters representing the identified trend must undertake a gladiator-type civil society combat to the death until they are victorious, not for the benefit of their own society or nation but to fulfil the interest of the West. Islamophobia, in its current manifestation in the Muslim majority states, emerges from this fomented contestation that is driven by problematizing Islam and Muslims in their own society. Thus, the events of 9/11 are seen not as singular act of individual terrorist or possibly a blowback from the Afghanistan operations; rather in the religious norms of Muslims and of Islam's imprint on society. Long discredited Orientalist and colonial theories are given a new garb by Benard and unleashed under the rubric of bringing about civil democratic Islam or, more accurately, the civilizing mission towards the new but old barbarians at the gates of civilization, the everyday Muslim him/herself. Talal Asad's observation is important and must be understood in relations to Benard's and Rand's project: 'A secular state does not guarantee toleration; it puts into play different structures of ambition and fear. The law never seeks to eliminate violence since its objective is always to regulate violence' (Asad, 2003, p. 8). The ambition to secure power by the fundamentalists, traditionalists, modernists and secularists in Muslim majority states centred Islamophobia as a strategy and to effectively monetize it to secure governance and authority by various groups that embraced one aspect or another of this framing. Islamophobia becomes the lens through which each group contests power and authority since all prescribe to an erroneous definition of the problem in the first place and accept their assigned role to remedy it. That Islam must be rescued from the misguided group or groupings was the developed talking point for each participant. All want to rescue Benard's Islam or the violent type of Islam, which means that the problem of violence, governance, economic stagnation, corruption, women's rights, human rights and environmental crisis are all located in Islam's supposed failure to thrive and a civil war is the way to remedy it.

While Benard's plan to foment a Muslim civil war emerged after the events of 9/11 nevertheless the process actually began to take shape as early as the 1980s with the Iranian revolution and the Russian invasion of Afghanistan (Ansary, 2014; Coll, 2004; Coll, 2018; Rashid, 2010). Islam's role in both was very critical and Sunni Muslim groups, sects and organizations were globally mobilized as instrumental foot soldiers to contain Shia Islam and defeat the 'evil empire', the USSR. (Here, it is important to remember that from the end of the Second World War until the collapse of the Soviet Union, Islam and Islamic groups globally were recruited by the US, Europe and major Arab and Muslim states to neutralize communism, socialism and Arab nationalism, and I would argue that it was a very successful strategy.) The end of the 1980s witnessed the success of the strategic deployment of Sunni Islam in both confrontations and the need to shut down the operation required a reorientation or another 'religion-building' project considering that the Jihad movement was itself a CIA and Muslim majority nation-state global partnership to achieve a strategic policy objective – the bleeding of the Soviet Union in Afghanistan and containment of the Iranian revolution in the Persian Gulf. During the decade of the 1980s or even before, the 'fundamentalists' (various groups fall under this problematic rubric) were celebrated as representing the global and friendly Islam, because they fulfilled the foreign and domestic policy needs of US, Europe and various Muslim majority nation-states that were committed to the two-front campaign against Iran and the Soviet Union. The 'traditionalists' and 'secularists' (various groups fall under this designation as well) represented the unwanted or marginalized version of Islam in Muslim majority nation-states because they did not serve the identified policy objectives or at least did not commit themselves fully to the CIA-sponsored strategic global project. Consequently, Islamophobia was woven into the fabric of each Muslim state policy as they attempted to work through the global alignment set in motion to confront Iran and the Soviet Union.

The end of the Cold War and the Iraq–Iran war brought about the need to shift away from 'Jihadi' Sunni Islam and into a de-escalation of the educational, political, economic, social, media and religious infrastructure that had kept humming for over two decades. At the of the Afghan and Iran operations, the massive training infrastructure set up in Iraq and on the Pakistan–Afghanistan border, as well as the large number of volunteers, needed to be de-programmed and re-oriented back into normal society and away from the particular version of Islam that had been drilled into them and that was needed for the war effort. Transitioning smoothly from war to a post-war posture for many of these Muslim front-line troop volunteers was interrupted by the Iraqi invasion of Kuwait and the subsequent arrival of US troops into Saudi Arabia and the region in general. Had Iraq's invasion of Kuwait not taken place or if the US had not intervened in Arab–Arab conflicts, it is possible that the last three decades would have been different and the rise of Al-Qaeda would not have come about! Desert Storm, or what is referred to as the first Gulf War, interrupted the de-programming campaign and led to re-consolidation and re-mobilization of the CIA and Arab and Muslim world intelligence services that had crafted Jihadi Islam, but this time around targeting the powers that incubated them in the first place. Contestation over the Gulf War is at the centre of the re-emergence of the 'fundamentalist' Islam that Benard's plan seeks to counter without giving actual recognition of how it came into existence in the 1980s and beyond. The argument of Islam's 'failure to thrive' is Benard's lazy and Islamophobic way to define a problem rooted in wrong-headed and one-dimensional policy choices that was further complicated by Iraq's invasion of Kuwait.

The Arab 'volunteers' returned from Afghanistan triumphant, believing that they took on the Soviet Union, a superpower, and defeated it, but not realizing that they were part of a larger global operation that involved almost all the intelligence services of the Western world, Arab and Muslim countries, and the deployment of massive military and financial resources towards the multi-year operation. Iraq's invasion of Kuwait and the subsequent US and Western countries' deployment of troops in the region resulted in the same Arab volunteers and their allies across the Muslim world contemplating taking on the only remaining superpower and its allies in Muslim majority nation-states. The first test for this re-tooled effort came in the aftermath of the December 1991 Algerian election. Witnessing the Islamic Salvation Front registering a resounding victory in the first round of elections, on 11 January 1992 the Algerian military stepped in and nullified the results, arrested leaders of the movement and unleashed a reign of violence in civil society against anyone affiliated with or supporting the movement. For the ensuing four or more years, Algeria witnessed bloodshed, terrorism and never before seen violence directed at civilian populations. Rather than contextualize the problem around contestation of power and a military coup nullifying democratic election, Islamophobia was unleashed by the Algerian government against the Islamic Salvation Front (FIS) and anyone who dared to take their side (Martinez, 2000; Mundy, 2015). The Algerian army resorted to violence to settle the power struggle, which brought about the re-mobilization of those volunteers that came back from Afghanistan. Thus, the roots of the Algerian civil war can be traced, on the one hand to Afghanistan's war and, on the other, to the failure of a post-colonial democratic programme in the country whereby the military posited itself as a custodian of the secular and modernist project, the idea of rescuing democracy from itself!

Facing a renewed challenge to their legitimacy and power, the post-colonial and modern Muslim nation-states (with few exceptions) mobilized Islamophobia discourses and cast their opposition in an Orientalist and stereotypical fashion. Not to sweep the threat under the rug, the emergence of violence and terrorism was very much a feature of the 1990s but it would be a mistake to assign the responsibility solely to those who returned from Afghanistan. It was a complex process that witnessed regimes in the region attempting to consolidate power at a moment of rising expectations from a population that got tired of corruption, economic stagnation and a post-colonial one party or one family rule. More relevant, the expansion of forms of mass media and communication enabled people to see what other regions in the world were going through (Eastern Europe democratization, Central and South America and Southern Africa) and to compare their conditions to what is taking place across the world, which informed rising economic and political expectations. Resorting to Islamophobia, rather than introducing meaningful and serious reforms, was the choice for regimes across the Muslim world, which resulted in coordination, training and close sharing of information between intelligence services. 'Political Islam' became a problem and strategies to counter it began to take shape across the Arab and Muslim world that heavily depends on Islamophobic content as well as embracing another type of Islam, an apolitical type. Benard's 'traditionalists', who were on the outside looking in during the Cold War, Afghan and Iran–Iraq war eras, became the preferred Islam and were invited to theorize religious-based remedies for countering the other types of Islam. The search for the correct, pristine and apolitical Islam began in the mid-1990s and has not yet stopped since the prevailing conditions that gave rise to Muslim involvement in political affairs has not changed or shifted much since the 1980s. It actually got worse!

Islamophobia and the search for pristine Islam

The subject of the contemporary Muslim world is often entertained rudimentarily with a sole focus on Islam and utilized as a singular causality without any reference to the long and complex history that shaped or formed the subject matter itself and the people connected to it in vast territories and diverse societies. As such, the subject of Islam is treated as ahistorical and confining the understanding or supposed research to an examination of the legal text to explain everything that takes place. Consequently, the issue is not the importance of Islam's primary texts, theology and law but the reductionist nature of approaching Muslim societies through an ahistorical examination of the inter-play between text, societies and the diverse set of contexts across generations. This reductionist view makes it possible to ignore the specificities of Muslim societies under consideration while permitting for the wholesale stereotyping of causes and outcomes and connecting it to Islamic texts alone. The issues that are often stereotyped are overwhelmingly disconnected from Islam's itself and its textual sources but it makes no difference since the dominant lens overtakes and shadows any other sound and scholarly grounded approaches. All events and actions are reduced to one causality, the 'fixed and regressive'[7] nature of Islamic text and a demand to alter it and embark on a reform course of action that intends to replicate Europe's historical reformation trajectory, which is often treated as the singular universal norm.

Exploring Islamophobia in the contemporary Muslim world must be undertaken with the long list of imprints that bears on Muslims, which are often utilized to drive the otherization discourse. A profound difference exists in the Islamophobia problem in Muslim majority nation-states, which amounts to the insistence on affirming a non-existent abstract Islam in the process of demonization and otherization of the experienced and lived Islam of the existing population. The imagined abstract notion of Islam, I would add also an idealized non-existent Islam, is set against and utilized to construct a series of negations that revolve around the actual and practiced form of Islam at any given moment, whether looking back into history or examining contemporary unfolding events. An Islamophobe in Muslim majority states always affirms the greatness of the abstract and non-existent Islam while unleashing the most offensive and bigoted attacks on the real, practiced and lived Islam. Thus, the Muslim Islamophobe posits himself/herself as the spokesperson of the pristine, uncorrupted, abstract and idealized Islam, i.e. the perfect Islam facing the wrong and corrupted Islam of the people or at least those who take Islam seriously and seek social justice through it. The boundaries of the wrong Islam always shifts according to the interest of those positing themselves as representing the ideal, pristine and uncorrupted Islam. Furthermore, the Islamophobes in Muslim majority nation-states maintain that Islam, capitalism, secularism and modernity are commensurate with each other and only those who are infected with the wrong understanding of Islam prevent the actualization of the real progress intended in the pristine message of Islam. This point is often lost on people who rally behind the forces that construct this binary and often are happy when their sect, brand or approach to Islam corresponds to the one promoted by the custodians of a particular nation-state project. The affirmation of a sect, brand or approach to Islam by state actors is a double-edged sword and is never lasting since the scope of acceptability is constructed around state priorities and totally external to all

Islamic groupings even when it appears that they are perfect and constitute an identical match. Thus, the only Islam that is permitted by the modern nation-state is that which affirms the unconditional power and authority of the state, nothing more and nothing less is demanded.

Indeed, recent events in Egypt, Tunisia and Turkey unearthed deep-seated Islamophobic attitudes among a sizeable segment of the population claiming the 'nationalist secular' mantel and asserting exclusive 'sacred' right to undemocrat-ically contest power on its basis. While each of these states and others in the region have their own historical specificity, the common thread at present is the re-emergence of distinct anti-Muslim and anti-Islam attitudes that conflates con-testation of political policies, power and governing programmes with its sup-posed origination in a 'backward' and 'religiously authoritarian' paradigm located in a distant 'pre-modern' system: Islam itself is the problem and anyone epistemologically identified with it. In this context and for this segment, Islam is viewed as 'backward, traditional, irrational and opposed to modern civilization'; the same attitudes and perspectives were held by the colonial powers in the not so distant past and also by contemporary Islamophobes in the West. The Gulf States have also taken a trajectory that claims to contest political Islam while affirming their own right to claim authority via a process located in crafting a power-accommodating type of apolitical Islam. Islam becomes the agency through which power and authority are claimed and negated, i.e. in both cases Islam is part of a political project that is serving different groupings that are con-testing power in a post-colonial nation-state structure.

The purported spokespeople recycle every negative Orientalist trope directed at Islam and Muslims over the past 200 plus years. However, in the process of attacking Islam they end up inserting themselves as the true guardians of 'demo-cracy', 'modernity' and 'rationality' opposite the Islamic-oriented political parties that have won elections across the region and in the countries mentioned above. How should we understand this phenomena and what are the impacts on the local and international levels at a time when Muslim 'otherness' has become a norm in Europe and the US?

The emergence of Islam and Muslims in the political arena has caused a disrup-tion in the forum and structure of the modern nation-state in the post-colonial Muslim world. The ontological assumption in the modern Muslim nation-state is that religion has no role or if it does then it is must be subsumed under the secular project and subject to its hegemonic and epistemological limitation. In the *Forma-tions of the Secular*, Talal Asad maintained that 'secularism is not simply an intel-lectual answer to a question about enduring social peace and toleration. It is an enactment by which a political medium (representations of citizenship) redefines and transcends particular class, gender, and religion' (Asad, 2003, p. 5). Moreover, Asad's asserts that 'Modernity is a project – or rather, a series of interlinked pro-jects – that certain people in power seek to achieve', which in the case of the Muslim world are those elites who were trained by the colonial powers to adminis-ter the native populations in the colonies or the post-colonial elites that have been educated in the global North, internalized the Eurocentric epistemology and embarked on creating an imitative nation-state, whereby European experience and history is constituted as the universal norm (ibid., p. 13).

Thus, the theory and concept of the state for the post-colonial secularist elites is an imitative one and must follow the 'universal' norms set in European models with a profound hostility towards religion due to real experiences with the Church in the past. An important point that must be emphasized is that the emergence of the 'modern secular' nation-state in the Muslim majority states was set in motion under a colonial and anti-Islamic framing whereby Muslim history was problematized and cast as a distant relic not suitable for contemporary and 'progressive' formations. One can contest the idea that secularism in the Muslim world was a real undertaking since many newly formed post-colonial states included an explicit reference to Islam or Sharia' being the primary source of legislation, which clearly is a contradiction. A quest for legitimacy was behind the inclusion of such language in the Constitution at a time when Muslim societies continued to seek an explicit link to its rich Islamic tradition.

The idea that Islam is a relic, anti-progress and not fit for inclusion in the 'modern nation-state' became a foundational thesis and was strongly present in colonial discourses as well as constitutive and productive for the 'secular state' in Muslim majority countries (Mahmood 2006, pp. 323–347; Modood 2010, pp. 4–14). To be 'modern' meant to take an anti-Islam perspective to demonstrate a break with the 'regressive' past and not a mere separation of state from mosque. However, the idea of separation of Church from the state must be understood within the specific historical experience of Europe and the divine rights of kings, a non-existent dynamic in the Muslim world. Europe's structural problem with the Church should not become the main philosophical, ontological and epistemological driving logic for the demand for reforms in the Muslim world or any other parts of the globe for that matter (Asad, 2003, pp. 181–205). Elites in Muslim majority nation-states, who were educated and internalized the Western epistemologies with the penchant of problematizing Islam in the same way the Church was in European history and assigning to it the causes of decline, despotism and backwardness, ended up constructing a 'modern nation-state' that had embedded in it an anti-Islam 'secular theology' while building walls of structural exclusions to keep out 'the barbarians' at the gates of civilization, i.e. the Muslim subject him/herself.

Orientalists postulated that the cause of decline and lack of progress in Muslim majority states was Islam and its followers' adherence to despotic modes of governance as well as an inability to think 'modernly' and 'rationally'. The Muslim 'elites' educated in the West and set loose to recreate the modern nation-state in light of the existing thesis adopted these notions and incorporated it into the state structures (Provence, 2017, pp. 6–48).[8] Modern Muslim nation-states were imitative, colonial and epistemologically anti-Islam and anti-Muslim with an enforced despotic and undemocratic secularity. Yes, Islam, as a cultural identity, was allowed in civil society but was put under extreme controls and relegated to ceremony and distorted notions of 'traditionalisms' and 'spirituality' emptied of meaning and agency.

Could Muslims speak, the political (which includes the economic), and could they develop a programme reflecting their perspectives with agency on important matters including Islam's role in their own societies (Sayyid 2014)? At the heart of these issues is an attempt to contest Muslim agency and the ability to construct a different and independent narrative than what was ascribed to them in the colonial and post-colonial periods. If the world is Eurocentric, which it is, and constitutes the singular universal, then modern Muslim nation-states must be, according to this view, constructed on the basis of an anti-religious foundation, which means Muslims can speak only in Eurocentric and colonial terms. In this regard, Islam's role in the modern nation-state is measured in relation to European experiences with the Church and Muslims ability to enter into the 'modern' must adhere to the Eurocentric prescriptive and normative paradigm for the state (Feldman, 2012; Hallaq, 2014; 'Book Review of Salman Sayyid, Recalling the Caliphate: Decolonization and World Order', 2016; Sayyid, 2014).

In the case of Turkey, the opposition to the AK Party and its success in governing can't be simply explained away as a result of dissatisfaction with the political programmes as valid and correct if it is rooted in policy differences. However, the language and content of opposition is Islamophobic in nature for it focuses on the supposed defective Muslim genes that produce backwardness and anti-modernity discourses. A similar case can be made in relation to the ongoing debates in Egypt, Tunisia, Pakistan and a host of other nations that are attempting to construct a modern nation-state project through replication of European experience. However, that modernity and secularism are never problematized or analysed as well as the Eurocentric universals are taken for granted without contextualizing the specific history that gave birth to them in the first place.

Modernity, secularism and Eurocentric discourses can't be taken as universals for they represent a specific context that gave birth to a range of political expressions. Indeed, one can access these experiences but not as the sole normative and universal; rather part and parcel of a diverse set of global expressions that may be utilized to understand, compare and, when appropriate, to use. Here, Islamophobia takes the form of a singular focus on the image of Islamic party members, the supposed backwardness of the headscarf, beards, incoherence of their language and, more critically, the supposed uncivilized and unrefined 'humans' they appear to be in public gatherings: all of these originate in colonial, Orientalist and Eurocentric thesis concerning the supposed Muslim otherness. The focus is not on policy debates or differences but on Muslim subjectivity with all the problematics contained therein. One can take issue with policies and I do have a profound problem with neoliberal economic programmes that are utilized by Muslim political parties and the acceptance of a military industrial complex type of economies coupled with 'war on terrorism' discourses against opposition. These are not rooted in Islam per se but represent policy formation and ideas that can and should be debated vigorously. In more than one way, Muslim political parties are themselves part of modernity and, despite often arguing against it in general terms, they end up developing programmes and implementing economic policies that adhere to its specific requirements.

Islamophobia takes root in attempted implementation of secularism while at the same time crafting programmes to shape and control the expressions of Islam in the modern Muslim nation-state. Democracy and elections for the secular elite are valid only in so far as they keep Islam out as well as preventing any Muslim asserting agency based on deeply held epistemologies from gaining power. The Islamophobic 'secular theologians' maintain that Muslims who assert agency in contesting the political on a democratic basis must be opposed and frustrated, because if they succeeded they will manage to bring the 'traditional backwardness' into the 'modern-rational-progressive' and in doing so will bring the positivist state to an end. Islamophobia in Muslim majority nation-sates is rooted in a contestation over who has the right to define the society and what sets of ideas, real or imagined, can be brought to bear in this effort. Coming back to Talal Asad's framing of the secular is important:

> the secular' should not be thought of as the space in which real human life gradually emancipates itself from the controlling power of 'religion' and thus achieves the latter's relocation. It is this assumption that allows us to think of religion as 'infecting' the secular domain or as replicating within it the structure of theological concepts.... Secularism doesn't simply insist that religious practice and belief be confined to a space where they cannot threaten political stability or the liberties of 'free-thinking' citizens. Secularism builds on a particular conception of the world.
>
> (Ibid., p. 191)

An article by Imogen Lambert (2017), 'The Case of Liberal Islamophobia', published on the Muftah website, uses Talal Asad's argument to assert that 'secularity is not purely the separation of religion and state, or freedom of religion in the public sphere. It is, instead, state control over religiosity and its power to distinguish the religious from the profane'. This is an important distinguishing feature of the modern notion of secularism. Lambert correctly observes that 'it is a mode of governance that regulates religion' which

> can be traced back to the formation of the modern Arab state and the manner in which the region's authoritarian regimes attempted to quell opposition from Islamic groups (notably the Muslim Brotherhood) by appropriating religion and bringing religious authorities under their control. This can be seen in how Egyptian President Gamal Abdel Nasser exerted control over mosques and Al-Azhar, as well as Bashar Al-Assad's alliance with the urban Grand Ulema.
>
> (Lambert, 2017)

Thus, the Muslim who arrives to power through democracy is not to be trusted, for his/her ultimate political goal is to recreate the backward, despotic and irrational past. Thus, the argument goes, the Muslim must be prevented from disrupting the progressive march towards the modern and civilized: saving democracy from itself by urging and supporting military interventions and military coups to safeguard the anti-Islam secular post-colonial project.

Public debates in Egypt, Turkey and Tunisia as well as other Arab and Muslim majority states have taken a most profound turn towards Islamophobic discourses, which locates the differences in Islam itself. In taking this track, the participants have provided ample source material for the global Islamophobic industry since the statements and perspectives emerging from the local context in each state are recycled in the West to illustrate the veracity of negative claims made against Islam and Muslims. What we have here is that Islamophobic content originating in the West from the past is utilized by internal secular forces to contest civil society after failure in governance, which is then recycled back to Western Islamophobes. More alarmingly, the current engagement and cooperation between some Muslim majority nation-states and individuals that are part of the Western Islamophobia industry.

Conclusion

Islamophobia in Muslim majority nation-states has historical genesis dating back to the nineteenth and early twentieth century and the attempts to embrace modernity in a rapidly shifting world order. Embracing modernity by Muslim elites was the needed antidote to economic stagnation, military defeats on various fronts, ethnic and religious fragmentation, and corruption. Muslim elites thought it to be possible to barrow and replicate European scientific advancement without undermining the ontological and epistemological foundations of Muslim society. Here, a major error in assumption arose that viewed that it was possible to transfer scientific knowledge and know-how without the epistemology that gave rise to it in the European context. Moreover, the primary focus for Muslim elites then, as it is still now, was on acquiring military scientific knowledge and know-how to close the power gap. Embracing modernity and forging a modern Muslim nation-state called for imitating the only living model, the European experience, which opened the door to invite experts to the Muslim world and send student delegations to learn and translate the existing body of scientific knowledge. In the same period, the rapidly expanding colonial powers sought to penetrate the vast Muslim territories and lay claim to existing resources and dominations of trade routes.

Thus, Modernity and the secular nation-state came into the Muslim world through a convergence between Muslim elites who sought education and know-how in the military scientific arena and the colonial powers that pursued domination, territorial and resources of the Muslim world. The tension between religion and modernity that is foundational to the secular nation-state project was absorbed by the emerging Muslim elites who, for the most part, abandoned Islamic epistemology, or if they did maintain any relations it was tenuous at best and confined to religious observance and ceremony. The reformists in the late nineteenth and early twentieth centuries adopted modernity and the epistemological structures behind it even though they differed on the specific role that Islam can play in the modern nation-state. Islam became a predicament that must be addressed in the same way that the Church was the problem solved by the emergence of the European modern and secular nation-state.

The early to mid-twentieth century Muslim world was ravaged by the birth of the modern nation-state centred on dislodging Islam, as a primary epistemic for the society, and replacing it with a Eurocentric imitative project. Leading the charge was post-Ottoman Turkey, Iran and Egypt who set in motion a violent reform programme that contested every aspect of the Islamic tradition and commensurate identities. Transforming and transfiguring the Muslim society into a modern and secular one meant contesting the foundations of the society and all external manifestations. In order to fit into a modern, secular, hoped-for society, women's hijabs, niqabs and other aspects of religiously articulated clothing requirements must be abandoned (Kilic *et al.*, 2008, p. 397). Men's beards, turbans and loose-fitting clothing, and other aspects of modes of conduct based on spiritual courtesies, must be abandoned to bring about the benefits of modernity. Legal, administrative, structural, economic, social, educational and familial reforms were set in motion but all founded upon the notion that Islam is the problem that is keeping society away from progress and development.

Today's Islamophobia in Muslim majority nation-states is a direct outcome of the contestations for the nature of the society, the state, economy, military and the basis to formulate responses to the complexities that confront or are created by modernity or if you may post-modernity. The early twentieth-century reforms have put Islam at the heart of the contestations in building the modern and secular Muslim nation-state project. Adoption of the barrowing or transplanting of modern scientific know-how and technology transformed the role of the military in Muslim states from securing the borders of the country to the mantle of defenders of the secular project itself. Custodians of the secularism or various renditions of the same concept is the response of the military in carrying out coups in Muslim majority nation-sates while being assisted by the ex-colonial motherland power of the past or the present post-colonial interventionist powers. Simply put, the modern Muslim secular post-colonial nation-state is built on two foundational pillars, the Eurocentric reformist and colonial nurtured, educated and empowered elites. The two clustered elites both problematize Islamic epistemology and tradition while laying claim to their own distinctive form of Islam to legitimize power and authority on its basis. Contesting and regulating the hijab, niqab, beard, turban, modes of teaching, dress and other external manifestation of Muslimness in Muslim majority nation-state is rooted in questions of epistemology and the source of meaning and future horizons for the society. The modern nation-state is an exclusivist and self-referential edifice that precludes other possibilities and Islam is posited as the challenge in crafting such secular state by an elite that does not identify with Islam or, if it does, then is only permitted on narrow terms, i.e. the private domain.

Islamophobia is a problem of Muslim elites that are generationally disconnected from the foundations of their own Islamic tradition while experiencing and engaging a full complement of Westernization, globalization, militarization and pernicious forms of capitalism. Islam or Muslims' intrusion into civil society vexes the elites and contests their prerogative to administer the modern Muslim majority nation-state within the scope of the universal norms; the Eurocentric universal norm. Modernization and secularism were constructed around an anti-Islam epistemic and the increasing levels of religious adherence starting in late 1970s have brought the tension to the fore anew, which was further complicated by the end of the Cold War, Western intervention in regional conflicts and the current open-ended war on terrorism that problematized the Muslim as a global category and a distinct class of humans. Just like the colonial era connected the colonial powers to internal elites seeking reformation, the current period is witnessing a coalescing between similar clusters that take an anti-Islam trajectory while giving lip service to the notion that Islam is peaceful or other renditions of this type of message. The same logic underpinning the contestation of the early twentieth century are at work in the Islamophobia era and the mission to civilize of old is transformed into a mission to counter the propensity to violence by the supposed Muslim subject. Here, the purported violence is of Muslims, as a group, and not as single agents causing harm. Muslims must be civilized away from violent tendencies through a wholesale sophisticated campaign to civilize them through new educational programmes, translated children stories, media projects, technology hubs and camps as well as civil society orientations that once again replicate the Eurocentric modality, which I may say is facing its own failures considering the re-emergence of fascism and economic chaos. Islamophobia serves as a most convenient veneer to conceal the real global and local problems while keeping a most oppressive and destructive status quo. Islamophobia in Muslim majority nation-states is secularism and colonialism in a new lease of life, allowing for problem projection on Islam and its supposed inability to address contemporary challenges.

Notes

1 Each modern Muslim majority nation-state (secular or otherwise) includes an article in the Constitution that Islam is the official religion of the state and Sharia is the primary source of legislation. This inclusion makes Islam a central theme in state formation but the rest of the adopted Constitution or articles thereof are often an amalgamation of barrowed or direct translation from French, British, Swiss, German and US codes, which creates a peripheral role for Islam and religion. One can argue that religion or religious ideas are embedded in Western legal codes but this would be a different discussion altogether than the role of Islam and Sharia in Muslim majority modern post-colonial nation-states.

2 I define Islamophobia in Western context as:

> Islamophobia is a contrived fear or prejudice fomented by the existing Eurocentric and Orientalist global power structure, which is directed at a perceived or real Muslim threat through it the maintenance and extension of existing disparities in economic, political, social and cultural relations is made possible, while rationalizing the necessity to deploy violence as a tool to achieve 'civilizational rehab' of the targeted communities (Muslim or otherwise). Islamophobia reintroduces and reaffirms global racial hierarchies through which resource distribution disparities are maintained and extended.

3 The work of Professor Beshara Doumani, Brown University, on local history, social history and waqf institutions in the late Ottoman period is a must read for anyone approaching the subject. See Doumani, B. (2017) *Family Life in the Ottoman Mediterranean: A Social History*. Cambridge, Cambridge University Press.

4 Franz Fanon's work on the impacts of colonization is a must read and no discussion is complete with reading *Peau noire, masques blancs* (1952; Black Skin, White Masks) which provided 'a multidisciplinary analysis of the effect of colonialism on racial consciousness', and was based on his work under French colonial administration in Algeria. Fanon's most widely known book and published before his death, *Les Damnés de la terre* (1961; The Wretched of the Earth), likewise is necessary to engage with the subject matter.

5 I recommend the reports and studies developed by the Collectif contre l'islamophobie en France (CCIF) in France as it provides a comprehensive coverage of Islamophobia in the country. Retrieve materials on their website: www.islamophobie.net.

6 For the Tunisian elections see the National Democratic Institute Final Report on the 2014 Legislative and Presidential Elections. Retrieved from: www.ndi.org/sites/default/files/Tunisia%20Election%20Report%202014_EN_SOFT%20(1).pdf, date of access: 14 August 2018.

7 I am using the notion of 'fixed and regressive' framing from the Islamophobic and Orientalist claims about Islam and Muslim societies, which I completely disagree with based on multi-layered studies on various aspects of Islam's vast tradition. Islamic tradition is complex, vast and at the core represents a wide stream of scholarly debates, disagreements and counter positions on almost every subject imaginable. Islamophobes and Orientalists tend to use a single text or point to the original primary text but not to all the accompanying commentaries, interpretations, case law or court records and tools to regulate the approach and methods of accessing given sources.

8 Reading about the first Egyptian student delegation to France is important and the primary focus of studies: Rifa'a Rafi' al-Tahtawi, Trans. Newman, D. (2011) *An Imam in Paris: Al-Tahtawi's Visit to France 1826–1831*. London, Saqi Books.

Bibliography

Ansary, T. (2014). *Games without Rules: The Often Interrupted History of Afghanistan*, Public Affairs, New York.

Asad, T. (2003). *Formations of the Secular: Christianity, Islam and Modernity*. Stanford University Press, Stanford.

Bazian, H. (2014). 'The Terrorist Designation Game: A Tool to Consolidate Power and Saving Islam from Islam!', www.hatembazian.com/content/the-terrorist-designation-game-a-tool-to-consolidate-power-and-saving-islam-from-islam/, date of access: 14 August 2018.

Bazian, H. (2015). 'The Islamophobia Industry and the Demonization of Palestine: Implications for American Studies', *The American Studies Association, American Quarterly* (2015) pp. 1057–1065, www.hatembazian.com/content/the-islamophobia-industry-and-the-demonization-of-palestine-implications-for-american-studies/, date of access: 14 August 2018.

Benard, C. (2003). *Civil Democratic Islam: Partners, Resources, and Strategies*, Rand Corporation, Santa Monica.

'Book Review of Salman Sayyid, Recalling the Caliphate: Decolonization and World Order' (2014). *Religious Studies Review*, Vol. 42, No. 2.

Coll, S. (2004). *Ghost Wars: The Secret History of the CIA, Afghanistan, and Bin Laden, from the Soviet Invasion to September 10, 2001*, Penguin, New York.

Coll, S. (2018). *Directorate S: The C.I.A. and America's Secret Wars in Afghanistan and Pakistan*, Penguin, New York.

Doumani, B. (2017). *Family Life in the Ottoman Mediterranean: A Social History*, Cambridge University Press, Cambridge.

Egyptian Streets (2015). 'Grand Imam of Al Azhar Tells Leader of Far-Right French Party to "Correct" Views on Islam', 29 May, https://egyptianstreets.com/2015/05/29/grand-imam-of-al-azhar-tells-leader-of-far-right-french-party-to-correct-views-on-islam/, date of access: 14 August 2018.

Eltahawy, M. (2009). 'Ban the Burqa', *New York Times*, 2 July, www.nytimes.com/2009/07/03/opinion/03iht-edeltahawy.html, date of access: 14 August 2018.

Esposito, J. and Mogahed, D. (2008). *Who Speaks For Islam?: What a Billion Muslims Really Think*, Gallup Press, New York.

Feldman, N. (2012). *The Fall and Rise of the Islamic State*, Princeton University Press, Princeton.

France 24 (2014). 'Tunisia's Essebsi Says Ready to Form Pluralist Govt', 26 November, www.france24.com/en/f24-interview/20141125-tunisia-essebsi-exclusive-ennahda-islamist-party/, date of access: 14 August 2018.

Ghazali, O. (2018). 'Free Lyrics of Mohammed Salah's Beard!', *Ahram*, 18 March, www.ahram.org.eg/NewsQ/642429.aspx, date of access: 14 August 2018.

Grosfoguel, R. and Mielants, E. (2006). 'The Long-Durée Entanglement between Islamophobia and Racism in the Modern/Colonial Capitalist/Patriarchal World-System: An Introduction', *Human Architecture*: *Journal of the Sociology of Self-Knowledge*, Vol. 5, No, 1, Article 2, http://scholarworks.umb.edu/humanarchitecture/vol. 5/iss1/2, date of access: 14 August 2018.

Hallaq, W. (2014). *The Impossible State: Islam, Politics, and Modernity's Moral Predicament*, Columbia University Press, New York.

Hourani, A. (1983). *Arabic Thought in the Liberal Age, 1798–1939*, Cambridge University Press, Cambridge.

Kilic, S., Saharso, S. and Sauer, B. (2008). 'Introduction: The Veil: Debating Citizenship, Gender and Religious Diversity', *Social Politics: International Studies in Gender, State & Society*, Vol. 15, No. 4.

King, S. (2003). *Liberalization against Democracy: The Local Politics of Economic Reform in Tunisia*, Indiana University Press, Bloomington and Indianapolis.

Kurzman, C. (2002). *Modernist Islam, 1840–1940: A Sourcebook*, Oxford University Press, New York.

Lambert, I. (2017). 'The Case of Liberal Islamophobia', *Muftah*, 15 September, https://muftah.org/case-liberal-islamophobia/#.W3Ee6n4na8U, date of access: 14 August 2018.

Mahmood, S. (2006). 'Secularism, Hermeneutics, and Empire: The Politics of Islamic Reformation', *Public Culture*, Vol. 18, No. 2.

Martinez, L. (2000). *The Algerian Civil War*, Columbia University Press, New York.

Modood, T. (2010). 'Moderate Secularism, Religion as Identity and Respect for Religion', *The Political Quarterly*, Vol. 81, No. 1.

Mundy, J. (2015). *Imaginative Geographies of Algerian Violence: Conflict Science, Conflict Management, Antipolitics*, Stanford University Press, Stanford.

Muntasir, S. (2018a). 'Just Saw a Letter to Mohamed Salah', *Ahram*, 11 March, www.ahram.org.eg/NewsQ/641343.aspx, date of access: 14 August 2018.

Muntasir, S. (2018b). 'Just Saw a Letter to Mohamed Salah', *Ahram*, 14 March, www.ahram.org.eg/NewsQ/641763.aspx, date of access: 14 August 2018.

Pipes, D. (2015). 'Will Dubai's Good Times Last?', *Asia Times,* 31 December, www.atimes.com/article/will-dubais-good-times-last//, date of access: 14 August 2018.

Pipes, D. (2017a). 'Please Join Me in Dubai & Abu Dhabi in 2 Months', 26 August, www.danielpipes.org/17612/invitation-uae, date of access: 14 August 2018.

Pipes, D. (2017b). 'Daniel Pipes Fact Finding Expedition to Dubai & Abu Dhabi 4–11 November, 2017', *UAE Heritage Study Programs*, 4–11 November, http://uae. heritagestudyprograms.com, date of access: 14 August 2018.

Provence, M. (2017). *The Last Ottoman Generation and the Making of the Modern Middle East*, Cambridge University Press, London.

Rashid, A. (2010). *Taliban: Militant Islam, Oil and Fundamentalism in Central Asia*, 2nd Edition, Yale University Press, New Haven.

Rifa'a Rafi' al-Tahtawi, Trans. Newman, D. (2011). *An Imam in Paris: Al-Tahtawi's Visit to France 1826–1831*, Saqi Books, London.

Sayyid, S. (2014). *Recalling the Caliphate: Decolonisation and World Order*, Hurst, London.

Taylor, A. (2015). 'In Egypt to Meet Moderate Muslims, France's Far-Right Leader is Scolded for Her Views on Islam', *Washington Post*, 29 May, www.washingtonpost. com/news/worldviews/wp/2015/05/29/in-egypt-to-meet-moderate-muslims-frances-far-right-leader-is-scolded-for-her-views-on-islam/?utm_term=.53e609615003, date of access: 14 August 2018.

Weymouth, L. (2013). 'An Interview with Tunisia's Beji Caid Essebsi, Leading Voice of the Secular Opposition', *Washington Post*, 12 December, www.washingtonpost.com/ opinions/an-interview-with-tunisias-beji-caid-essebsi-leading-voice-of-the-secular-opposition/2013/12/12/f40f6690-6344-11e3-aa81-e1dab1360323_story.html?utm_ term=.dc3599d444f1, date of access: 14 August 2018.

Wiles, E. (2007). 'Headscarves, Human Rights, and Harmonious Multicultural Society: Implications of the French Ban for Interpretations of Equality', *Law & Society*, Vol. 41, No. 699.

3 Islamophobia in the contemporary Albanian public discourse

Rezart Beka

Introduction

Albania is a Southeastern European Muslim majority country[1] that after the fall of the communist regime, in 1991, entered a phase of intense identity-building that included the revision and renegotiation of traditional national narratives, religious identities and cultural belongings. The construction of a new nation-building narrative rendered the question of the Muslim identity of the Albanian population and the place of Islam and Muslim culture in the Albanian society the focus of an intense national debate. The Albanian intellectual elite perceived itself as responsible for the forging of the new national narrative and since then it has been at the forefront of the intellectual attempts to construct the main features of the new post-communist Albanian identity. Although in the post-communist period Albania experienced, to a certain extent, an Islamic revival, nevertheless its effects proved limited given the pronounced secularization of the Albanian population and the general indifference of contemporary Albanians towards religion. Therefore, as Clayer (2003) states, in the post-communist period, Albanian Muslims found themselves in the paradoxical position of 'a numerical majority in a kind of intellectual, social and political 'minority' situation' (p. 294). Consequently, the articulation of the new nation-building discourse remained mainly in the hands of the secular and Christian Western-oriented cultural elites.

For the greater part, the post-communist national narrative has revolved around 'the political myth of return to Europe' (Sulstarova, 2016, pp. 52–68) or 'Eurotheism' (Dani, 2016, p. 417) in which Albanian identity has been presented as quintessentially European and Christian whereas the integration of Albania in the European Union as the fulfilment of the national *telos*. As we shall see, the centrality of the 'European paradigm' in the public sphere has led to the creation of a post-communist exclusionary national discourse in which Islam and the Muslim culture are precluded from exerting any significant public role in society and are presented as the main obstacle for the full realization of the European identity. It is in the context of constructing this particular understanding of the political myth of return to Europe that the Albanian public intellectuals have made use of Islamophobic themes and applied them to the Albanian context in ways that often depart or diverge from their articulation in the Western discourse. In this way, Islamophobia has increasingly become an influential element in the building of the new national discourse on Muslims, and has significantly permeated the social, political and cultural spheres. The public discourse on religion in Albania is nuanced and multifaceted. The aim of this chapter is mainly that of underlining the main features of the Albanian post-communist discourse of return to Europe and that of highlighting the ways in which Islamophobic conceptual frameworks are mobilized by the Albanian cultural elite in order to support the exclusionary nature of the central paradigm of 'return to Europe' and to exclude Islam from exerting any role in the post-communist debates on the identity formation and nation-building narrative.

Islam and the myth of return to Europe

The political myth of return to Europe constitutes the main instrument through which the Albanian cultural elite have articulated their vision of Albania's national *telos* and of religion's place in society. In the contemporary Albanian public discourse, Europe constitutes the normative framework of any national and identity discourse. The political project of the European Union and of the Albanians' integration in it is presented not only as the 'return' of Albania to its natural historical destiny but also as the 'eschatological fulfilment' of all Albanians' historical aspirations. The renowned Albanian literary writer, Ismail Kadare, has provided the most developed and influential articulation of the idea of 'return to Europe'. In one of his writings, Kadare (2006a, pp. 20–23) portrays the Europeanness of Albanians as an intrinsic and a primordial feature of the Albanian society that, for him, is clearly reflected in the Albanian particular geographical position, the whiteness of the Albanian race, its medieval European and Mediterranean history, its indigenous customary laws and the rich medieval Christian literature.[2] In a typical Orientalist fashion, Kadare posits an irreducible polarity between the Orient and the West where both civilizations are ascribed with mutually exclusive civilizational essences. In this Manichean understanding of the world, the Orient is constructed as the 'Other' par excellence, stagnant, barbaric and backward, while the West is projected as the incarnation of reason, civilization and progress.[3] From early on in his writings, Kadare has portrayed the Ottoman invasion of Albania and the consequent flourishing of Oriental elements in Albanian culture as a 'spiritual and material catastrophe', 'obscurantism', 'cultural barbarism', 'an oriental ignorance', in short 'the apocalypse in the true meaning of the word' (Kadare, 1981, pp. 14, 146–147).

In Kadare's writings, the European identity is constructed as something historically fixed and immutable. European identity is presented in religious terms as inherently Christian. The inner core of European identity resides in Christianity and the progressive values of European Renaissance. Christianity, especially Catholicism, is perceived as an essential element of being European, therefore, rediscovering the Christian roots of Albania becomes a constitutive element of the myth of return to Europe. For Kadare, Catholicism represents for

Albanians the religion of the forefathers, the only genuine and original Albanian religious and cultural identity, while Islam is presented just as an historical accidence imposed by the Oriental Ottomans upon the Albanian culture – an imposition that has never penetrated into the heart of Albanian cultural identity.[4] The return to Christianity and the gradual abandonment of Islam and of the Oriental elements of Albanian culture will constitute, according to Kadare, 'a great historical rectification that would hasten Albania's union with the mother continent: Europe' (as cited in Clayer, 2003, p. 207).

As Kadare explains:

> The Albanians, the people I belong to, have lost Europe twice: the first time in the 15th century, together with all the other Balkan peoples, and the second time after the Second World War, when they fell under the Communist rule. I am not overstating the case when I say today that after the breakdown of Communism, the Albanians live with the anxiety of a third loss of Europe. This would be fatal to them, would be equal to their death.
>
> (As cited in Sulstarova, 2015, p. 28)

Here, the Ottoman and the communist experiences are presented as a loss of identity and a deviation from the Albanian natural historical course. In this context, the Ottoman experience signifies the extirpation of Albania from its natural European soil and its transformation into an Asian and Oriental state. The Ottomans and the communists represent the Other of Europe, the Orient. As a consequence, this presupposed Oriental experience is perceived by Kadare as 'a misfortune and a calamity' and the cultural aspirations of Albanians are presented as a perpetual striving 'to cut the connection with the East' (as cited in Sulstarova, 2015, p. 34). For him, Christianity constitutes for Albanians 'the open door towards the West', while Islam 'has never been a symbol of Europe' (as cited in Sulstarova, 2015, p. 346). This new national narrative embodied in the political myth of 'return to Europe' excludes Islam as a constitutive element of Albanian national identity. It presents Islam 'as an outsider within Europe and as a possible inhibitor to the European integration of Albania' (Sulstarova, 2015, p. 24). Therefore, as Merdjanova (2013, pp. 118–119) explains, in the contemporary Albanian public discourse, Islam is depicted as the 'archetypal "Other"' and Muslims are faced either with the choice of forging an indigenous European Islam, that claims to be in harmony with European values, or to convert to Christianity.

Muslim visibility in public space

It is in the context of the myth of 'return to Europe' that the construction of a proper European image for Albania has taken a central role in the Albanian public discourse. In the post-communist period, Albanian intellectual elites have generally considered the downplaying or the erasure of the visible presence of the Ottoman and Islamic legacy from the public sphere as a necessary step for building a European image for Albania. This approach is reminiscent of the inter-war Albanian secularist intellectuals and Muslim reformists' attempts to portray Albania as a European country by proposing the establishment of a modern and European–Islam in harmony with the Western civilizational values of rationality, science and progress.[5] Both in the inter-war and post-communist period the majority of practicing Muslims have considered the intellectual elite's attempt to build, at any cost, a European 'face' for Albania as a complex of inferiority towards the foreign perception and as deleterious for the social unity and inter-religious harmony.

It is in this context, that the decision of the Albanian government in 1992 to join the Organization of Islamic Conference (OIC) caused an uproar within Albanian intellectual circles.[6] For them, this political move constituted a departure from the European heritage of Albania and reinforced its stigmatization as an Islamic country. At that time, Kadare and Bosquet (1999, p. 151) expressed his concern that this political move will push Albania away from its reunification with Europe. For the previous ambassador of Albania in the Vatican, Neshat Tozaj (1995), the membership of Albania in the OIC will transform it into a 'depot of Islamic munitions' and will reinforce its stigma as an Islamic country. Furthermore, according to him, this decision constitutes a betrayal of the noble cause of the heroic gestures of the national hero Skanderbeg to transform Albania into 'a fence for European Christianity' (p. 6).

In their attempt to construct a European image for Albania many public intellectuals have aligned themselves with the global Islamophobic discourse on the visibility of Islam in the public sphere. In their writings, they conflate Europe with Christianity and define Europe as 'the exclusion of Islam' (Plasari, 1992a). For them, being European is a notion that 'was born out of the confrontation with Islam' (Plasari 1992a), therefore if Albanians would not be able to get rid of their image as an Islamic country then Europe would be justified in its refusal to accept Albanian's integration into European Union. In this context, the Albanian literary critic Pirro Misha (2003) states: 'A country like Albania does not have any interest to be perceived as an Islamic country. Especially in view of the present global context' (p. 127). Therefore, he laments the fact that the symbols of the Muslim veil and beards have become normalized in Albanian public life. Whereas media analyst Mustafa Nano (2002) does not hesitate to express his annoyance at the presence of *aẓān* (the call to prayer) in the Albanian public soundscape. In his recent writings, he has described the conversion of Albanians to Islam as 'The biggest misstep in history ever done by Albanians' (Nano, 2017). For all these public figures, the visibility of Islam in the public sphere and the persistence of what is perceived as the Oriental cultural elements of Albanian society constitute an obstacle towards the construction of a proper European image for Albania.

The construction of this image is also at the centre of the recent promotion of Mother Teresa, the humanist and Catholic nun of Albanian origins, to a new national figure. The personality of Mother Teresa has been instrumental for the attempt of the Albanian political class and public intellectuals to construct a new post-communist nation-building narrative in which Albania is presented with a Christian face and a European pedigree. The transformation of Mother Teresa to a national symbol is a direct consequence of an intended and intensive top-down approach adopted by the official institutions of the Albanian state. The symbol of Mother Teresa has become predominant in the Albanian public sphere. Schools, public squares, hospitals and the only national airport have been named after her. The day of her sanctification has been declared a public holiday and Mother Teresa's portrait or statue has become the semi-official image of Albania.[7] Despite the fact that Mother Teresa defined her mission in purely religious terms as 'quenching the thirst of Jesus Christ in the cross for love and souls' (as cited in Kolodiejchuk, 2007, p. 347) and despite the fact that she was convinced to have been called by God to 'become Indian, live with them and become them in order to arrive at the heart of people' (as cited in Kolodiejchuk, 2007, p. 61), this has not prevented the Albanian political class and cultural elite from appropriating and reinterpreting her personality for political ends.

This process of 'motherteresification'[8] of the Albanian public sphere and the transformation of Mother Teresa into a national figure is closely related with the political and cultural project of constructing an European image for Albania at the expense of Islam and Muslim elements of Albanian culture and society. As Endresen (2015) has aptly remarked:

> The semi-official and official cult of Mother Teresa as 'the mother of the nation' [...] reflects the historical tendency of many Albanian nation-builders to dissociate the nation symbolically and rhetorically from its Islamic legacy, outwardly seeking to reverse the historical Islamization process, and emphasizing the nation's 'Christians roots' – all with the aim of legitimating Albanians as belonging to 'Europe'.
>
> (pp. 18–19)

In this way, Islam and Muslims are constructed as alien to Europe. They are excluded from the nation-building narrative and are perceived as inhibitors of the reunification of Albania with Europe. This is the reason why many Albanian Muslims have considered the top-down involvement of the political institutions in the promotion of Catholic nun Mother Teresa into a national figure as a violation of secularism and as an unjust favouritism of one religion at the expense of another.[9] Nevertheless, for the Albanian political class, Mother Teresa seems to embody all the necessary qualities needed to present Albania as a quintessentially Christian and European country.

Reinterpreting the national hero in Huntingtonian lenses

Huntington's thesis of the clash of civilizations has received a wide acceptance in the Albanian public discourse. Huntington's ideas have been conceived as a valid framework for the understanding of the global geopolitical developments and for the articulation of the place of Islam in the contemporary Albanian society. For the Albanian intellectual Aurel Plasari (2002), the events of 9/11 have definitely proved the veracity of Huntington's thesis of the clash of civilization. For him, this event displayed the reality of the contemporary world in its 'naked' truthfulness and it corresponded exactly with that described by Huntington.[10] Based on the idea of a clash of civilizations, Albanian public intellectuals have generally portrayed the country as on the verge of a crucial and historical decision, i.e. taking side with the Western civilization and fulfilling in this way its historical aspirations or remaining within the Asiatic and Islamic civilization and betraying in this way its European primordial identity.

Huntington's ideas have been instrumental in the process of the reconceptualization and reinterpretation of George Castriot Skanderbeg (1405–1468), the Albanian national hero, in ways that fits the Eurotheism of Albanian cultural elite. Skanderbeg was an Albanian Christian lord, who after reaching the highest ranks of the Ottoman army, deserted and engaged himself in a long war against the Ottomans in Albania. As historians have noticed, traditionally the official Albanian discourse tended to downplay the religious elements of his life in favour of his political and state-building activities as well as in order to present him as a unifying figure for the multidenominational Albanian society (Dani, 2016, p. 418; Nixon, 2012, pp. 145–153; Puto, 2012, pp. 18–23). Nevertheless, the first attempts to interpret Skanderbeg's life on religious grounds, as an anti-Islamic figure, a Christian hero and a defender of Christianity and Europe from Islam and the Ottoman empire, appears at the beginning of the twentieth century, within a small circle of Roman Catholic intellectuals (Dani, 2016, pp. 421–422). In the inter-war period, this interpretation of Skanderbeg remained marginal to the Albanian historiography and in the communist period was further marginalized only to be strongly suggested again in the post-communist era. This shift was prompted 'not so much by genuine historiographic studies but rather by the endeavour to rediscover the European identity of the Albanians' (Dani, 2016, p. 417). In this way, in the post-communist period, the religious elements of Skanderbeg's life are highlighted in order to better serve the political myth of return to Europe.[11]

In the present context, Skanderbeg's life is generally interpreted within the framework of the antemurale myth in which his activities are presented as a bulwark against the Islamic and Ottoman threat to Christianity and Europe.[12] The post-communist narrative on Skanderbeg portrays him as a precursor of the future clash of civilization world-view who decisively took side with Christianity and European values against the Islamo-Asiatic civilization. Skanderbeg's war against the Ottomans is re-conceptualized as a war between East and West or between European Christianity and Asiatic Islam. For this reason, according to many Albanian public intellectuals, he should be considered as a precursor of the North Atlantic Alliance (NATO) (Kadare, 2005, p. 16). Departing from the traditional national narrative that portrays his heroic gesture as directed towards the construction of the Albanian nation and the common good of its people, in the post-communist period Skanderbeg is presented as fighting principally for the sake of Europe and Christianity. His life is invested with a messianic role and a religious aura. Skanderbeg is re-conceptualized as a European Christian lord engaged in holy crusades against Islam and the Ottomans. Under his guidance, it is said that Albanians have gathered together 'in the biggest Christian state in the Balkans' (Plasari, 1992b, p. 21). The title *Athleta Christi*, given to him by Pope Calixtus III (1378–1458), becomes a representative symbol of his personality. The crusade against the Turks, conducted by Skanderbeg side by side with other European countries, demonstrates, according to the Albanian public intellectuals, that the Albanians' cultural and political identity is quintessentially Christian and European.

According to this perspective, Skanderbeg's life constitutes a normative model for the way in which contemporary Albanians should position themselves within the presupposed ongoing conflict between the Christian West and the Oriental Islam. This reconstruction of the significance of his life excludes Islam and the Ottoman legacy from being an essential part of Albanian identity. Through the Huntingtonian intellectual framework, Albanian Islamophobic discourse has presented Skanderbeg in a confessional and Eurocentric manner which limits its relevance only to the Christian or secular Western-oriented segments of the Albanian population. This restriction of the comprehensiveness of Skanderbeg's personality permits Albanian intellectual elite to exclude Islam from the post-communist nation-building narrative and present Albania as a quintessential Christian and European country.

Islamo-communism and the Oriental 'other'

The neologism 'Islamofascism' came to public prominence in 2006 when the American President, George W. Bush, described the United States as 'at war with the Islamic Fascists who will use any means to destroy those of us who love freedom' (as cited in Santos, 2014, p. 611). The use of this term generated controversy and became the focus of an intense public debate within the United States. Generally, US Muslim leaders and academicians criticized the term for being historically inaccurate and sufficiently vague to generalize it on all Muslims, whereas neo-conservatives and various Islamophobe figures found the term adequate and considered it as the right name for the enemy (Pipes, 2006). As Hibbard (2009, p. 196; 2010, p. 10) has argued, the term Islamofascism corresponded to the specific understanding, by the Bush administration, of the war on terror that situated it in the ideological realm and conceived it as the perpetual battle between the forces of progress and modernity (i.e. the West) against the forces of evil and tyranny (i.e. Islamic fundamentalism). This approach neglects the socio-economic and geopolitical reasons that might be at the root of the emergence of Islamic fundamentalism in the Middle East. It abstracts Islamic fundamentalists from their immediate context and transforms them into ideological representatives of anti-Western values.

In the Albanian context, the ideological nature of the discourse on Islamofascism finds its application, paradoxically, in the debate on Islamo-communism. Many Albanian intellectuals have attributed the establishment of communism in the country to the Islamicity of Albanian society and to the Muslim family provenance of the communist dictator Enver Hoxha. For Arshi Pipa (1993, pp. 25–26), the Albanian dictator was influenced in his action by his Muslim upbringing whereas for the Albanian Catholic priest At Zef Pllumi, Albanian communism was an 'Islamic fundamentalism disguised under the mask of communism' (as cited Cara, 2007, pp. 22–23). For another Catholic intellectual, Ardian Ndreca (2012), Albanian communism was of Islamic origin and this is shown by the special animosity of the communists against the Catholic Church. Whereas, for the Albanian philosopher, Artan Fuga (2001, pp. 79–83), Islam shares with the authoritarian thought the same philosophical logic of homogeneous structures where the existence of any other contending categorical pole is strictly negated. In his view, communists utilized this compatibility with religion as a cultural substratum in order to establish itself in the Albanian society. Although this line of thought has been criticized in some Albanian intellectual circles, nevertheless it has increasingly become an established discourse in the Albanian public sphere.[13] Unlike the usage of the term Islamofascism, which was coined as an 'analytical term' to depict Islamic fundamentalism, the term Islamo-communism is articulated in the Albanian context as an essential feature of Islam as a whole.

Apart from its bad theology and over-caricaturization of religious notions, the idea of Islamo-communism relies for its credibility on the myth of Oriental despotism. As Joseph Massad (2015, pp. 18–19, 27–28, 50–54) has argued, Oriental despotism is an eighteenth-century Orientalist construction that played a double role in the European history, i.e. from one side that of self-constituting Europe as civilized and democratic against the 'despotic' Orient and from the other side that of serving the European imperial domination by legitimizing, on cultural grounds, the establishment of despotic forms of government in the colonies. The idea of Islamo-communism conceives tyranny or its endurance as a constitutive element and ontological condition of the Muslim subjectivity and disregards the socio-economic or geopolitical contingent circumstances that enabled the establishment of communism in Albania.[14] Instead, it favours a culturalist and essentialist approach that sees Islam as the only or the main explanatory factor for the establishment of communism in Albania. For Halliday (1993, pp. 151–157), this essentialism and ahistorical understanding of Islam has been one of the main characteristics of classical Orientalism. In this way, the role that Islam or religion in general have played in fomenting anti-communist sentiment in society is entirely negated. However, in the Albanian context, the main function of the idea of Islamo-communism is that of providing legitimacy for the binary vision that informs the political myth of 'return to Europe' where, in an essentialist way, all the negative historical experiences are ascribed to the Oriental archetypal 'Other', be it Islam or the Ottoman legacy. This is contrasted with Christianity or the West, perceived as the embodiment of all the progressive values of Albanian society and as an indicator of the authentic Albanian and European identity.

Christian identity and the racialization of Muslims in Albania

In the Albanian public discourse, Christianity is often conflated with European-ness and it is presented as the embodiment and the source of European culture and values. European identity is portrayed as intrinsically connected with Chris-tianity, which is articulated as a kind of racial and ethnic feature that is supposed to differentiate Europeans from the rest of the world. In this way, many con-temporary Albanian intellectuals tend to conceive Christianity as an inborn and essential trait of being Albanian and identify it with the core of national identity that is presupposed to orient Albanians naturally towards the West. Most of the cultural and religious elements, like Islam or the Ottoman cultural legacy, that are part of the Albanian social texture, are considered to lack this primordial trait and are believed to have been unable to penetrate or affect the essential Christian and Western-oriented elements that is believed to characterize ethnically the Albanian population.

A clear example of this perspective is visible in the speech that the President of the Republic of Albania, Alfred Moisiu, delivered in 2005 at the Oxford Forum in London. In the speech, entitled 'Religious tolerance in the tradition of the Albanian people', Moisiu explains the phenomenon of religious tolerance in Albania by arguing that although from a synchronic perspective Albanians are divided into Muslims and Christians, from a diachronic perspective 'all Albanians are Christians' (Moisiu, 2005). In his view, the Islamization of the Albanian population did not affect the core of their primordial Christian identity because in Albania 'Islam is not an indigenous religion' or 'an autochthonous faith' but a phenomenon that came very late in Albanian history and preserved the language and the rituals of the Oriental powers that brought it in the country (Moisiu, 2005). Therefore, for Moisiu, religious tolerance in Albania is a result of the inherent Christian identity of Albanians and of their superficial adherence to Islam.

As he states:

> As a norm (Islam in Albania) is a superficial Islam. If you scratch slightly, in every Albanian you will discover their Christian core ... This means that inside every Albanian, regardless of how they define themselves today, exists a homogenizing factor and this factor is precisely the period of fifteen centuries of Christianity that all of them have in the tradition of their predecessors.
>
> (Moisiu, 2005)

Here, Christianity is presented as the original core of Albanian identity; it repres-ents the European nature of Albanian society whereas Islam constitutes just an exogenous layer that has been added but has not affected the primordial essence of Albanian identity. Under the various layers of any Albanian does exist a prim-ordial and authentic Christian core. In this way, Christianity assumes a kind of ethnic dimension that is presupposed to characterize the ontological essence of every Albanian regardless of their religious or ideological convictions.[15] Since the early 1990s this conceptualization gave rise to the contemplation of the possibility of a conversion *en masse* of the Albanian population given that such an act could be presented as a return to a genuine authenticity and as a restoration of the true Albanian identity. In fact, at that time many Albanian intellectuals, like Kadare, expressed the conviction that Albania's return to Europe requires the gradual abandonment of Islam and the conversion to Christianity (Kadare, 1991, p. 51). As Kadare states, 'the Albanian path towards Europe should be taken without the baggage of Islam, which is not worth it, and only delays the arrival' (as cited in Elbasani and Puto, 2017, p. 63) Another public intellectual, Mustafa Nano, concords with Moisiu in the idea that Albanians are not real Muslims and claims that the process of de-Islamization is already happening and that 'Western rulers with a little strategic exertion […] can quickly convert Albanians into their ancient religion (i.e. Christianity)' (Nano, 2002).[16]

This perspective is at the basis of the contemporary racialization of Muslims in Albania. The main conceptual framework through which in Albania religion is 'raced', and Muslims are racialized, rests in the romantic notion of 'pure blood'. According to this discourse, Christianity, particularly Catholicism, is portrayed as the guarantor of the Albanian identity. Ethno-cultural authenticity is imagined as in a symbiotic relationship with Catholicism.[17] The predominantly Catholic regions of Northwest Albania are presented as containers of the 'unadulterated Albanian blood' and identity. These regions are believed to have remained pure from the Asian and Islamic influence; therefore, they have played the role of the incubator of the true Albanian identity that is defined as quintessentially Christian and European. As the Catholic priest, Dom Ndoc Noga explains, 'The religion of Albanians has always been Christianity. The other religions have existed and have been imported with the only objective to eradicate Christianity, but with the immediate effect of polluting our pure Albanian blood' (as cited in Dani, 2016, p. 428 and Sulstarova, 2013, p. 236).

Despite the fact that Albanians are mostly ethnically homogeneous, nevertheless, based on the racist notion of pure blood, some public intellectuals have articulated the idea that Albanian practicing Muslims, or Muslim actors in the public sphere, should not be considered ethnically Albanian but descendants of the Asian Ottoman colonizers who settled in the country during the Ottoman 'yoke'.[18] The pejorative term 'Ottoman remnants' is increasingly being articulated against practicing Muslims who advocate the endorsement of Islamic values in the public sphere. It is said that Muslims possess 'different memories and nostalgias' (Kadare, 2006b, p. 10) that differentiate them ontologically from the rest of genuine Albanians. The innate characteristic, that supposedly defines their identity, is anti-Europeanism and the nostalgia for the Ottoman Oriental legacy. The presupposed Oriental and anti-European 'memories and nostalgias' of the Albanian Muslims are described as innate traits of Islam. They constitute 'the call of blood' of the Oriental predecessors that resides within Albanian Muslims. Therefore, Albanian Muslims are often presented as a foreign body and a threat for the nation. As Kadare puts it, the memories and nostalgias of these descendants of the 'Asian colonizers' 'are not only different from those of the Albanian nation [...] but they are in complete contradiction with the national interest, and no contemporary nation can permit this' (as cited in Sulstarova, 2013, p. 222). For the ex-ambassador of Albania to the Vatican City, Willy Kamsi, 'Albania and the Albanian people are Europe' and those who oppose this fact are 'descendants of the old Asian colonists ... that want to be imposed on the overwhelming majority of Albanians, with whom they share the religion but not ethnicity' (as cited in Sulstarova, 2015, p. 34). For the mere fact of practicing Islam, the ethnic identity of Albanian Muslims is put into question and they are described as 'polluted blood' and the main inhibitors of Albanian political and cultural project of 'return' to Europe.

Conclusion

The analysis has shown that the Muslim question has become a pivotal concern in the Albanian public discourse. The cultural elite has tended to present Islam and Muslim culture as incompatible with the European aspirations of the Albanian society. Moreover, Islam is perceived as the main obstacle to the full integration of Albania in the 'European family'. The new nation-building discourse is built on a binary vision where Islam plays the role of the 'archetypical Other' against which the new European and Christian identity of Albania is construed. The exclusion of Islam from the new nation-building discourse has been enabled by a selective reading of the Albanian history, the renegotiation of old nationalistic political myths and narratives as well as the construction of new identities. The role of global Islamophobic themes has been that of providing Albanian public intellectuals with the necessary intellectual tools to frame the issue of Islam in Albania in ways that exclude it from being an essential part of the national identity. The Islamophobic notions have been adjusted and remodelled in accordance with the specificities of the Albanian context to better serve the particular exclusionary or binary vision that informs the political myth of return to Europe.

Notes

1 For the religious configuration of the Albanian population in the inter-war and post-communist period respectively see Nathalie Clayer (1997, p. 117) and Sulstarova (2015, p. 32).
2 For a succinct critique of these elements see Sulstarova (2006, pp. 45–47).
3 This conceptualization is a continuation, although in an exacerbated form, of the Albanian National Renaissance discourse. For the historical precedent of such a discourse see Elbasani and Puto (2017, p. 56).
4 For the prevalence of this idea in the Albanian public discourse see Puto (2006, p. 28).
5 These reforms included, among others, the ban on Muslim veil, the democratization of the process of ijtihad, the centralization of the religious hierarchy, the modernization of the educational system, etc. For more, see Clayer (2008, pp. 128–156; 2010, pp. 53–69).

6 For the reply of Albanian state authorities to the critics see Barbullushi (2011, pp. 149–150).

7 In fact, in 2007, the Albanian media reported the state initiative to issue new national ID cards with the portrait of Mother Teresa inscribed in it. This idea was not welcomed by the Albanian Muslims and prompted the negative reaction of the official authorities of the Albanian Muslim Community (AMC). For this reason, the project was never implemented. For more on the controversy see Endresen (2015, pp. 10–11).

8 The term, originally coined by Olsi Jazexhi, is used by Cecilie Endresen (2015) in order to explain 'the way Mother Teresa has been turned into a national symbol of Albania and a visible feature of the public sphere' (p. 2).

9 For the various public reactions against the promotion of Mother Teresa to a national hero see Endresen (2015, pp. 11–13).

10 For a more detailed analysis of Plasari's ideas see Sulstarova (2013, pp. 245–254).

11 For a detailed analysis of the reinterpretation of Skanderbeg figure in the post-communist period see Dani (2016, pp. 426–468).

12 For the dominance of the antemurale myth in the contemporary Albanian public discourse and in the Balkans in general see Nixon (2012, pp. 157–160). For the ways in which the antemurale myth is interpreted and endorsed by various contemporary Albanian religious denominations, including the Muslim community, see Endresen (2012, pp. 228–232).

13 For a criticism of the notion of Islamo-communism see Baleta (2002, 2006) and Hoxha (2014).

14 According to Kullashi (2003, p. 139), the idea of Islamo-communism transforms Islam into a political scapegoat that enables the people and groups responsible for the establishment of communism in Albania from taking political responsibilities for the atrocities committed by the communists.

15 For a more thorough analysis of Moisiu's speech see Brisku (2006, pp. 59–62).

16 However, in his recent writings, Nano seems to have reconciled oneself with the fact that Albanians are and will remain Muslims. As he says: 'Only a stupid can believe that Albanians can be re-convert (to Christianity), that they will return massively to the early religion, to the first ever-religion, that of Isa. This is a closed chapter in history' (Nano, 2017).

17 See for more Dani (2016, pp. 417–418) and Sulstarova (2013, pp. 93–97).

18 Such statements are present in the writings of Kamsi (2004, pp. 16–19) and Kadare (2006b).

Bibliography

Baleta, A. (2002). *Kush dhe çfarë fshihet pas trillimit komunizëm islamik*. Tiranë: Botime Ora.

Baleta, A. (2006). *Përballjet me Islamofobitë*. Tiranë.

Barbullushi, O. (2011). The Politics of 'Religious Tolerance' in Post-Communist Albania: Ideology, Security and Euro-Atlantic Integration. In M. Pace (Ed.), *Europe, the USA and Political Islam* (pp. 149–150). Basingstoke: Palgrave.

Brisku, A. (2006). Oksidentalizimi i së shkuarës dhe orientalizimi i së tashmes: Identiteti 'evropian'i shqiptarëve sipas shkrimtarit Ismail Kadare e Aleksandër Moisiu. *Revista Përpjekja*, 12/23.

Cara, A. (2007, 4 August). Kurrgjë më shumë se liria. *Gazeta Shekulli*.

Clayer, N. (1997). Islam, State and Society in Post-Communist Albania. In H. Poulton and S. Taji-Farouki (Eds), *Muslim Identity and the Balkan State* (pp. 115–139). London: Hurst & Company.

Clayer, N. (2003). God in the 'Land of Mercedes': The Religious Communities in Albania since 1990. In P. Jordan, K. Kaser, W. Lukan, S. Schwandner-Sievers and H. Sundhaussen (Eds), *Albanien: Geographie – Historische Anthropologie – Geschichte – Kultur – Postkommunistische Transformation* (pp. 277–231). Wien: Peter Lang.

Clayer, N. (2008). Behind the Veil: The Reform of Islam in the Inter-War Albania or the Search for a 'Modern' and 'European' Islam. In N. Clayer and E. Germain (Eds), *Islam in the Inter-War Europe* (pp. 128–156). London: Hurst & Company.

Clayer, N. (2010). Adapting Islam to Europe: The Albanian Example. In Ch. Voss and J. Telbizova-Sack (Eds), *Islam und Muslime in (Südost) Europa. Im Kontext von Transformation und EU-Erweiterung* (pp. 53–69). München-Berlin: Verlag Otto Sagner.

Dani, D. (2016). *Shpikja e Mesjetës: Vetja dhe Tjetri në Medievistikën Shqiptare.* Tiranë: Pika pa sipërfaqe.

Elbasani, A. and Puto, A. (2017). Albanian-Style Laïcité: A Model for a Multi-Religious European Home?. *Journal of Balkan and Near Eastern Studies*, 19/1.

Endresen, C. (2012). *Is the Albanian's Religion Really 'Albanianism'? Religion and Nation According to Muslim and Christian Leaders in Albania.* Wiesbaden: Harrassowitz Verlag.

Endresen, C. (2015). The Nation and the Nun: Mother Teresa, Albania's Muslim Majority and the Secular State. *Islam and Christian-Muslim Relations*, 26/1.

Fuga, A. (2001). *Shtigje drejt guvës së gjarprit.* Tiranë: Botime Ora.

Halliday, F. (1993). Orientalism and Its Critics. *British Journal of Middle Eastern Studies*, 20.

Hibbard, S. (2009). Islamo-Fascism and America's Long War. *Journal of Islamic Law and Culture*, 11/3.

Hibbard, S. (2010). 'Islamo-Fascism' as an Ideological Discourse. *Journal of Islamic Law and Culture*, 21/1.

Hoxha, Ç. (2014, 15 November). A kishte frymëzim fetar komunizmi? Retrieved from www.e-zani.com/2014/04/01/kishte-frymezim-fetar-komunizmi/, date of access: 29 July 2018.

Kadare, I. (1981). *Vepra letrare 12: Autobiografia e popullit në vargje; Reportazhe e shënime udhëtimi; Intervista.* Tiranë: NaimFrashëri.

Kadare, I. (1991). *Printemps albanais. Chronique, lettres, réflexions.* Paris: Fayard.

Kadare, I. (2005). *Dantja i pashmangshëm.* Tiranë: Onufri.

Kadare, I. (2006a). *Identiteti evropian i shqiptarëve.* Tiranë: Onufri.

Kadare, I. (2006b, 3 July). Biseda për Evropën. *Gazeta Shekulli.*

Kadare, I. and Bosquet, A. (1999). *Dialog me Alain Bosquet.* Tiranë: Onufri.

Kamsi, W. (2004). Jezuitët, Shqipnia dhe Europa, Kleri katolik shqiptar dhe parimet e demokracisë perëndimore (Ed.), *Konferencë Kombëtare* (pp. 16–19). Tiranë: Instituti i Kërkimeve Politike 'Alcide de Gasperi'.

Kolodiejchuk, B. (2007). *Madre Teresa: Sii la Mia Luce.* Milano: BurSaggi.

Kullashi, M. (2003). *Përplasja e identiteteve.* Pejë: Dukagjini.

Massad, A. J. (2015). *Islam in Liberalism.* Chicago and London: Chicago University Press.

Merdjanova, I. (2013). *Rediscovering the Umma: Muslims in the Balkans between Nationalism and Transnationalism.* Oxford: Oxford University Press.

Misha, P. (2003). Tolerancë fetare apo papërgjegjshmëri?. *Politika & Shoqëria*, 6/1.

Moisiu, A. (2005, 9 November). Toleranca Ndër-fetare në Traditën e Popullit Shqiptar, Retrieved from https://albemigrant2011.wordpress.com/2014/04/13/fjala-e-ish-presidentit-alfred-moisiu-ne-forumin-e-oxfordit-9-nentor-2005-londer-angli/, date of access: 29 July 2018.

Nano, M. (2002, 6 June). Në kërkim të rrënjëve, ose në kërkim të vetvetes. *Shekulli*, Tiranë.

Nano, M. (2017, 11 September). Politically Incorrect: Çfarë ka që nuk shkon sot me Islamin shqiptar?, *Gazeta Mapo*. Retrieved from www.mapo.al/2017/09/politically-incorrect-cfare-ka-qe-nuk-shkon-sot-me-islamin-shqiptar/1, date of access: 29 July 2018.

Ndreca, A. (2012, 15 November). Quando ci siamo persi l'Albania, che da cristiana è diventata musulmana, *Tempi*. Retrieved from www.tempi.it/quando-ci-siamo-persi-lalbania-che-da-cristiana-e-diventata-musulmana#.UzFSXBCsQrp, date of access: 29 July 2018.

Nixon, N. (2012). Nga herë e tashmë Evropian: Figura e Skënderbeut në nacionalizmin bashkëkohor shqiptar. *Revista Përpjekja*, 28–29.

Pipa, A. (1993). Turqit e rij të Shqipnisë së re. In A. Klosi (Ed.), *Quo vadis Shqipëri?*. Tiranë: Albania.

Pipes, D. (2006, 14 August). More on the Term 'Islamic Fascists'. Retrieved from www.danielpipes.org/blog/2006/08/more-on-the-term-islamic-fascists, date of access: 29 July 2018.

Plasari, A. (1992a, September). The Line of Theodosius Reappears: Which Side Will the Albanians Take? Retrieved from file:///Users/rezartbeka/Desktop/Plasari,%20The%20theodosius%20line%20reappears.pdf, date of access: 29 July 2018.

Plasari, A. (1992b). *Vija e Teodosit rishfaqet: Nga do t'ia mbajnë shqiptarët?* Tiranë.

Plasari, A. (2002, 8 September). Hotch-Potch ose dita e botës lakuriq. *Gazeta*, 55.

Puto, A. (2006). Fryma romantike dhe nacionaliste ne debatin për 'identitetin shqiptar'. *Revista Përpjekja*, 12/ 23.

Puto, A. (2012). Nga Skënderbeu mitik në atë historik. *Revista Përpjekja*, 28–29.

Santos, G. (2014). Islamofascism. In Charles Gallagher and Cameron Lippard (Eds), *Race and Racism in the United States: An Encyclopedia of the American Mosaic* (vol. 1, pp. 611–612). Santa Barbara, CA: Greenwood.

Sulstarova, E. (2006). Evropa e ngurtë e Kadaresë. *Revista Përpjekja*, 12/23.

Sulstarova, E. (2013). *Arratisje nga Lindja: Orientalizmi shqiptar nga Naimi tek Kadareja*, 3rd Edition. Tiranë: Pika pa Sipërfaqe.

Sulstarova, E. (2015). Islam and Orientalism in Contemporary Albania. In A. Elbasani and O. Roy (Eds), *The Revival of Islam in the Balkans: From Identity to Religiosity* (pp. 23–42). Basingstoke: Palgrave Macmillan.

Sulstarova, E. (2016). *Islamizëm do të thotë lindje*. Tiranë: Pika pa sipërfaqe.

Tozaj, N. (1995, 10 January). Shqipëria, një depo e municionit islamik? *Zëri i popullit*.

4 Post-coloniality, Islamization and secular elites

Tracing Islamophobia in Pakistan

Syed Furrukh Zad Ali Shah

Introduction

There is a considerable growth of literature in the West about the culture, politics and discourses of Islamophobia, which focuses on varied themes derived from historical rivalries and contemporary patterns of transnationalism and globalization. The emotive and cognitive demonization of Muslims as the 'other' and the 'enemy' is projected frequently through cultural, political and media discourses, reverberating moral panic in these societies. Within Muslim majority societies, manifestations of similar stereotyped expressions and prejudiced anxieties are also noticeable, which point to the presence of Islamophobic currents, though in different socio-political terms and historical connections. This chapter is divided in four parts: the first part discusses contemporary Islamophobia culture, the second part examines post-colonial Islamophobia episteme, the third part elaborates Islam in the Pakistani context, where religionization of politics and Islamization of politics has taken place since independence, and the last part traces Islamophobia and secular elites along with their ideological linkages and manifestations in Pakistan.

Contemporary Islamophobia culture[1]

Islamophobia as a term and subject of academic and public interest became well known with publication of the Runnymede Trust Report (1997), although the biases and hatred attached to the concept can be traced back to centuries-old rivalries between the Islamic–Orient and Western–Christian worlds. Present day usage treats it as a distinct category of racism. By its very nature, Islamophobia is the result of deeply ingrained intolerance, animosity, bigotry, prejudice and enmity wrapped in xenophobia and racism towards those who are seen and assumed as Muslims and their faith (Schiffer and Wagner, 2011). It is manifested within a range of biased perceptions, discriminatory practices and exclusionary attitudes, by inventing the 'Islamic' scapegoat and excluding it from social solidarity bonds of nationalist imagining to maintain their hold on opportunity structures, societal resources and social spaces. The presumed identity of their subject group is derived from various cultural–historical stereotypes in purely negative terms. Here Islamophobia emerges as 'an expression of sweepingly negative view of the religion and the culture of Islam' (Hafez, 2014). Islamophobes usually place Islam and Muslims beyond the folds of their so-called 'organic' society, and civilizational ascendency, not according their victims a legitimate space in the public sphere. From an ideological perspective, it appears to be the global ideology, similar in theory, function and purpose to racism and colonialism that sustains and perpetuates negative ascriptions and subaltern positions to their victims as an inferior social entity. Allen (2010) contends that it is an ideology that informs and shapes our speech, attitudes and thoughts, resulting in exclusionary and discriminatory practices, including violence and abuse. Shryock also opines that Islamophobia as a unifying concept brings together different possibilities in such a manner that a reliable stereotyped profile of Muslim can easily be generated. In tracing the history of this concept, he puts forward the argument, which is generally acknowledged among scholars, that the association of Islam and terrorism was pervasive in Western cultures long before 9/11 (Shryock, 2010). However, this construction of the Muslim 'other' as the presumed 'enemy' has precisely been invented in the aftermath of the Cold War along with the demise of Soviet communist threat. Therefore, it can be argued that the identification of Muslims as a religious group is not a new invention, but their growing visibility in terms of numbers and socio-cultural assertion in Western social landscape.

This current rise of global Islamophobic culture can be attributed to media, which acts as a virulent manufacturer and propagandist disseminator, generating moral panic in multi-ethnic societies (Bayraklı and Hafez, 2015). Various studies have witnessed its prevalence, significantly observable in individuals, societal and institutional expressions, manifestations and practices in Western societies (see Adida, Laitin and Valfort, 2012; Bayraklı and Hafez, 2015; European Monitoring Centre on Racism and Islamophobia, 2006; Faliq, 2010; Fekete, 2012; Lambert and Githens-Mazer, 2010). These practices involve racial discrimination, social segregation, cultural labelling of backwardness, violence and abuse, policing and surveillance of Muslim communities as 'suspect', media representation of 'Muslim terrorist', anti-Muslim political campaigns, mosque vandalism and hate crimes.

Therefore, there is considerable variation in Islamophobic expressions, manifestations and cultures across societies, which is not only limited to Western societies but is present in various shapes and shades in the non-Western world. India and China as states and societies exemplify this Islamophobic culture with regard to their Muslim minorities. Although the genesis of this culture can be conflated with Western constructions as well as deep-rooted societal conflicts between communities in post-colonial world order, this Western invention of the Muslim 'enemy' Islamophobic culture has proliferated globally. Although it has happened due to the rise of global communication media and other channels of dissemination, it can also be linked to the discourse of a Westernized post-colonial secular elite, who has been made to perceive religion and its adherents with bias, suspicion, fear and hatred. In many cases it is subtle and implicit, 'respectable and enlightened' (Hafez, 2014), whereas in its public manifestations it is discriminatory, violent and explicit. There is no denying the fact that such Islamophobic culture also exists in Muslim majority societies, which is expressed by a Westernized post-colonial secular elite, embedded in European critique of religion during Enlightenment and contemporary global culture of religious radicalism. This embodies the elites' attempts to deny the legitimate space and opportunity structures in politics for governance and role of religion in shaping cultural contours of the society. A cursory glance over Muslim majority societies across the globe stands testimony to it, such as Pakistan, Indonesia, Egypt, Nigeria, Bangladesh, Uzbekistan etc. This may appear counter-intuitive, yet it distinctly manifests itself in Muslim majority contexts within post-colonial episteme.

Post-colonial Islamophobia episteme

The epistemological grounds for implicit 'respectable' and 'enlightened' Islamophobia can be traced within post-colonial theory. According to Grosfoguel, epistemic racism and its derivative Eurocentric fundamentalism shape a contemporary global system that places Western knowledge, beauty, traditions, cosmologies and spiritualties at a higher pedestal (Grosfoguel, 2006; 2010). The non-Western ones are rendered inferior and subaltern, because only the West carries the legitimacy to produce 'authentic knowledge' with access to 'universality', 'rationality' and 'truth'. Within this hierarchical conceptualization of the world-system, Islamophobia can be viewed as 'subalternization and inferiorization' of Muslims by a hierarchy that constructs stereotypes and extends prejudices about them in media, academics and the larger global public sphere (Grosfoguel, 2010). As Said demonstrated, essentializing discourses to denigrate Muslims are acceptable in the West, because what is said about their mind, character or culture on a whole, cannot now be said about Africans, Jews, other Orientals or even Asians (Said, 1997). Franz Fanon also elaborated on this privileged position of narrative hegemony, which places 'others' outside the epistemological boundaries set by Europe (Fanon, 2008). This has occurred during colonialism that has inadvertently (re)produced hegemonic relations and structures of thought in colonies. The power flew from the metropole to the periphery, submerging itself in psychic, cultural, intellectual and power structures for control and manipulation in manifest and implicit forms. However, the foremost impact of colonialism is in terms of its centric approach, where Europe occupies the centre stage to manufacture and manage not only the material, but also the ideological structures and forces.

The origins of Eurocentrism are traced to European Renaissance and Enlightenment due to a violently progressive historic, political and economic march of Western imperialism. This view assumes that due to superior values of European civilization, it carries a triumphalist vision. Eurocentrism thereby posits that its history is the universal history, which aims to serve as the reference point against which all other histories for human progress are to be judged, expecting that the same linear model is to be adopted for modernization (Mingnolo, 2000). This claim is further based upon the premise that modernity is an automated and integral product of European genius, which owes nothing to the non-European world. Post-colonial structures and Westernized secular elites in the peripheries have traditionally been immersed within these trappings, which de-historicize the global history as singular and one-dimensional. The marginalized groups are seen through these established structures, images, representations, consequences and constructs of European colonization of the non-European world from the fifteenth century to twentieth century. Nonetheless, colonialism has been a recurrent and widespread feature of human history with its various forms in different parts of the globe and ages, which has always created complex, entangled and traumatic experiences, both for the colonizers and the colonized (Loomba, 2005). The oppressive politics of knowledge production and image construction are the mechanism and strategies through which subjugated non-European races were and are ascribed troubled identities and social places in exploitative hierarchical relationships. Popular social and academic narratives, embedded in theories of civilizational superiority by European colonial powers like France, Britain, Belgium, The Netherlands and Germany, are employed to justify colonization and progress with Eurocentric models of modernity. An essentialist Orientalist-style discourse is not only propagated by Western academics, but also by post-colonial secular elites, wherein religion is presented as a threat, devoid of its local history and socio-cultural convenience. This is observable when such discursivities are deconstructed, which are less obvious, hidden behind or embedded within Western debates related to secularism, liberalism and tolerance (Allen, 2010).

The episteme of post-colonial Islamophobia culture is premised on this hegemonic Eurocentric approach that looks at European liberal democratic order as natural of a progressive human march, wherein Muslims and their cultures are seen as retrogressive and backward. Consequently, European comprehension of its 'others' on its own terms, assumptions and scales regardless of how people beyond these Westernized ontological and epistemological frames perceive themselves, naturalizes the polarization between the privileged Europe and subaltern groups, leading to the construction of prejudices and of inferiority. One of the central tenets of Islamophobic culture is the essentialization of Muslims as a single entity with obvious disregard to their ethnic, cultural, national, historical or even religious complexities. This generalization leads to the construction of a single demonizing 'other', who requires discipline and management through intelligence profiling, regulated surveillance and increasing securitization. Although, post-colonial theory resists and attempts to dismantle these corrosive discursive and cultural domains, yet media narrativization and sections of global academia have sought to employ and perpetuate these reductive frames of reference (Lawson, 1992). These persistent and prevalent hegemonic cultural cataloguing practices and structures continue to produce conflicting relations among Muslim and Western societies through creating binary divisions of 'us' versus 'them', along with denoting factually inaccurate all-inclusive essentializing labels to these relationships (Treacher, 2005). The subalternization of excluded groups and their values, beliefs, traditions, histories and *weltanschauung* (world-view) are silenced through non-representation into the established power structures. Islam and Muslims are cast out from the 'standardized' elite versions of global histories (Chaturvedi, 2000). Their location in narrative industry is that of a marginal figure who is talked about but is not talked to or heard.

Islam in Pakistani context

Presently Pakistani society is deeply divided along religious, ideological and political lines due to a number of internal and external factors, including ramifications of colonialism, its chequered post-colonial political history, growing religionization of politics, resurgence of Islamism in the region, and longstanding conflicts in Kashmir and Afghanistan. These factors have contributed to the creation of fissures within the polity and the triggering of religious radicalism, extremism, sectarianism, fundamentalism and terrorism. Islam, which is practiced among an overwhelming majority of the population, has come to be seen as a menace by a small minority of Westernized secular elites who exhibit currents of 'implicit', 'respectable' and 'enlightened' Islamophobia, which can be understood as 'discursive' manifestations of the phenomenon.

Within Pakistan, there have been strong local traditions of pluralism and cosmopolitanism, reflected in its folklore, art, culture and literature, associated with mysticism and Sufism of the region. Over the centuries, Muslim Sufi saints, philosophers, poets and scholars of this part, including Dattaa Ali Hajeveri, Moin-ud-din Chisti, Bu Ali Qalandar, Amir Khusro, Waris Shah, Baba Fareed, Khawaja Latif Bhattai, Lal Shabaz Qalandar, Khushal Khan Khattak, Sultan Bahoo, Bhulay Shah and Mian Muhammad Bhakh fostered inclusivist, tolerant and universalist Islamic religious traditions (Bennett and Ramsey, 2012; Islam, 2002) in the multi-religious Indian sub-continent. Geographically, this area of Indus Valley incubated various religions for centuries, like Buddhism, Hinduism, Islam and Sikhism, along with other smaller religious groups. Historically, after Greek and Aryan invaders, Arabs, Persians, Mongols and Turks made their way through this enormous geographical landmass, leaving indelible cultural footprints. These can be gauged in the rich mosaic of languages, cultures and religions, which existed together for centuries. The religion was not treated as a divisive factor, rather different religious communities used to observe religious traditions beyond their faith barriers. Hindus, Sikhs and Christians used to attend Muslim saints' shrines and gatherings regularly, which still continues in multi-religious communities living together. Such religious harmony was fractured by politicization of religion during European colonialism in the Indian sub-continent, emerging as the basis of 'new Islamicity' through institutionalization of Muslim communities (Malik, 2008). This reconstruction of history traces power struggles between some factions of Hindus and Muslims during Arab, Persian and Turkish rules, as manifestation of permanent religio-cultural divide (Qureshi, 1977). Since British colonization of the sub-continent, religion has been employed as the paramount identity marker and a major mobilizing factor, initially to seek a separate homeland and later for Islamization in the new state as part of nation-formation and state-building purposes.

It is to be recognized that the Pakistan Movement was founded and launched by European-educated Muslim secular elites, originating from feudal, business and professional classes. They employed religious identity to garner the support of masses from the beginning due to the fear of Hindu domination (Sayeed, 2001). It is interesting to note that these secular elites derived their nationalist ideology from religious identity rather than territory. Jinnah, the founder of Pakistan, was a profound liberal, secular and Westernized, who believed in and practiced fervently religious harmony and cooperation. In the early years of his political career, he was endowed with the title of 'ambassador of Hindu–Muslim unity' by Sarojini Naido, known as the nightingale of India. His 11 August 1947 speech envisioned the new state, where all the people who would come to dwell within its boundaries, whatever their personal religious beliefs may be, as Pakistani. Haider (2011) argues that Jinnah's resort to religion was essentially not a committed ideology but to afford 'a semblance of unity and solidity to his divided Muslim constituents'. Although a large number of religious clerics stood against partition, some noteworthy religious elites joined the movement.[2] After independence from British colonial rule, the secular elites of the newly founded state decided to manage it on religious-cum-ideological basis. Objective Resolution (1948) adopted by the Constituent Assembly of Pakistan envisioned a democratic state according to principles enunciated by Islam (Mehdi, 2013). Thus, post-independence ideological discourse envisioned Pakistan as an Islamic state. Herein, the religious narrative of Hindu–Muslim divide influenced a significant section of society especially in the wake of mass atrocities committed across borders, and in the process made the radical mind set more empowered in the absence of nation-state structures. Over a period of time, these resulted in episodic religious violence that was condoned by weaker state-enforcement regimes. To these were added frequent instances of religious minorities, employed by political parties to garner political support and mobilization. Moreover, Cold War rivalries and geostrategic imperatives further fuelled extremism and radicalization, which witnessed murderous sprees.

Within this context, the religious-cum-ideological narrative became deeply embedded within state institutions and societal structures, including the pulpit and the media. The state had moved from religionization of politics to politicization of Islam, wherein the secular elites were gradually replaced by power elites who continued with the Islamization project. However, this did not happen in vacuum, rather a number of international events and ideological confrontations paved the way for this gradual transition. Conflict with India, the Arab–Israel War, the Iranian revolution and Afghan Jihad within Cold War rivalries led to a resurgence of religion in politics (Mandaville, 2014). Alongside this, local Islamists, most notable of which was *Jammat-e-Islami*, founded by Maududi, continued the political struggle for Islamization of the state and the society. Moreover, the state's governance deficit and the military's drive for legitimacy contributed further in bringing religion in. The 1973 Constitution of Pakistan further declared Islam as the official religion of the state, wherein it was declared that no law should be enacted which is repugnant to the injunctions of Islam. Later on, Zia's Islamization project brought Sharia courts to the existing judicial system along with a number of legal instruments (Mehdi, 2013). His military rule exacerbated Islam for any and every political objective, which significantly radicalized sections of society and emboldened the religious character of the state in every possible regard. Even the short-lived democratic regimes of liberal–socialists and national–conservatives in the 1990s continued with Islamic narratives, slogans and policies. The military dictatorship of Musharraf in the wake of 9/11 in alliance with the West ostensibly lambasted religious sections for political gains and legitimacy and proved counter-productive, creating mayhem within the polity. This points to the fact that recourse to Islam since pre-independence has produced inevitable ramifications for policy-makers to run the state.

Islamophobia and secular elites

Mills in his classic book, *The Power Elites* (1956), identifies distinct power-wielding groups in the American political system that are the outcome of advanced industrialized societies through rationalization processes. The mechanisms of political power are concentrated within this tiny minority, which employs it for political influence and manoeuvring in a given system. They are far more organized, operating within a dense web of interconnections and hierarchies. Although throughout history various groups have had the tradition of establishing, coordinating and systemizing their relations for their rights and gains, since the emergence of the nation-state and its representative character, a number of such elite groups have surfaced on the political terrain to exert influence on government public policy formation, decision-making and implementation-mechanism processes in a more organized manner. Varied by size, influence and interests, these groups employ real power in modern political systems through multiple strategies such as lobbying, campaigns, activism, advocacy and networking. Some of these groups coordinate on the basis of common interests, be these political, economic, social, religious or ideological, wielding pressure on a government seeking benefits for society, depending upon how state institutions function and how various preferences are configured. As Gellner (1983) asserts, post-colonial nationalisms provide the basis for nation-construction and state-building so that it can constitute a vehicle for collectivism, populism and social cohesion. They can be located in state and non-state organizations, professional associations, advocacy groups, social networks and political parties. Representing the democratic potential of modern societies, their socio-political activism consists of offering alternative forums to promote collective ideals. These operate in what Habermas terms as the public sphere, an arena where various societal factions contest the dominance of the ruling elite.

Pakistan, with a 97 per cent Muslim population and a declared Islamic Republic, has a smaller, yet formidable section of society that corresponds to Islamophobic currents. These Westernized secular power elites share similar anti-Islam sentiments, rooted in traditional Western discourses of secularism and modernity. Furthermore, modern resurgence of political Islamism and its conflation with violence also demonizes the religion in general, which is embedded in local cultural traditions and social customs. Religion that is seen as anti-modern and irrational has to be disposed of if society is to be reformed and modernized. Although these secular elites are dispersed across various societal structures and levels, their social status, educational credentials and economic class are closely immersed to echelons of power, therefore these are considered as power elites. Within Pakistan, as in other developing societies, these secular elites are structurally differentiated and socially heterogeneous, characterized by dynamism and activism that strives to create a social space in which articulation of public demands and resistance against the monopolizing power of the state is conducted. There is a plethora of conceptualizations and discourses of pluralism, secularism and notions of private sphere, which are situated within Eurocentric traditions of Western civility. While a counter-cultural notion of civil traditions and political rights is contested in post-colonial theory that challenges hegemonizing Western narrations of individual liberty and citizen empowerment, it has far less theoretical and political import in non-Western societies (Nisar, 2013). Therefore, these secular elites are far more under the influence of colonial legacies of European imperialism, which developed clear differentiations between imperial and native organizational patterns, societal institutions and value systems to its own advantage. This pattern persisted in the post-colonial state where new political elites continued to keep this differentiation between native societies and their cultural traditions to those of Eurocentric models. This colonial governmentality effectively resulted in patron–client relationships around modernity versus a tradition nexus sustained by such elites that continued to look down upon the native value system and customary practices as incompatible with West-centric modernity (Mamdani, 2012). Therefore, these local cultures, whether religious or not, were viewed with suspicion and disregard.

Islamophobia in the Pakistani context can be explained as respectable and enlightened implicit Islamophobia, which rests on various similar notions that secular liberal Islamophobes in Western contexts delve upon. As contrived prejudice fomented by the existing West-centric global power structure, it rationalizes a perceived Islamist threat by constructing them as folk devils, causing moral panic. Islamophobes therefore reaffirm a global racial structure that seeks to conflate Islam as a belief and cultural system with that of Islamism, which is seen as a totalitarian political ideology, comparable to fascism and communism. As an inferior social system to that of West, it is seen as monolithic, barbaric and archaic, which promotes extremism and supports terrorism. Islamophobia here can be understood as a cognitive and emotive expression of general negativity towards Islam as a stigmatized belief system, and a stereotyped out-group phenomenon towards ostensibly practicing Muslims. Such group-focused enmity and negativity is a specific aspect of respectable and enlightened Islamophobia (Hafez, 2014), which designates a subordinate social status and seeks group exclusion from the public sphere for multiple sociological and historical reasons. This negativity alludes to liberal authoritarianism, imperial dominance and cultural conservatism. Stereotypes, cognitive biases and emotive prejudice shape their views and attitudes towards Islam and Muslims in particular. Hence, in specific contexts they would come to equate Islam as a major driver of religious extremism, fanaticism, radicalism and terrorism.

In lieu of politicization of Islam in the Pakistani context, the social space for a genuine dialogue for the role of religion and Islam has largely shrunk, which has led to radicalism among secularists and religious. In general, Islam, like any other religion, is seen to be based upon irrationality, pursuing a course of obscurantism, and is antithetical to modern consciousness and way of life. Brutal local customs that restrict female freedom and gender equality are tended to be the product of Islam and practicing Muslims. Mahmood (2009), for example, in his various books and articles, emphasizes that Islam practiced in the sub-continent is the major source of 'cultural suffocation' and largely responsible for all prevalent misogyny in Pakistani society. Similarly, Azhar (2015) traces female subjugation and social inequality in the 'repressive' Islamic patriarchal system wherein Muslim women exist as 'slaves'. To realize their existence as free human beings they need to throw away the religious chains that usurp their essential humanity. Through this specific understanding of religion and the culture of Islam, they propagate a sweepingly negative view of ordinary Muslims and their religious faith. They are placed beyond the folds of contemporary global civilizational ethos, wherein a legitimate space for expressing and performing their religion, encoded in local cultural traditions, are denied in the public sphere. From an ideological perspective, it appears to be the global ideology, similar in theory, function and purpose to racism and colonialism, that sustains and perpetuates negative ascriptions and subaltern positions to their victims as an inferior social entity. In the political sphere, Islam is designated as a totalitarian political ideology that is comparable to fascism. The dread of Sharia, the diluted Islamic legal code, is perpetuated by portraying it as anti-social and anti-civilization, which is meant to regulate all aspects of life, from economics and politics, to science, social issues, interpersonal relations and sexuality. Such ideas are not publicly expressed due to the religious extreme present on the other side of the scale, but are kept within like-minded groups, where these are ferociously debated and held. Hassan (1977), a renowned Pakistani socialist thinker and activist, draws linkages between Islam, primitivism and irrationality, which is inherently incompatible with modernity. Relying on binaries drawn from European Orientalist discourse, static stereotyped constructs about Islam and Muslims are perpetuated that are overly primitive, violent and sensual. Like their Western counterparts, they would ultimately rely on extremist agenda and radical propaganda, and therefore would struggle to keep Islam and practicing Muslims out of the social solidarity bonds. This inadvertently functions to preserve the Western dominance and authority over non-Western cultures and philosophies. To them, resurgent Islamism is a strategic tool, ultimately leading to a repressive anti-modern clerical/theocratic regime.

It can be understood as a consequence of power-struggle whereby these secular elites lost influence in power hierarchy due to the rise of Islamism in public sphere and resultant religious cum sectarian conflicts in the polity.

Interestingly, the political role of Islamism in Pakistan is largely restricted due to their poor electoral performance, yet their connections with the deep state in Pakistan have been regarded as significant evidence of their anti-democratic profile and propensity towards authoritarianism. Islamism, therefore, is branded as a destructive ideology and anti-modern philosophy, which produces only alienated, extremist and radicalized groups and individuals, through propaganda, indoctrination and infiltration. This has been employed by military dictator General Pervaiz Musharraf who sought for political manipulation through 'enlightened moderation', framing and labelling prevailing Islamic practices as 'fundamentalist and militant', yet at the same time promoting and securing them an instrumental role in state politics. Correspondingly, secular forums that invoke enlightenment rationality and secularism pursue cultural racism wherein the Western ontology and epistemology stands hegemonic. This stands in contrast to their democratic credentials and liberalist philosophy, denying the legitimate space for religious practices that has been largely the case in Western secular societies. Religio-cultural practices such as Sharia-sanctioned punishments and gender-related issues of veil and segregation, which are validated by some Muslim scholars and are carried out in some Muslim societies, are employed to validate essentializing discourses about Islam. Here the linkage of Islam with backwardness, fanaticism, irrationality, extremism and violence is naturalized through constant reiteration and reinforcement. Like the Black subject of Fanon, practicing Muslims cannot fit squarely in the liberal democratic society. As an 'awkward' figure and a subaltern 'other', they are stereotyped as passive, preposterous and primitive. Their religion is associated with wrongness and villainy, which is assumed to be incompatible with modernity. This is evidenced by the increasing wave of religiosity among Islamists, who search for 'authentic' Islam and fall into the radicalization trap. These consequences of Islamophobia are far more observable in consolidating religious cultures of Muslim societies like Pakistan, Iran, Sudan and Afghanistan. Muslims, past and present, fall into this hegemonic colonial categorization that labels, classifies, essentializes and narrates them. Islamophobia discourses are derivative of these factors, which are manufactured, constructed and operationalized through multiple structures, practices and narratives, where the thin line between liberal critique of religion and prejudiced essentiality is often breached and negated.

Conclusion

Thus, it can be concluded that secular elites in post-colonial Muslim societies share prejudices towards Islam and practicing Muslims, apart from its civic critique. Islamic symbols, beliefs, normativities and politics produce disdain and prejudice, aimed at excluding Islam from spheres of dominance. Although in

Pakistan Islam has frequently and fervently been employed by the state establishment to develop ideological foundations of the post-colonial polity, such religionization of the society and Islamization of politics have multiplied the governance issues and societal fissures, whereby Islam, as a cultural and faith system, has come to be seen as a menace by liberal secular elites in the society. The violent disdain and utter disregard of religion and religiosity by secular elites is framed around Western disregard of religion in general and particularly towards Islam and Muslims as backward, irrational, intolerant, oppressive, fanatic and violent: the entire spectrum of negativities which are characteristic of an implicit and discursive, respectable and enlightened Islamophobia.

Notes

1 The author has completed his doctorate studying cultural politics of Islamophobia in Europe. The first two sections include references from his dissertation.
2 Like Shabir Ahmed Usmani, Maulana Zafar Ahmad Anshari and Pir Manki Sharif, who joined the Pakistan Movement and supported the nascent state in its making.

Bibliography

Adida, C., Laitin, D. and Valfort, M. (2012). 'Muslims in France: Identifying a Discriminatory Equilibrium', IZA. Retrieved from http://ftp.iza.org/dp6953.pdf, date of access: 9 June 2018.

Allen, C. (2010). *Islamophobia*. Farnham, Ashgate.

Azhar, A. (2015). *Dhund kay Paar*, originally in Urdu, translated as 'Beyond the Fog'. Toronto, Shaun Graphics & Publishers.

Bayraklı, E. and Hafez, F. (2015). *European Islamophobia Report*, SETA: Foundation for Political, Economic and Social Research. Retrieved from www.islamophobiaeurope.com/reports/2015/en/EIR_2015.pdf, date of access: 9 June 2018.

Bennett, C. and Ramsey, C. (2012). *South Asian Sufis: Devotion, Deviation and Destiny*. London, Continuum International Publishing.

Chaturvedi, V. (2000). *Mapping Subaltern Studies and the Postcolonial*. London, Verso.

European Monitoring Centre on Racism and Xenophobia (2006). *The Annual Report on the Situation Regarding Racism and Xenophobia in the Member States of the EU*. Budapest, EUMC.

Faliq, A. (2010). 'Islamophobia and Anti-Muslim Hate: Causes and Remedies', *The Cordoba Foundation: Cultures in Dialogue*. Retrieved from www.thecordobafoundation.com/attach/ARCHES_Vol%204_Edition%207.PDF, date of access: 9 June 2018.

Fanon, F. (2008 new ed. English translation of 1952). *Black Skin, White Masks*. London, Pluto Press.

Fekete, L. (2012). *Pedlars of Hate: the Violent Impact of the European Far Right*, Institute of Race Relations. Retrieved from www.irr.org.uk/wp-content/uploads/2012/06/PedlarsofHate.pdf, date of access: 9 June 2018.

Gellner, E. (1983). *Nations and Nationalism.* New York, Cornell University Press.

Grosfoguel, R. (Fall 2006). 'Many Faces of Islamophobia', *Human Architecture: The Journal of the Sociology of Self-Knowledge*, 1 (1).

Grosfoguel, R. (Fall 2010). 'Epistemic Islamophobia and Colonial Social Sciences', *Human Architecture: The Journal of the Sociology of Self-Knowledge*, 8 (2).

Hafez, K. (2014). *Islam in 'Liberal' Europe: Freedom, Equality, and Intolerance*, (Trans. Alex Skinner). Lanham, Rowman and Littlefield.

Haider, Z. (2011). 'Ideologically Adrift'. In Lodhi, M. (ed.) *Pakistan: Beyond the Crisis State*. New York, Oxford University Press.

Hassan, S. (1977). *Musa say Marx Tak*, originally in Urdu, translated as 'From Moses to Marx'. Karachi, Zaki Sons Printers.

Islam, R. (2002). *Sufism in South Asia: Impact on Fourteenth Century Muslim Society*. Oxford, Oxford University Press.

Lambert, R. and Githens-Mazer, J. (2010). *Islamophobia and Anti-Muslim Hate Crime: UK Case Studies*, European Muslim Research Center. Retrieved from http://library. college.police.uk/docs/Islamophobia-Lambert-2010.pdf, date of access: 9 June 2018.

Lawson, A. (1992). 'Comparative Studies and Post-colonial "Settler" Cultures', *Australian-Canadian Studies*, 10 (2).

Loomba, A. (2005). *Colonialism/Postcolonialism* (2nd ed.). London, Routledge.

Mahmood, A. (2009). *Sakafti Ghuttan aur Pakistani Muaashara*, originally in Urdu, translated as 'Cultural Suffocation and Pakistani Society'. Karachi, City Press.

Malik, J. (2008). *Islam in South Asia: A Short History*. Leiden, Brill.

Mamdani, M. (2012). *Define and Rule: Native as Political Identity*. Massachusetts, Harvard University Press.

Mandaville, P. (2014). *Islam and Politics*. New York, Routledge.

Mehdi, R. (2013). *The Islamization of the Law in Pakistan*. New York, Routledge.

Mills, C. W. (1956). *The Power Elites*. New York, Oxford University Press.

Mingnolo, W. (2000). *Local Histories/Global Designs: Coloniality, Subaltern Knowledges, and Border Thinking*. Princeton: Princeton University Press.

Nisar, T. (2013). *The Discourses on the Civil Society and the State in the Context of European and Post-Colonial Narratives: Re-Conceptualizing the Civil Society in Pakistan*. Rome. Doctoral Dissertation. Retrieved from http://eprints.luiss. it/1278/1/20131217-nisar.pdf, date of access: 9 June 2018.

Qureshi, I. H. (1977). *The Muslim Community of Indo-Pakistan Sub-Continent, 610–1947: A Brief Historical Analysis*. Karachi, Ma'aref.

Said, E. (1997). *Covering Islam: How the Media and the Experts Determine How We See the Rest of the World*. New York, Random House.

Sayeed, K. B. (2001). *Pakistan: The Formative Phase 1857–1948*. Karachi, Oxford University Press.

Schiffer, S. and Wagner, C. (2011). 'Anti-Semitism and Islamophobia: New Enemies, Old Patterns', *Race and Class*, 52 (3).

Shryock, A. (2010). *Islamophobia/Islamophilia: Beyond the Politics of Enemy and Friend*. Indianapolis, Indiana University Press.

The Runnymede Trust (1997). *Islamophobia: A Challenge for Us All*. London, The Runnymede Trust.

Treacher, A. (2005). 'On Post-Colonial Subjectivity', *Group Analysis: The Group Analytical Society London*, 38 (1).

5   The politics of Islamophobia in Turkey

Ali Aslan

Introduction

This chapter analyses the dominant years of the politics of Islamophobia in Turkey, which roughly covers the years from the last decades of the nineteenth century to the late 1990s. It takes the definition of Islamophobia as the construction of Islam and Muslims as the enemy. Based on that definition, it argues that Islamophobia played a constitutive role in the establishment and construction of the modern Turkish state. First of all, the politics of Islamophobia served to replace the Ottoman Empire with the secular–nationalist Turkish Republic. Following the completion of this political transition, Islamophobia was deployed to produce a secular–nationalist reality, which included the forming of a secular–nationalist society in its domestic realm, backing a Westphalian regional order and a Western-centric global order on its outside. The politics of Islamophobia remained dominant in Turkish politics until the 2000s.

This study discusses the political function of Islamophobia in Muslim majority societies, concluding that Islamophobia is an important problem in Muslim societies as well, especially as it pertains to countries that underwent a radical modernization process. Second, this study examines the theoretical foundations of Islamophobia and asserts that only those criticisms towards Islam and Muslims that make the latter the enemy can be considered as Islamophobia. Finally, the study applies those theoretical findings to the Turkish case. Here, it first seeks to manifest how Islamophobia was utilized in transforming the political form and ideological basis of the political community towards the nation-state and secular–nationalism before the republic was established. Then, it analyses how the secular republican elite deployed Islamophobia in the reproduction of the secular–nationalist nation-state to hold on to power until the late 1990s.

The political function of Islamophobia

Islamophobia is often defined as 'unfounded hostility towards Islam, unfair discrimination against Muslim individuals and communities, and exclusion of Muslims from mainstream political and social affairs', (Elahi and Khan, 2017,

p. 7) 'anti-Muslim racism', (Bayraklı and Hafez, 2018), 'anti-Islamic and anti-Muslim sentiment' (Ogan *et al.*, 2014) 'indiscriminate negative attitudes or emotions directed towards Islam and Muslims' (Bleich, 2011, p. 1582) or 'fear of Islam' (Shryock, 2010). All these descriptions point at the process of antagonization of Islam and Muslims or 'making Muslims the enemy', (Gottschalk and Greenberg, 2008) especially in the Western world after the Cold War.[1] Indeed, there is a long history of conflict and enmity between Muslims and Christians (or Westerners) which goes back to the Middle Ages. However, the intra-European wars in the first part and the presence of the Soviet threat in the later years of the twentieth century decreased the political importance of Islam and Muslims. The collapse of the Soviet Union and communism, along with the unification of Europe, put the spotlights back on Islam and Muslims (Huntington, 1993). This process of antagonization of Islam and Muslims gained momentum after 9/11 and recently continued with the ISIS threat (Morgan and Poynting, 2012). The rising population of Muslims in the last decades and the pouring of refugees from conflict areas and civil wars into Europe after the Arab Spring exacerbated the situation.

Indeed, the study of Islamophobia has created a vast literature on the subject. However, this literature appears to be lacking the study of Islamophobia in Muslim majority countries. Islamophobia is also an important problem in Muslim societies. The colonial past and radical secularist policies implemented by the state elites have created a fertile ground for Islamophobia in Muslim countries. In the process of modernization, which was carried out by the state elites in an authoritarian way, Islam and Muslims were made the enemy. The dosage of Islamophobia differed among Muslim societies with respect to how radical the modernization process was perceived and handled. In extreme cases, Islamic past and symbols were wiped out, religious–conservatives were denied basic rights and freedoms and were politically repressed as a consequence (Atabaki and Zürcher, 2004). In a nutshell, there was an attempt to destroy the political existence of Muslims in Muslim societies through brutal means in the last century.

This chapter highlights the rather systematic and institutional character of Islamophobia, which is backed by the state and is ingrained in the official ideology. It is a norm that resides at the centre of politics. This is because politics is essentially about transforming the identities of others by integrating them into an overarching identity (through immigration laws, for example)[2] in an open political struggle or within the framework of democratic politics. Islamophobic policies come into play when political actors fail to hegemonize by integrating others into themselves or reject to add them into themselves or else put pressure on them to give in. Consequently, they tend to make them the enemy (Laclau and Mouffe, 1985).

For instance, in Turkey, the secularist political forces, which strived to produce a modern political community on the basis of a secular–nationalist identity, always kept Islamophobic politics as an option. When the republican elite failed to transform the identity of Muslims to secular–nationalism, which was substantialized by the six arrows or principles of the Republican People's Party (CHP) – republicanism, populism, nationalism, laicism, statism, and revolutionism – that served as the official ideology of the Turkish state, (Parla, 1995) or bring religious–conservative sections of society under the overarching secular–nationalist identity, they had a tendency to present them as enemies of the regime. This was also the case when the republican elite, which sought to set positivistic science and nationalism as new bases for the legitimacy of the political order, failed to nationalize and rationalize Islam in order to hegemonize it under a secular–nationalist political project (Sakallıoğlu, 1994). Accordingly, Islam and Muslims were kept outside the 'official us'. To give an example, for quite a long time in Turkey, women wearing headscarves were not allowed to enter into the Parliament and become part of the ruling circle, not to mention that they could not even become public servants (Shively, 2005). Moreover, political parties with no ties to violence or terrorist activities were closed down with the accusation of being hubs of anti-secularist activities.[3] The secularist identity had therefore decided the dividing line between the centre that harboured those who were part of the ruling group and enjoyed public life and the periphery that included those who were being ruled and relegated into private life (Mardin, 1973). This was neither periodical nor temporary; although its visibility rose in times of increasing polarization and declined in other times, it always remained there.

These qualities underline the fact that, in the politics of Muslim countries, Islamophobia is a constitutive element that lays out the foundations of the new political community. It is deployed in the political struggle over the construction and reproduction of a political community. This is actually not much different in non-Muslim societies. Despite the fact that Islamophobia is often associated with marginal political actors or portrayed as a political anomaly in many non-Muslim societies, it is also observed that mainstream political actors can easily and increasingly resort to the same exclusionist discourse and practices. Islamophobia can turn into a norm that is utilized in organizing the totality of the political community. The basic political function of Islamophobia in Muslim minority countries is to cleanse the political body from Islam and Muslims and keep them outside the political community by turning them into the enemy.[4] Moreover, this serves to draw boundaries and differentiate the modern world from the 'backward' or 'dangerous' Muslim world. For instance, senior British diplomat Robert Cooper argues that there are postmodern, modern and pre-modern worlds with specific rules of conduct and therefore calls for a liberal imperialism and admission of double standards in foreign policy towards the less civilized worlds (Cooper, 2003).[5] The traces of this attitude that harbours double standards – such as offering Turkey a 'privileged partnership' instead of a full membership status – can be detected within European Union (EU)–Turkey membership negotiations as well ('Merkel Says Still against Turkey Joining the EU', 2015).

Although Islamophobia is a constitutive element of the political community in Muslim societies, it displays itself in a different manner. In contrast to non-Muslim majority societies, Islamophobia is adopted in Muslim societies to repress or wipe out the elements that might produce difference and hinder integration with the outside, namely with the modern Western world which is deemed as the 'friend'.[6] That is why Islamic symbols were demolished and religious–conservatives were denied basic political rights and freedoms and rendered politically invisible. And that's why it causes fear and angst in the political circles that seek integration with the modern world as Islamic symbols and Muslims gain larger visibility and presence in public life.[7] While Islamophobia establishes division lines with the outside and serves as a 'wall' between us and them in the non-Muslim case, it is deployed for integrating the political community with the outside and serves as a 'bridge' between us and them in Muslims countries.[8]

The basic tenet of Islamophobia in a Muslim society such as Turkey is, therefore, rejection of the political existence of the Islamic civilization and Muslims in order to integrate with the modern Western civilization. Accordingly, Islam is provincialized and reduced to a particularistic position. Religious–conservative sections of society, on the other hand, are subjected to policies of assimilation and otherization. In doing that, Islam is argued to belong to the pre-modern era or not applicable in the modern world. In other words, it is claimed that Islam is culturally backward, conflicting with modern science, strategically incompetent and a hindrance to progress in our time. The institutional outcome of this historical–cultural break is replacing Islamic political concepts and institutions with modern Western concepts and institutions.[9]

One of the major institutional changes is replacing empires, which claimed universal sovereignty, with particularistic territorial nation-states. In terms of Islamophobia and among its many other functions, the nation-state serves double purposes in a Muslim country like Turkey. On one hand, as a political tool, the nation-state facilitates the integration of Muslim majority communities into the modern world (the secularist dimension). On the other hand, it ensures that Muslim majority communities produce a political difference with the outside with their own sovereign polities (the nationalist dimension). The nation-state thus helps to tackle one of the important problems of modern international relations, which is the handling of the problem of inside/outside (Walker, 1993).

Islamophobia through the lenses of Carl Schmitt

To analyse above-mentioned problem properly, we have to focus on one of the major definitions of Islamophobia, which is 'making Muslims the enemy' and discuss what it means to make someone or some group of people the enemy. Since the meaning of any concept could be understood in relation to its opposite, the enemy can only be understood by comparing it with its polar opposite, the friend. As Carl Schmitt puts forward: 'The distinction of friend and enemy denotes the utmost degree of intensity of a union or separation, of an association or dissociation' (Schmitt, 2007, p. 27). Rather, the enemy is the one who is outside of 'us' or outside the political collectivity we form. The enemy does not have to be morally evil, aesthetically ugly or culturally backward (Schmitt,

2007). To be evil, ugly or backward does not make someone our enemy, although we resort to these non-political categories when producing our enemy. It does not need a specific content, since any content that can produce an intense separation between us and them is capable of creating an enemy. Therefore, the enemy is rather a matter of the intensity of the differences between the inside and the outside of a political collectivity and, as the intensity of the differences increases, the level of animosity mounts accordingly (Morgenthau, 2012). The enemy, thus, refers to other collectivities of people who are outside the boundaries of the nation-state.[10]

According to Schmitt, either the enemy should be other political collectivities or the enemy within a society could only exist before the state is formed, that is in the state of nature or the state of war in which everyone is against everyone else (Hobbes, 1962). However, as we observe in the discussion of Islamophobia, the enemy could also be within the state. Can the enemy be within the state? This raises the issue of social cohesion in the state. There are three degrees of social cohesion on the basis of the nature of the inter-relations between fellow citizens that can be found in society (Schmitt, 2000). At the top of it lies consensus on social values and principles. The whole society may gather around a certain set of ethical–political values. Members of a society perceive each other as 'friends' and each defines his identity and interests not independently from the others in the society. This transcendental form of society characterizes a rather communitarian and Hegelian type of political community (Taylor, 1984).

This is followed by another situation where society is divided into multiple social groups on the basis of value or identity differences. Here, members of a society perceive each other as 'rival' or 'adversary'. Despite individuals defining their identity, values and interests differently than others, they at least share some form of interests such as accepting the rules of competition among each other. Here, the consensus is merely over the rules of conflict, which are the basic elements of any political order. In this instrumentalist type of society, one can at least find a political order that allows for fair and open elections and a peaceful transfer of power among rival political forces. This poses a rather agonistic democratic order (Mouffe, 2000).

Both political orders, in which everybody views others as friends or rivals, require an enemy outside its borders. The enemies are those other political collectivities that do not share our cultural values, national identity or ethic-political principles. If there is not an enemy outside the borders, the enemy is produced within the borders. Here, we find a form of society in which members of the society perceive each other as 'enemy'. In this situation, individuals or social groups neither share a common identity and interest nor the rules of competition among each other. Rather, what members of the society share is a common understanding based on not attacking each other, *pacta sund servanda*. One can argue that, in this situation, the key to political order is the presence of a balance of threats that keeps the society from dissolving or plunging into a bloody civil war. This poses a rather anarchic and antagonistic political situation that can only be observed in international politics (Walt, 1987).

The society may evolve into any of these three generic political situations. Friends can become rivals and rivals can turn into enemies. This devolution to a Hobbesian situation can sometimes be limited to some sections of the society. Social groups, especially ethnic and religious minorities, may face a situation in which they are portrayed as the enemy of the society and the state. Indeed, every political order for it rests on a specific definition of us or an identity involves some sort of exclusion. They are constructed as outsiders and pushed to the outside of the political community. Their political demands are disregarded and even some of their basic rights can be breached. As noted above, this is likely to happen when the inclusiveness of the state declines, especially as a result of finding an enemy outside the national borders. When the state fails to include social groups into the political community on the basis of a common enemy outside itself, it tends to antagonize and securitize their demands and rights. As mentioned above, the decline of the communist or Soviet threat led to the emergence and rise of Islamophobia in the West. Islamic symbols and some Muslim practices, such as the wearing of the headscarf or burqa and even circumcision, have suddenly become a security problem. Why were they not a security threat during the Cold War?

All in all, Muslims in Muslim minority societies should interact with others in constructing the values and rules of political life. They have to participate and take responsibility in sustaining the political order. In that interaction, the state, along with major political actors, attempts to gain the consent of Muslims and enter into bargaining with them – this is most likely since Muslims are a minority – by satisfying their demands and integrating them into their political project. Muslims have the right not to give their consent and to expect more, just as those political actors have the right to criticize Muslims in return. However, this critique of Muslims should not reach to the level of making Muslims the enemy. In that case, we can start talking about Islamophobia, especially if it extends to an essentialist opposition to Islam and Muslims. Muslims should be friends or rivals in those democratic political settings, not the enemy. This is also true for Muslim majority societies. The religious–conservative social groups should not be made the enemy and put outside the political community. To reiterate, this is only viable as the state or main political actors find a common enemy outside the borders. As the friend–enemy distinction with the outside wanes, it inevitably pops up within borders. The enemy is constitutive in building the political community.

The politics of Islamophobia in Turkey

To understand Islamophobia in a Muslim majority society, one should look at how it is related to the construction and reproduction of the political community. If Islam and Muslims are made the enemy and systematically kept outside the political community, we can say that Islamophobic policies are already underway. Since Islam serves as the central value system and religious–conservative social groups are in the majority, Islamophobia is more likely to occur in Muslim majority societies. This is because it is very difficult for political actors to produce an inclusive identity without coming to terms with Islam and religious–conservative social groups. This becomes a much more difficult task since political actors are supposed to modernize the country as well. This is especially more likely when modernization is equated with Westernization. In that case, the local value system and their representatives, meaning Islam and Muslims, become the natural enemy. In order to unite with the West or produce a Western identity, Islam and Muslims are taken as the outside and made the enemy. That is why, in many Muslim majority countries, political life is mainly determined by the polarization between the secularists and the conservatives.

Turkish politics is not an exception in this regard. In Turkish politics, the main line of conflict or division has been between the Turkish–Islamic tradition and the secularist Westernist politics since the nineteenth century (Mardin, 1973). From the nineteenth century onwards, the alliance of bureaucracy with local notables has strived to produce a modern or Westernized political community by secularizing politics (İnancık, 1941). This search for a secular Western-style politics had two dimensions. One of them was the transformation of the political form from ancient to modern by following the French example of 1789 through which the Islamic content was emptied out from the locus of power. In fact, this did not mean that the locus of power was supposed to be filled with a more appropriate, that is, secularist, content. Modernization, secularization or democratization of politics basically implies that 'the locus of power becomes an empty place',[11] it has to remain empty. For instance, elections in democratic politics are one of the major indicators or providers of the emptiness of the locus of power:

> At the moment of elections, the whole hierarchic network of social relations is in a way suspended, put in parentheses; 'society' as an organic unity ceases to exist, it changes into a contingent collection of atomized individuals, of abstract units, and the result depends on a purely quantitative mechanism of counting.
>
> (Zizek, 1989, p. 157)

Elections show that power belongs to no one or can belong to anyone.

This transformation involved the decline of the role played by religion or any other transcendental source of power that claims to fill the locus of power in political life; whereas the other dimension was about providing a secular ideological content to this new modern political form (Berkes, 1998). There are two crucial points here. The first is that the politics of secularism in Turkey inclined to Islamophobia since, in order to empty the locus of power, Islam and any other transcendental source of power in politics had to be delegitimized. The other point is that, since modernization was equated with Westernization, the secularist elite tended to make Islam and Muslims the enemy in their struggle to produce a secular–nationalist political order. With its political form – the modern nation-state – and its political content – the secular–nationalist identity – Islam and Muslims functioned as the enemy. The sacred alliance between the bureaucracy and local notables deployed Islamophobia in order to further their political interests, which was to seize the state power in order to Westernize the country.

From ancient to modern politics

The basic difference between the ancient and modern political forms is found at the ontological level. In pre-modern times, political order was claimed to be the reflection of cosmic order on Earth. Its legitimacy, therefore, came from the outside, from the metaphysical world. As long as it lived up to the transcendental truth, political order was regarded as stable and healthy and those in a position of rule were considered successful in their task so long as stability was sustained. Indeed, the central task of politics was to guarantee and maintain the correspondence between the metaphysical and physical worlds (Larkins, 2010).

In Turkish–Islamic political thought and practice, this was formulated with the concept of *nizam-ı alem* (the order of universe). *Nizam-ı alem* was carried out by keeping each component of political order – the Sultan, the ruling class, and the common people – in its proper place. This was deemed to be key to render justice, which was the central concept in Turkish–Islamic political thought. The main task of the Sultan, who was regarded as the extra-political figure, was to sustain justice by arranging the relations between the ruling class (*askeriyye*) and the people (*reaya*) (İnalcık, 1958).

In this hierarchic political form, therefore, the locus of power was not empty. It was filled with certain transcendental truth and a limited number of people were claimed to have access to this truth. Moreover, the representatives of this metaphysical truth in the physical world occupied places of power. They sustained the connection between these two worlds. Hence, the Sultan had a divine right to rule, he was believed to be awarded with *kut*.[12] The Sultan was identified with power and was designed as the natural ruler, whereas the rest were relegated to the position of the ruled (İnalcık, 1958).

Secularization of politics, in principle, involved emptying the locus of power. It introduced anarchy and a new division in the political universe, a division between the state and society. This encapsulated setting politics free from any higher authority, such as religion or morality. Politics became autonomous, an independent realm with its own rules and ethics. This process of freeing politics involved delegitimizing the metaphysical world, denying its role in sociopolitical life, and emptying the locus of power by forcing the Sultan to share power with the others through introducing the parliamentary system (shifting from absolute to constitutional monarchy) or eliminating the Sultanate altogether (shifting from monarchy to republic).[13] Since there was no transcendental truth outside us, political order could not be legitimized with reference to the metaphysical world and the place of power could not be identified with the Sultan. This created the problem of finding a new source of political authority. The political order, therefore, had to turn to itself in order to sustain its own legitimacy (Flynn, 2006). An immanent source replaced the transcendental source.

Anarchic and self-organizing politics replaced hierarchy (Rasch, 2004). This immanent source was determined to be popular sovereignty or the political community itself. The people's or national interest thus had to be the ultimate source behind every decision made by the state. Popular sovereignty and national interest have become the ground for legitimacy in politics.

This process of secularization of politics in the Ottoman Empire encompassed a long time period (İnalcık, 1968). It followed a double and interacting process of de-sacralizing politics and gradually limiting and destroying the Sultanate (in 1922) and then the Caliphate (in 1924). To legitimize the de-sacralization of politics, secularist forces resorted to two discourses in order to make Islam the enemy: the culturalist and the realpolitik discourses. The culturalist line of argument took pains to assimilate Islamic history into 'universal' European history and argued that Islam shared the darkness and ignorance of the European Middle Ages, that it was something to be feared of and kept outside. Islam was claimed to be the primary obstacle and regressive force in front of both individual and collective freedom and progress (Akşin, 2018).

The realpolitik line of argument, on the other hand, asserted that Islam was the major reason why the empire lagged behind the European powers. Islam was claimed to obstruct the introduction and the application of modern ways of warring and adaptation to modern international politics (Quataert, 2013). Not to mention that Islam hindered the introduction of modern sciences and mass education, which facilitated the industrial revolution in Europe. In contrast to these anti-Islamic arguments, the proponents of Islam contended that Islam was the only legitimate source and served as the truest guide for conducting politics and that the reason why the empire lagged behind was that the state and society ceased and failed to follow the Islamic rules (Okumuş, 1999).

De-sacralization of politics was coupled with the emptying of the locus of power and transformed it into a modern political form. The first step was the limitation of the Sultan's power. In order to ensure this, secularist forces, mainly the bureaucratic class that took modern education and succumbed into the materialist culture that was prevalent in European capitals at that time, strived to transform the absolute monarchy to a constitutional monarchy in 1876 (Mardin, 2000). After this attempt failed due to the resistance by Sultan Abdulhamid II, the anti-monarchist alliance of the bureaucrats and local notables gathered forces and pressed for the second time for a transition into constitutional monarchy in 1908 (Kansu, 2017). In the run-up to 1908, Abdulhamid was called the 'Red Sultan', which denoted his rule with an iron fist, and slogans from the French revolution of 1789, 'freedom, equality, and brotherhood', were chanted on the streets.[14] The Sultan was finally toppled by a military coup and replaced with a more benign figure. Accordingly, in the post-1908 period, the Sultan lost his standing, especially after 1913 as the Committee of Union and Progress took control over the empire and ruled singlehandedly (Hanioğlu, 2001). The secular alliance, in the end, crushed the Sultanate in 1922 and proclaimed the republic in 1923. The founding fathers of the republic argued that the people was the new basis for political authority in Turkey ('Egemenlik kayıtsız şartsız milletindir!'[15]).

Finally, popular sovereignty replaced *nizam-ı alem* as the source of political authority (İnalcık, 1998).

These transformations were supposed to bring about a modern democratic form of politics where the metaphysical world played no role in politics, the locus of power was emptied of the Sultan, and the qualitative difference between the ruling and the ruled was wiped out for good. In line with republican ideals, power was supposed to become accessible to everyone, since domination was no more acceptable (Laborde and Maynor, 2008). In this new political order, no one was supposed to have the right to rule before entering into and winning the competition for power. Moreover, power was supposed to belong to no one and the place of power could only be occupied for a temporary time until the next elections through which a new government was formed (Lefort, 1988). These colossal changes were supposed to introduce the phenomenon of 'democratic' conflict and contingency into Turkish political life. Yet, after the collapse of the monarchy in 1922, a secularist autocratic regime was institutionalized. It was a republican regime in theory, but an autocratic regime in practice. Thus, the ensuing conflict was between the supporters of a secularist autocracy who tended to make Islam and Muslims the enemy and those who sought to democratize politics. This conflict took place on two fronts.

Popular sovereignty and its rivals

At first sight, the order of 1923 seemed to have institutionalized a modern democratic political structure in Turkey. Yet, in practice, Turkey's political and ideological transformation from the nineteenth century to 1923 produced an autocratic regime, whose essence was to control the state and not to share power with others (Köker, 2004). The difference between what was written and what was practiced paved the way for an inexorable struggle over the basis of political authority.

Despite the fact that the republican regime declared popular sovereignty to be the new basis of authority, the republican elite that was composed of bureaucracy and local notables struggled to base political authority on alternative sources. The discourse of popular sovereignty was used to topple the old monarchical system, although it was not institutionalized in practice. That is why the political process that took place between 1908 and 1923 is depicted as a 'liberal' revolution. (Kansu, 2008). The reason for that was that people were still loyal to Islamic ethos and making them the basis of authority was deemed counterproductive to the secular transformation in the country (Mardin, 1991). The secular elite thus often argued that the country was not ready for a democratic transition and Turkey had special conditions that did not allow for an organized popular opposition (Heper, 2006). In their mind, the country would only be ready for a democratic transition when the society lost its ties with Islamic ethos and the local symbolic world, embracing the secular world-view. Islamophobia, turning Islam and Muslims into the enemy, functioned here as a factor that hindered democratization in the country.

Accordingly, the bureaucracy has put forward the state as the basis of political authority and engaged in rendering the society ready for a democratic transition. This required the introduction and the top-down application of secularist revolutionary laws or Ataturk's codes, such as changing the alphabet from Arabic to Latin, enforcing Western style of clothing, replacing local civil laws with Western civil laws, closing down religious seminaries, dervish convents, and madrasas, rendering secular education obligatory and forbidding the pilgrimage (hadj) (Zürcher, 2004). The primary contradiction of those codes was that people's opinion was not taken into consideration. In a genuine democratic regime or a republic where popular sovereignty is the norm, one would at least expect that the government would present the reforms to people's vote in a referendum before legalizing them. However, this did not happen.

Authoritarian politics led to an autocratic political institutionalization where the locus of power was kept filled with a secular–nationalist content and the ruling and the ruled were separated on that essentialist basis. This was a real step back from the secularization of political life in the country in terms of political form. In this new regime, bearing the secular–nationalist identity or pursuing secularist politics became the new basis for the separation of the ruling from the ruled, or of the one inside from the one outside the official us. Those who bore a secular–nationalist identity were deemed to be natural members of the ruling group, whereas others were relegated to the position of the ruled. This amounted to pushing religious–conservative social groups into outside of the political community. They were targeted as the enemy of the state. Therefore, the basis of sovereignty was not the people but the secularist regime or identity. The decisions of the state were taken on the basis of the secular–nationalist identity. Those decisions were considered legitimate as long as they were in line with the secular–nationalist identity and furthered the secularization or Westernization of the country. The national interest of the state, too, was determined within the boundaries of the secular–nationalist identity (Zarakol, 2011).

This non-democratic political context produced a single-party regime. The single-party regime did not allow for multiple political parties, prevented the conduction of free and fair elections, and kept the opposition from entering the Parliament and sharing power with the government (Tunçay, 1981). Doing the reverse would mean setting politics free, rendering the sovereignty of secularist politics questionable. Therefore, the republican regime in Turkey violated the basic principle of democratic politics, which involves abiding by the principle of keeping the locus of power empty. The locus of power was filled with the secular elite gathered around the Republican People's Party (RPP). They acted as if they owned the state and the sphere of democratic politics was kept closed to the opposition. The two attempts to switch to a multi-party democratic regime in 1925 and 1930 were short lived. The Progressive Republican Party (PRP) in 1925 and the Free Party (FP) in 1930 were closed down by the regime on account of being the hub of anti-secularist politics. The societal upheavals against the secularist revolutionary laws were repressed with the same Islamophobic argument – fight against religious reactionism or obscurantism – by the

Independence Tribunals (Zürcher, 2004). For the republican regime, the threat of Islam and the old imperial regime was still alive.

However, in the 1940s, the secular alliance between the bureaucracy and local notables started to be shattered. One of the primary reasons for that was that the logic of politics and economics, despite being shaped by mundane concerns, were no more in agreement.[16] The logic of economics desired to arrange a political system in order to create economic wealth and material benefit for everyone. The logic of politics, on the other hand, sought to arrange the political system in order to further the regime's secular ideological goals, thus keeping the control of the state. The notables, who tended to act according to the logic of economics within the RPP, also saw that the regime could not sustain itself if democratization was not introduced. The notables understood democratization as opening up a sphere of freedom for people both in the realm of politics, which meant switching to a multi-party system, and in the realm of civil society, which meant loosening the state's control of economic activities.

As a result of this friction in the secular alliance, the Democratic Party (DP) was established in 1946 by local notables who broke off of the RPP. Turkey switched to a multi-party system in 1946 and the DP won the first next elections in 1950 (Karpat, 1959). DP's election motto was revolutionary: 'Enough, it's people's turn!' The DP's main strategy was to shift the basis of authority in the political system (Demirel, 2016). Despite the fact that it represented the interests of local notables and the bourgeois (although not all of them, especially the so-called 'big business' were not convinced of the necessity to ally with the people against the secular bureaucracy) in general, it did not shy away from allying with the people. It used popular sovereignty for its political interests. As a party of local notables and the petty bourgeois, DP's first choice for the basis of authority was naturally the individual or the entrepreneur, not the people. Indeed, ideologically, DP was a liberal political party, not a democratic one. Thus, 1950 started a new era in Turkish politics, an alliance between the people and the notables versus the secular bureaucracy. In other words, the politics of popular sovereignty plus individual freedom versus the bureaucratic oligarchy became the major front of political conflict. Yet, we should note that the politics of popular sovereignty or national will was always in a secondary position to the politics of individual rights and freedoms within the anti-bureaucratic oligarchy alliance.

This new alliance softened the antagonism between secular and religious–conservative politics. This softened the secularist stance towards religion in the period between 1950 and 1960. For instance, it was decided that the call to prayer (*ezan*) was to be recited in Turkish in the 1930s in the context of the politics of de-Islamization and the DP reintroduced the practice of reciting the call to prayer in Arabic. Moreover, the party took the initiative to open up theology departments in universities and to establish religious vocational schools. Again, it decided to have radio shows on religious matters and that included the recitation of Qur'an.

The secular notables and religious–conservative masses came together for a common political purpose. This common political purpose was indeed the democratization of politics. Hence, the secular–religious antagonism, which had determined Turkish politics for many decades, was replaced by a new antagonism of democracy versus authoritarianism after the 1950s. This was the strategy of the democratic opposition since then. They argued that authoritarianism was the new enemy of a democratic political order. In response, the state bureaucracy kept Islam and Muslims as the enemy and placed the left as another enemy of the regime until 1989. However, the notables understood democracy as the increase of individual rights and freedoms against the state, whereas the religious–conservative masses viewed it as the domination of the national will in politics. Even though this caused frictions and periodical dissolutions within the democratic alliance, the presence of a common rival, meaning the authoritarian bureaucracy, kept the democratic alliance floating for a long period of time.

The bureaucracy's response to the shift to the multi-party system and the election victory of the democratic alliance was to end the process of democratization by way of a military coup in 1960. One of the major justifications of the coup was that the DP had become the hub of anti-secular activities, with, for example, the re-Arabization of the call to prayer and the allowing of religious figures and symbols in the public sphere. The DP's attempt to re-include Islam and religious–conservative social sections into the political community worried the secularist forces in the bureaucracy that still kept control of the state. Accordingly, the secularist elite created a new institutional design based on bureaucratic tutelage and that limited the role and sphere of democratic politics in the aftermath of the coup. Two steps were taken in the construction of the bureaucratic tutelage. One of them was to introduce new institutions such as the Constitutional Court, the National Security Board, the Military High Court, the Supreme Military Council, the Supreme Board of Radio and Television, the Supreme Council of Judges and Lawyers, the Board of Higher Education and the Higher Military Administrative Court. This set of new institutions served as a protective belt for the republican regime under the control of secular bureaucracy. Their basic political function was to limit or contain the transformative role of civil politics over the state. For the bureaucratic establishment, the obstruction of the arrangement of politics according to popular sovereignty has always been a primary political goal.

The other step was to keep the head of civil politics down. For this purpose, the 1961 Constitution divided the legislative into two branches, where the higher branch of the Parliament was designed to be populated by members of the secularist bureaucracy, such as retired judges and military generals. The 1982 Constitution that was produced after the 1980 military intervention, on the other hand, divided the executive into two parts by empowering the President with large powers against the Prime Minister and the Cabinet. The Turkish President, who was chosen by the Parliament among the retired bureaucrats or bureaucracy-friendly senior politicians, was considered to be a check-and-balance over civil politics within the institution of politics (Karpat, 2007).

When these two steps failed to contain politics or when civil politics failed to play its special role of providing stability for the continuation of the bureaucratic tutelage, either the military directly intervened into politics – with the 1960, 1971 and 1980 military coups – or the judiciary stepped in to neutralize politicians or political parties – with, for example, the closing down of the ruling Islamist Welfare Party (WF) in January 1998 by the Constitutional Court – which were perceived to cross the red lines of the regime and were shaped around the protection of the secularist republican order.

In all these military or judiciary interventions, one could observe the common accusations that civil politics led Turkey back to the darkness of the Islamist past or losing national independence since the Islamists or the Sultan were accused of allying with the occupying forces against the national forces during the War of Independence. These two fears based on Islamophobia have always been fed into the public's mind in order to garner public support for bureaucratic interventions into civil politics and to keep the public in line with the regime at other times. The secularist civil society played a significant role both in the 1960 and 1997 interventions ('Bir Dakika Karanlık ve 28 Şubat', 2014).

Secular–nationalist identity

The other front was over defining the political community or nation since, at least in principle, the basis of political authority was the people. To hold on to power, the republican elite had to do more than champion the bureaucratic authority against the authority of the national will or popular sovereignty. They had to hegemonize the social realm by producing the most inclusive identity, or the conception of political community. The political community that the republican elite based its rule on was constructed around a secular–nationalist identity.

The production of this secular–nationalist political community had several moments. The first moment encapsulated the integration of Turkey into the modern Western civilization and cutting off its ties with the Islamic civilization. One of the strategies for that involved the denial of the existence of multiple civilizations or degrading other civilizations, including the Islamic one, to particularity in the face of Western superiority or universality. The motto of that goal was 'to catch up with the modern civilization' (Belge, 2009). This led to the portrayal of Islam as belonging to the pre-modern past and questioning its viability in modern times. In this way, the republic, or modern Turkey, was cleansed of Islamic elements. If Islam could not belong to the modern times, modern Turkey was not argued to have or need to have ties with Islam.

Another strategy to integrate Turkey into the Western world was constructing a new past, which was bereft of Islam, for modern Turkey (Bora, 2015). This involved the de-emphasis on Turkey's Islamic past and the discovery and reinforcement of the pre-Islamic history of the Turks. This secularist narrative had different versions. One of them was that, in pre-Islamic times the Turks were claimed to have ancestral ties with the Sumerians, whom were also claimed to be the ancestors of modern (Western) civilization. Thus, according to this narrative, the Turks and the Westerners used to be together in the past, although the Turks deviated as they entered into contact with the Arabs and converted to

Islam. Now, the Turks were thus returning to their real home, joining with their Western brothers.

The second moment was to produce Turkey's difference on the basis of Western universality. In the past, the Ottoman Empire claimed to represent the universal by being the real heir of the Roman Empire (Necipoğlu, 1989). Thus, the Ottomans tended to particularize European powers by locating themselves at the position of universality. Starting with the seventeenth century, as they weakened, the Ottomans started to view the European powers as their equal. The difference was in general produced on the basis of being two different yet equal civilizations. From the nineteenth century onwards, the empire sought to enter into the European international society in order to get protection, especially against the increasing Russian threat. This attempt, which involved admitting half-heartedly the European superiority, failed. After 1923, the universality of the West was admitted wholeheartedly and it was reciprocated by the European powers in the Treaty of Lausanne (1924). Turkey was admitted as an independent sovereign state and a member of modern law of nations (Khadduri, 1956). It started to produce its difference on the basis of being an autonomous sovereign nation-state. In short, from the empire to the republic, the mode of difference with the outside was demoted from the level of civilization to the level of nation-state.

This new political community was a totality of three corresponding realities that were supposed to be constantly constructed through performative actions of the nation-state. This is because borders function very differently in the world of nation-states than the world of empires (Kratochwil, 1986). The borders are the existing limit points of the empire. They are rather the furthest post before the next move of enlargement. The borders are a gate to the outside world, not a wall that is used in the protection of the inside from the outside. Thus, for an empire, the outside is not absolute; it is rather contingent and relative. The whole world and human beings, in principle, belong to the empire, thus the whole world and humanity are perceived as the inside of the empire.

The nation-state differs significantly in this respect. For a nation-state, the outside world is absolutely outside. Only the territory and human beings under its sovereign jurisdiction are considered as inside. The boundaries are final. They are rather the wall against which national territories and citizens should be protected. For that reason, a nation-state has to construct two corresponding realities, one within its territories and the other in the outside: the national and the international.

These realities are to be constructed on the basis of a particular identity. Without an identity or ideology, the difference between inside and outside cannot be determined. The Turkish nation-state constructed these realities on the basis of the secular–national identity. In the domestic realm, the secular–nationalist nation claimed to represent the metaphorical totality of the society (Laclau, 2014). This hegemonic move led to two distinct policies. One was to integrate the people into this political whole by assimilating them through secularist revolutionary laws (Yıldız, 2007). This involved an enforced identity change. This policy of assimilation into secular–nationalist identity was met with strong popular reaction, especially under the single-party rule. With the failure of that reaction, the religious–conservative groups retreated behind their own communal boundaries. Here, they established religious communities and gave priority to their communal ties rather than their citizenship status. The state and society in general were deemed as alien places.[17] In order to re-establish ties with the society, the state put the so-called Turkish–Islamic synthesis into practice after the 1980 military coup (Taşkın, 2006). This policy tried to hegemonize Islam ('rationalizing Islam' was one of the major arguments in that context) within a nationalistic discourse and brought religious–conservative sections of the society into the 'national' political community (Çetinsaya, 1999). One of the basic reasons behind this policy was the presence of a common enemy, the communist Soviets, on the outside and also the strengthening of the leftist politics in the 1970s.

The other policy was to marginalize and make those people who resisted the policy of assimilation the enemy. The so-called 28 February Process in 1997 was a perfect example of how Islam and the religious–conservative sections of the society were made the enemy. The National Security Council gave a memorandum to the coalition government on 28 February 1997 that reminded the secularist red lines of the republican regime. The latter revolved around the protection of secularist revolutionary laws that were listed in the 174. Article of the Constitution as follows: (1) Unification of education under a secular institutional framework, (2) wearing a Western-style hat, (3) closing down of the Darvish convents, madrasas and tombs, (4) enforcing the conduct of marriage act only by state officials, (5) admission of international (Western) numbers, (6) admission of the Latin alphabet, (7) abolishment of traditional epithets and titles (such as *efendi*, *bey*, *paşa*) and (8) prohibition of wearing special costumes such as religious gown and turban by the imams and other personnel of religious affairs. The purpose of these laws was said to be 'uplifting Turkey to the level of modern civilization and protecting the secularist character of the Turkish Republic'.[18]

The memorandum also presented a to-do list for the incumbent coalition government of Islamist Welfare Party (WP) and the centre-right True Path Party (TPP). This list included, among others, not to challenge the revolutionary laws, closing down of the Darvish convents that conflict with the revolutionary laws, not to encourage those who wear religious gown and turban, advising to bring back the 163 Article of the 1982 Constitution (which was lifted by Turgut Özal in 1991) that consisted of punishing those who resorted to a religious discourse in politics, readjusting the education policies according to the law on the unification of education under a secular institutional framework, extending the compulsory education from five to eight years (which aimed at undermining the secondary section of religious vocational schools), closing down some of the religious vocational schools, containing the infiltration of 'fundamentalist' religious persons into the state, controlling the building of mosques, preventing the recruitment of those who were suspended from the military over accusations of anti-secularist activities in municipality services, closely monitoring the financial institutions and foundations under the control of religious orders, monitoring the messages of TV channels and radio stations that use an anti-secularist language to be kept in line with the Constitution, and increasing the control over Iran's activities that aim at destabilizing Turkey's secular regime and taking the necessary measures to contain them ('28 Şubat Kararları', 2002).

As a result of that military intervention in 28 February, many female students wearing the headscarf were not allowed to enter into universities and were forced to leave their education incomplete. Many religious–conservative people were blacklisted and were prohibited from ever getting a job in the state. Moreover, many financial institutions and civil society organizations were kept under pressure, if not closed down for good. This quasi-military coup was supported by secularist civil society organizations with slogans such as 'one minute of darkness for eternal light'.[19] All of these Islamophobic policies that purged Islam and religious–conservative people from the political community were claimed to bring the state back to its factory settings after years of management of the country with a counter-revolutionary perspective since the 1940s.

On the outside, there are two realities. One is regional, and the other international. The Turkish nation-state boosted a Westphalian regional order in its vicinity. This is because this state-centred order served to shape the imperial borders into nation-state borders. The boundaries in the region became absolute, providing a clear-cut division between the inside and the outside of the state. The transformation of boundaries through the Westphalian order was necessary in order to keep the secular regime floating. By recognizing other Muslim societies as distinct nations and equal sovereign entities, the traditional concept of Ummah, which stipulated the unity of Muslims, was discredited (Sayyid, 1997). The Westphalian order guaranteed not only military security but also the ontological security of each nation-state and the post-imperial nationalist regimes in the region. Moreover, the Westphalian order established space for the Turkish state to create a distance from the Arabs, whom, in the secular Turkish mind, represented the 'backward' Islamic civilization. Relations with the Arabs were thus always kept underdeveloped and distant (Aykan, 1994).

The Turkish nation-state also backed a Western-dominated international system. The reason for that was not only military security, but also the ontological security of the Turkish state. The existence of the Turkish state was tied to the Western-dominated international system. The Turkish state allied with the West against the Soviets to sustain its national security, but that alliance was also stipulated in order to reproduce its secular–nationalist identity (Bozdağlıoğlu, 2004). Indeed, the Turkish state, or rather the republican regime, got its legitimacy from the universality of the Western civilization. The decline of the West would always jeopardize the security of the secular–national conception of the nation in domestic politics. This was the case in the 1990s when postmodern ideologies and globalization became dominant. The questioning of modernity and the universality of the West put the secular regime in Turkey in a deep crisis (Erdoğan, 2009). The Turkish state in the Kemalist era, therefore, followed Western interests in international politics, as long as the Western powers did not violate or disregard Turkey's sovereignty and national existence as observed in the Cyprus problem (Uzer, 2011).

Conclusion

Islamophobia was central to the construction and reproduction of the political community in Turkey for about a century. There were two sub-periods in the golden age of the politics of Islamophobia. The first was the transition from the empire to the nation-state and from the monarchical regime to the republican regime. The second was the construction and reproduction of a secular–nationalist nation-state. In the first period, Islamophobia was utilized to empty the locus of power from its dynastic content and demolish the empire. In the second period, Islamophobia was deployed to create a nation-state on the basis of a secular–nationalist identity. This identity led to a secular–nationalist society in the domestic realm, backed by a Westphalian regional order and a Western-centric global order in its outside.

This secular–nationalist political order, which attempted to make Islam and Muslims the enemy or as its outside, was opposed by the democratic alliance that was formed by religious–conservative masses and some sections of the bourgeois. These political forces opposed the authoritarianism of the secularist republican order and struggled to institutionalize democratic politics after the 1940s. However, they failed to institutionalize a democratic regime and dislocate the republican elite from the state until the 2000s. The republican elite carried out the politics of Islamophobia very skilfully to push back on the democratic alliance.

After the 1990s, the politics of Islamophobia started to backfire due to domestic and international developments. In the domestic realm, the religious–conservative periphery poured into the cities and became very influential in politics. Whereas in the international realm, the international society, and especially the European Union, increased their pressure on the autocratic republican regime, criticizing its radical secularist (and also anti-Kurdish) policies. The regional instability, which was triggered by the collapse of neighbouring states, also made it very difficult for the secularist Turkey to continue its traditional foreign policy in the region. All these factors paved the way for the dislocation of the republican elite from the state, and thus the decline of the politics of Islamophobia in Turkey in the following decade.

Notes

1 Yet the history of this phenomenon goes back to the end of the nineteenth century, see Bravo Lopez (2011).
2 Attempts to create a 'European Islam' is one of the ways of hegemonizing Islam and Muslims. See Enes Bayraklı, Farid Hafez and Leonard Faytre, 'Engineering a European Islam: An Analysis of Attempts to Domesticate Muslims in Austria, France and Germany', *Insight Turkey*, Vol. 20, No. 3, 2018, pp. 131–156.
3 The notorious 163. Article of 1982 Constitution was providing the basis for those anti-democratic decisions. 'Türkiye'de kapatılmış partiler', *NTV*, 11 December 2009.
4 The French law on secularity and conspicuous religious symbols in schools bans wearing conspicuous religious symbols in French public or government-operated primary and secondary schools. 'French Secularism on Trial', *New York Times*, 2 December 2013.

5 See Anghie (2005) for a critique of this categorical thinking on international order.
6 In politics the friend is a social category on which different political actors come together on the basis of sharing ideational and material interests. According to this view, we have same identity and same interests with our friends. See Wendt, 1999.
7 For instance, when Turkey's relations with the Western powers deteriorate, the secularists got alarmed and put forward the argument that Turkey's axis is shifting in foreign policy. 'TESEV'in bulgularıyla eksen kayması', *Habertürk*, 15 June 2010.
8 'Muasır medeniyetler seviyesine ulaşmak' (catching up with the modern civilization), which implies integration with the West or Westernization, is the motto of the republican elite. See Belge, 2009, pp. 29–43.
9 This process of provincialization cannot be limited to the Islamic world. All non-European civilizations were subjected to the same cultural–political process. See Chakrabarty, 2000.
10 That's why anarchy is the constitutive concept of modern international relations, see Morgenthau, 1948; Waltz, 1979.
11 This is the quintessential character of modern democratic politics. See Lefort, 1988, p. 17.
12 The meaning of *kut* is very close to Aristotle's concept of political virtue or Machiavelli's concept of virtù. See Inalcık, 1993, pp. 1–18.
13 Parliamentarism in essence added a new distinction, which is the government and the opposition, to the old distinction of the ruling and the ruled. It served to include the opposition into power. Alongside the periodical elections, Parliament, as another modern political institution, helped empty the locus of power by dividing power between the government and the opposition. See Luhmann, 1990.
14 The secularist forces added 'justice' to those three concepts. However, in time the secularists ceased to refer to justice in politics.
15 That means 'sovereignty belongs to the people'.
16 The other major reason was Turkey's relations with the US. In the post-Second World War period, Turkey had to carry out some of the basic requirements of democratic politics in order to be considered a member of the Atlantic Alliance against the Soviets.
17 Necip Fazıl Kısakürek, who is one of the leading intellectual figures in Islamist politics, cultivated these themes of alienation with the existing political order. See Duran, 2005, pp. 129–156.
18 See the Turkish Constitution of 1982, www.tbmm.gov.tr/anayasa/anayasa_2011.pdf.
19 In those demonstrations many secularists, among other things, put off their lights for a minute at nine in the evening to display their displeasure with the government. See 'Sürekli aydınlık için bir dakika karanlık', *Bianet*, 9 December 2014.

Bibliography

28 Şubat kararları, (2002, 28 February), Bianet.
Akşin, S. (2018). *Kısa Türkiye Tarihi*. İstanbul: Türkiye İş Bankası.
Anghie, A. (2005). *Imperialism, Sovereignty and the Making International Law*. Cambridge: Cambridge University Press.
Atabaki, T. and Zürcher, E. J. (Eds) (2004). *Men of Order: Authoritarian Modernization under Atatürk and Reza Shah*. London and New York: I. B. Tauris.
Aykan, M. B. (1994). *Turkey's Role in the Organization of the Islamic Conference, 1960–1992*. New York: Vantage Press.
Bayraklı, E. and Hafez, F. (Eds) (2018). *European Islamophobia Report 2017*. İstanbul: SETA.
Bayraklı, E., Hafez, F. and Faytre, L. (2018). Engineering a European Islam: An Analysis of Attempts to Domesticate Muslims in Austria, France and Germany. *Insight Turkey*, 20(3).

Belge, M. (2009). *Mustafa Kemal ve Kemalizm. Modern Türkiye'de Siyasi Düşünce: Kemalizm.* İstanbul: İletişim.

Berkes, N. (1998). *The Development of Secularism in Turkey.* London: C. Hurst & Co.

Bir dakika karanlık ve 28 Şubat, (2014, December), Bianet.

Bleich, E. (2011) What is Islamophobia and How Much is There? Theorizing and Measuring an Emerging Comparative Concept. *American Behavioral Scientist,* 55(2).

Bora, T. (2015). *Medeniyet Kaybı: Milliyetçilik ve Faşizm Üzerine Yazılar.* İstanbul: Birikim.

Bozdağlıoğlu, Y. (2004). *Turkish Foreign Policy and Turkish Identity.* London and New York: Routledge.

Bravo Lopez, F. (2011). Towards a Definition of Islamophobia: Approximations of the Early Twentieth Century. *Ethnic and Racial Studies,* 34(4).

Çetinsaya, G. (1999). Rethinking Nationalism and Islam: Some Preliminary Notes on the Roots of 'Turkish-Islamic Synthesis'. *Modern Turkish Political Thought,* 89(3–4).

Chakrabarty, D. (2000). *Provincializing Europe: Postcolonial Thought and Historical Difference.* Princeton, NJ: Princeton University Press.

Cooper, R. (2003). *The Breaking of Nations: Order and Chaos in Twenty-First Century,* New York: Groove Press.

Demirel, T. (2016). *Türkiye'nin Uzun On Yılı: Demokrat Parti ve 27 Mayıs Darbesi.* İstanbul: İstanbul Bilgi Üniversitesi.

Duran, B. (2005). *Cumhuriyet Dönemi İslamcılığı, Modern Türkiye'de Siyasi Düşünce – 6: İslamcılık,* İstanbul: İletişim.

Elahi, F. and Khan, O. (Eds) (2017). *Islamophobia: Still a Challenge for Us All.* London: Runnymede.

Erdoğan, N. (2009). *Neo-Kemalizm, Organik Bunalım ve Hegemonya, Türkiye'de Modern Siyasi Düşünce: Kemalizm.* İstanbul: İletişim.

Flynn, B. (2006). *The Philosophy of Claude Lefort: Interpreting the Political.* Evanston, IL: Northwestern University Press.

French Secularism on Trial, (2013, 2 December), *New York Times.*

Gottschalk, P. and Greenberg, G. (2008). *Islamophobia: Making Muslims the Enemy.* Lanham, MD: Rowman and Littlefield Pub.

Hanioğlu, Ş. (2001). *Preparation for a Revolution, the Young Turks, 1902–1908.* Oxford: Oxford University Press.

Heper, M. (2006). *Türkiye'de Güçlü Devlet Geleneği.* İstanbul: Doğu Batı.

Hobbes, T. (1962). *Leviathan.* Oxford: Oxford University Press.

Huntington, S. P. (1993). *Clash of Civilizations. Foreign Affairs,* 72(3).

İnalcık, H. (1941). *Tanzimat Nedir?. Dil ve Tarih Coğrafya Fakültesi Dergisi.* Tarih Araştırmaları Cildi, s. 237–263.

İnalcık, H. (1958). Osmanlı Padişahı. *Ankara Üniversitesi SBF Dergisi,* 13(4).

İnalcık, H. (1993). Turkish and Iranian political theories and traditions in Kutadgu Bilig. In İnalcik, H. (Ed.), *The Middle East and the Balkans under the Ottoman Empire: Essays on Economy and Society.* Bloomington: Indiana University Turkish Studies and Turkish Ministry of Culture Joint Series.

İnalcık, H. (1998). *Türkiye Cumhuriyeti ve Osmanlı. Doğu Batı.* Ankara, s. 9–22.

Kansu, A. (2008). *Hürriyet, Musavat, Uhuvvet, Adalet – 100. Yıldönümünde 1908 Devrimi'ni Anlamaya Çalışmak.* Toplumsal Tarih.

Kansu, A. (2017). *1908 Devrimi.* İstanbul: İletişim.

Karpat, K. H. (1959). *Turkey's Politics: The Transition to a Multi-Party System.* Princeton, NJ: Princeton University Press.

Karpat, K. H. (2007). *Türkiye'de Siyasal Sistemin Evrimi*. İstanbul: İmge.

Khadduri, M. (1986). Islam and the Modern Law of Nations. *American Journal of International Law*, 50(2).

Köker, L. (2004). *Modernleşme, Kemalizm ve Demokrasi*. İstanbul: İletişim.

Kratochwil, F. (1986). Of Systems, Boundaries, and Territoriality: An Inquiry into the Formation of the State System. *World Politics*, 39(1).

Laborde, C. and Maynor, J. (2008). *Republicanism and Political Theory*. Oxford: Blackwell.

Laclau, E. (2014). *The Rhetorical Foundations of Society*, London: Verso.

Laclau, E. and Mouffe, C. (1985). *Hegemony and Socialist Strategy: Towards a Radical Democratic Politics*. London and New York: Verso.

Larkins, J. (2010). *From Hierarchy to Anarchy: Territory and Politics before Westphalia*. New York: Palgrave Macmillan.

Lefort, C. (1988). *Democracy and Political Theory*. Cambridge: Polity Press.

Luhmann, N. (1990). *Political Theory in the Welfare State*. Berlin: Walter de Gruyter.

Mardin, Ş. (1973). Center-Periphery Relations: A Key to Turkish Politics? *Daedalus*, 102(1).

Mardin, Ş. (1991). The Just and the Unjust. *Daedalus*, 120(3).

Mardin, Ş. (2000). *The Genesis of Young Ottoman Thought*. Syracuse, NY: Syracuse University Press.

Merkel Says Still against Turkey Joining the EU, (2015, 8 October), Reuters.

Morgan, G. and Poynting, S. (2012). *Global Islamophobia: Muslims and Moral Panic in the West*. London and New York: Routledge.

Morgenthau, H. J. (1948). *Politics among Nations: The Struggle for Power and Peace*. New York: Alfred A. Knopf.

Morgenthau, H. J. (2012). *The Concept of the Political*. New York and London: Palgrave Macmillan.

Mouffe, C. (2000). For an Agonistic Model of Democracy. In Sullivan, N. E. (Ed.), *Political Theory in Transition* (pp. 113–130). New York and London: Routledge.

Necipoğlu, G. (1989). Süleyman the Magnificent and the Representation of Power in the Context of Ottoman-Hapsburg-Papal Rivalry. *The Art Bulletin*, 71(3).

Ogan, C., Willnat, L., Pennington, R. and Bashir, M. (2014). The Rise of Anti-Muslim Prejudice: Media and Islamophobia in Europe and the United States. *The International Communication Gazette*, 76(1).

Okumuş, E. (1999). İbn Haldun ve Osmanlı'da Çöküş Tartışmaları. *Divan*, 1.

Parla, T. (1995). *Türkiye'de Siyasal Kültürün Resmi Kaynakları – 3: Kemalist Tek Parti İdeolojisi ve CHP'nin Altı Ok'u*. İstanbul: İletişim.

Quataert, D. (2005). *The Ottoman Empire, 1700–1922*. Cambridge: Cambridge University Press.

Rasch, W. (2004). *Sovereignty and Its Discontents: On the Primacy of Conflict and the Structure of the Political*. London: Birkbeck Law Press.

Sakallıoğlu, Ü. C. (1994) Kemalism, Hyper-nationalism and Islam in Turkey. *History of European Ideas*, 18(2).

Sayyid, S. (1997). *A Fundamental Fear: Eurocentrism and the Emergence of Islamism*. London: Zed Books.

Schmitt, C. (2000). State Ethics and the Pluralist State. In Jacopson, A. J. and Schlink, B. (Eds), *Weimar: A Jurisprudence of Crisis*. Berkeley, CA: University of California Press.

Schmitt, C. (2007). *The Concept of the Political*. Chicago and London: The University of Chicago Press.

Shively, K. (2005). Religious Bodies and the Secular State: The Merve Kavakci Affair. *Journal of Middle East Women's Studies*, 1(3).

Shryock, A. (Ed.) (2010). *Islamophobia/Islamophilia: Beyond the Politics of Enemy and Friend*. Bloomington, IN: Indiana University Press.

Sürekli aydınlık için bir dakika karanlık, (2014, 9 December), Bianet.

Taşkın, Y. (2006). *Muhafazakar Bir Proje Olarak Türk-İslam Sentezi, Modern Türkiye'de Siyasi Düşünce – 5: Muhafazakarlık*. İstanbul: İletişim.

Taylor, C. (1984). Hegel: History and Politics. In Sandel, M. (Ed.), *Liberalism and its Critic*. New York: New York University Press.

TESEV'in bulgularıyla eksen kayması, (2010, June 2015), Habertürk.

Tunçay, M. (1981). *Türkiye Cumhuriyeti'nde Tek-Parti Yönetiminin Kurulması 1923–93*. Ankara: Yurt.

Türkiye'de kapatılmış partiler, (2009, 11 December), NTV.

Uzer, U. (2011). *Identity and Turkish Foreign Policy: The Kemalist Influence in Cyprus and the Caucasus*. London: I. B. Tauris.

Walker, R. B. J. (1993). *Inside/Outside: International Relations as Political Theory*. Cambridge: Cambridge University Press.

Walt, S. M. (1987). *The Origins of Alliances*. Ithaca and London: Cornell University Press.

Waltz, K. (1979). *Theory of International Politics*. Reading, MA: Addison-Wesley.

Wendt, A. (1999) *Social Theory of International Politics*. Cambridge: Cambridge University Press.

Yıldız, A. (2007). *Ne Mutlu Türküm Diyebilene*. İstanbul: İletişim.

Zarakol, A. (2011). *After Defeat: How the East Learned to Live with the West*. Cambridge: Cambridge University Press.

Zizek, S. (1989). *The Sublime Object of Ideology*. London: Verso.

Zürcher, E. J. (2004). *Turkey: A Modern History*. London and New York: I. B. Tauris.

6 Islamophobia in satirical magazines

A comparative case study of *Penguen* in Turkey and *Charlie Hebdo* in France

Müşerref Yardım and Amina Easat-Daas

Introduction

In September 2005 the Danish newspaper, *Jyllands Posten* published 12 Islamophobic cartoons as part of their editorial spread that discussed criticisms of Islam, including an alleged sense of self-censorship and limitation of the freedom of speech for fear of offending Muslims. These images published alongside the editorial predominantly featured the Prophet Muhammad and were largely provocative in nature and this was felt in Denmark and beyond. The cartoons were reprinted by other media institutions across Europe, including *Le Monde, France Soir, Libération* and *Charlie Hebdo* in France, and in the predominantly Muslim world; *Al Fagr* in Egypt, *Al Shihan* and *Al Mehwar* in Jordan, and *Shams* in Saudi Arabia. Thus, these Islamophobic acts were not exclusive to the Western world, but instead permeate what are typically seen as Muslim countries. Nonetheless, given their offensive and inflammatory character, the cartoons sparked controversy among Muslims across the world. It is estimated that protests against the publication of these images lasted well up to February 2006 (Kublitz, 2010).

The satirical images used by *Jyllands Posten* drew on stereotypical Orientalist tropes, such as those that frame Muslims as the 'Other', intolerant and non-liberal. Allegedly these criticisms of Muslims were borne out of a presumed Muslim inability to comprehend the humour of the images. The cartoons emphasized the subaltern nature of Muslim populations in Europe and beyond (Bonde, 2007, pp. 35–37). The use of satire as a means of emphasizing the alterity of Muslims and Islam is not a new phenomenon, rather examples of such practices can be seen as far back as in Dante's *Divine Comedy*, within which central figures in Islam are damned with other 'deviant' characters (Palacios, 1919).

The use of humour and satire as an Islamophobic tool is effective in that it implies, rather than overtly states, the diametrically opposed and 'Otherized' construction of Muslims and Islam. Furthermore, in its assertion of all that is 'other', these satirical publications (re)affirm the perceived image of the Western self; satire becomes a subtle expression of societal norms and expectations beyond those which are explicitly stated. Such satirical imagery has somewhat become a mirror of time in its ability to represent history, heritage and political agendas of the society in question (Akıner and Mencet, 2016, p. 190, Yardımcı, 2010, p. 1). The images have a speedy and dramatic effect (Kar, 1999, pp. 19–22). In short satirical cartoons offer collective critical messages and have clear implicit functions in the sociological sense (Okutan, 2013, p. 9).

Moreover, the exponential growth of the internet and technology has facilitated an evolution in the consumption of mass media material. Satirical cartoons that were once limited to circulation via print media only are now routinely shared across social media platforms and thus have a vastly increased reach. In this regard, and in conjunction with reasoning discussed further in this chapter, it is apparent that comparatively studying the role of satirical magazines in France and Turkey represents a timely and necessary site of enquiry.

The publication and reprinting of the Danish Islamophobic cartoons was justified and legitimized under the banner of satire, freedom of speech and freedom of expression. For example, in the wake of the Danish cartoon affair the European Union issued a parliamentary text expressing its support for *Jyllands Posten* quoting freedom of expression as a central value of the European Union (Résolution du Parlement Européen, 2006). Essentially, rather than problematizing the Islamophobic content of the Danish images, the European Union parliamentary statement gave a *carte-blanche* to those, both in the West and the Muslim world, wishing to publish copy-cat Islamophobic imagery.

Satirical magazines, such as *Charlie Hebdo* in France and *Penguen* in Turkey, among others, have responded to this call in subsequent years by publishing material that incites anti-Muslim and anti-Islamic rhetoric and action. As such, this contribution seeks to specifically establish and compare the nature of Islamophobia in these two nationally leading publications, *Charlie Hebdo* and *Penguen*.

The French language publication, *Charlie Hebdo*, was founded in 1970 and publishes typically non-conformist material, critical of politics, current affairs and notwithstanding, religion. Although the publication had a hiatus between 1981 and 1992, *Charlie Hebdo* boasted its highest circulation figures in 2015, amassing a staggering 7 million copies following the attacks it faced (Chazan 2018). The magazine has a strong French secular positioning (one that is notably distinct from Anglophone understandings of the term). Similarly, *Charlie Hebdo* frames itself as being extreme left in terms of its political leanings and as having an anti-racist orientation. However, these self-identifications by the magazine have been repeatedly brought into question. The problematization has been especially apparent in the literature that emerged following the January 2015 terror attacks on the publication headquarters and employees (central to this chapter, is the notion that *Charlie Hebdo* asserts strong Islamophobic tendencies, apparent in the material that it publishes).

Similarly, Turkish satirical publication *Penguen* seeks to amalgamate political stance and humour, with varying degrees of what may be perceived as success. The illustrative language used by *Penguen* in both political and social criticism shows its limited restraint in the use of sacred symbols. For example, in a regular column entitled 'Compulsory Religious Education', based on answering the incoming questions by a grandfather figure, *Penguen* makes light of religious symbols. In general, cartoons using religious symbols include explicit or implicit messages through elements such as mosques, rosaries, beards and headscarves. In particular, humour objectifies religious artefacts. Rather than being perceived as humorous, among the religious the images provoke offence, which on occasion even leads to protest or the seeking of legal redress. Conversely, when there is limited public protest, condemnation or judicial sanctions, objectification of the religious goes unnoticed by many (Okutan, 2013, pp. 20–21). In a nutshell, the magazine *Penguen* is implicitly embedded within the 'us versus them' dichotomy on the flawed axis of 'West/East'. We define the position of *Penguen* as a form of 'auto-Orientalism' and Islamophobic.

In his seminal 1978 text, Orientalism, Said describes the 'Orient' as follows:

> The Orient was almost a European invention, and had been since antiquity a place of romance, exotic beings, haunting memories and landscapes, remarkable experiences.... The Orient is not only adjacent to Europe; it is also the place of Europe's greatest and richest and oldest colonies, the source of its civilizations and languages, its cultural contestant, and one of its deepest and most recurring images of the other. In addition, the Orient has helped to define Europe (or the West) as its contrasting image, idea, personality, experience.
>
> (Said, 1978, pp. 9–10)

Thus, we see that the Orient and Orientalism stem from a perceived exoticism and 'otherness' of the Muslim and Eastern world. Yet, he goes on to explain that this oppositional construction is illusory, rather the Orient, its cultures, languages and ideas feed into the very base construction of the West (Said, 1978, p. 10). The myth of Oriental 'otherness' however is maintained in order to legitimize the subjugation and colonialization of the East. Central to this chapter, and contrary to the interrelated realities of cultures, Orientalism typically focuses on the external Western gaze on the Orient, its peoples and practices. In this chapter, via the consideration of *Penguen* in Turkey, we further problematize the Western gaze and argue that attitudes that previously emanated from the West may now also be found in traditionally Muslim societies. Furthermore, we consider Orientalism, be it from the Muslim or non-Muslim societies, to be a significant and influential factor in the nature of Islamophobia seen today across the globe.

Our rationale behind this comparative case study is based on two central hypotheses, first, we assert that in spite of dramatically differing trajectories, the nature of Islamophobia across the world is increasingly converging. Notwithstanding, although we adopt a predominantly convergence theory-based approach, we recognize the significant role and influence of context-specific factors in the production of Islamophobia.

Furthermore, we argue that Western Orientalist tropes dominate this increasingly proliferating global anti-Muslim discourse, thus there is a Western ideological hegemony. Similar Islamophobic ideas are apparent in political arenas, cultural norms and media, especially satirical magazines. This convergence in anti-Muslim discourses penetrates both the traditional, and flawed, binary geo-graphically and ideologically 'Western' and 'non-Western' societies. In short, like other contributors to this volume, we assert that Islamophobia is not simply a Western phenomenon, rather it is non-geographically bound and therefore can be located in traditionally Muslim societies.

While the assertion of an increasingly global Islamophobia and our problema-tization of Western and non-Western cultural binaries might pave the way between any number of cases, our rationale behind seeking to comparatively analyse the nature of Islamophobic rhetoric in *Charlie Hebdo* and *Penguen* stems from the influence of French culture, and especially French secularism, on Turkish society. This French influence became particularly apparent during the establishment of the Turkish Republic in 1923 and the strength of this influence has evolved over time throughout Turkish modern history. Notwithstanding, the French influence on Turkey has also shaped modes of anti-Muslim prejudice in the country. It is our central argument that the parallels between French and Turkish Islamophobic discourses are especially apparent in satirical magazines, and that furthermore these parallels emerge among elite subsections of Turkish society, rather than broadly being adopted across the nation.

In this contribution, we begin by presenting an overview of the nature of Islamophobia in *Charlie Hebdo*, followed by an original and in-depth discussion of state of Islamophobia in *Penguen*. Finally, the chapter concludes with the comparison of the two cases and asserts that there is significant convergence between the nature of Islamophobic tropes instrumentalized within *Charlie Hebdo* and *Penguen*. Furthermore, these tropes are both informed by Orientalist ideologies.

Islamophobia and *Charlie Hebdo*: a background

The French weekly, *Charlie Hebdo*, is widely acknowledged in popular culture for its Islamophobic orientations. Furthermore the Islamophobic tropes it repro-duces, from Orientalist cartoons or crude drawings of the Prophet, do not represent novel forms of Islamophobia, rather *Charlie Hebdo's* Islamophobic tradition is seen as imitation, thus meaning that *Charlie Hebdo* is nothing more than an Islamophobic mouthpiece in an already crowded media sphere.

There is no shortage of imagery from within the publication that projects Islam and Muslims as being backward or intellectually inferior to the hegemonic French culture, be it through the visual representation of Muslim males as aggressive tyrants, creating moral and physical threat and therefore national panic, or the portrayal of veiled Muslim women being hyper-fertile thus placing an undue demographic and economic burden on the nation.[1]

In sum, Islam and Muslim identity are seen to be markers of moral, demo-graphic and economic threat. Such connotations have Orientalist and imperialist foundations but highlight the bases of contemporary, Western European Islamo-phobia. The images employed by *Charlie Hebdo* are often highly gendered and typically place veiled women or bearded men at the centre. The images rely on provocation and sensationalism and do little to foster inter-community relationships in France, where already given its turbulent colonial past, France's relationship with its Muslims can often be described as strained.

Yet, in spite of the less than subtle nature of such imagery, *Charlie Hebdo* contests being labelled as Islamophobic, in much the same way it disputes the allegations of being xenophobic or anti-religious more generally. Instead the publication self-proclaims an extreme left identity and dismisses those who criticize it or its humour as simply not being capable of understanding French culture, humour and values.

In January 2015, the *Charlie Hebdo* Parisian headquarters faced heinous and unjustifiable terror attacks, which resulted in 12 fatalities and left 11 injured. The abhorrent attacks were alleged to have been spurred on in retaliation to the Islamophobic nature of the publication. The events of January 2015 fuelled a wider anti-Muslim and Islamophobic response across the globe. In the period following the attacks, the French Islamophobia monitoring and campaigning organization the *Collectif Contre L'Islamophobie en France* (CCIF) reported an increase in Islamophobic hate crime reported to their organization. This spike in Islamophobic hate crimes arose in spite of widespread condemnation by Muslims in France and across the world. Furthermore, such increases in Islamophobic violence appear to be commonplace following major terror attacks.

Beyond the direct physical and verbal aggressions towards Muslims, Muslim sites of worship and those presumed to be Muslim, wider and potentially more harmful discourses were at play; in the period that followed the attacks worldwide proclamations of *Je Suis Charlie* came to the fore, but what did it mean? Numerous scholars have attempted to grapple with this very question (based on these articles, along with our own insights we would argue that, contrary to popular arguments that these global expressions were synonymous with freedom of expression, in part, worldwide identification of *Je Suis Charlie* contributed to 'Othering' Muslim populations, in that Muslims are framed as a monolith that is inherently opposed to these aforementioned values).

This oppositional framing of Muslim communities is both flawed and arose in spite of French and European Muslims, among others, openly speaking out against the attacks committed on *Charlie Hebdo*. Fassin (2015) problematizes popular reaction following the attacks in stating

> the emphasis and indignation concentrated on Muslims. Their unwavering condemnation of violence as foreign to Islam, which all those interviewed, including religious leaders, repeatedly expressed, did not seem to be enough. They had to identify with the satirical magazine, notwithstanding the fact that it had insistently denigrated them.

His insights shed light on the way in which the French model calls for assimilation, rather than integration of French Muslims; in turn, non-assimilation leads to ostracization that may subsequently contribute to and seemingly legitimize Islamophobic sentiment.

In short, the Islamophobic rhetoric articulated through the use of visual imagery in *Charlie Hebdo* functions on multiple levels; on a more explicit level Islamophobic images employed by the publication are clearly anti-Islamic and anti-Muslim. These images are informed by Orientalist legacies and serve to contribute to modern day misconceptions regarding Islam and Muslims. On a more complex and nuanced level, the ideological and philosophical underpinnings that *Charlie Hebdo* claims to adhere to are employed to emphasize the imagined alterity of Muslim.

Humour in Turkey: from past to day

Throughout Turkey's Westernization project, the alleged historical clash between secularism and religion has been regularly depicted in Turkish satirical magazines. Establishing ideological superiority of secularist ideals through Orientalist tropes and the use of irony is visible in the majority of cartoons published in Turkish satirical magazine (Arsal, 2000, pp. 74, 123). Such cartoons ridicule the religious and directly mock Islamic beliefs, and are therefore examples of 'auto-Orientalism'.[2] For example, with the initiation of Tanzimat reforms, an apparent distinct dilemma emerged in the national imagine: the balance between the materialism and perceived modernity of the 'West' represented in the political reforms, and the spirituality of the 'East', represented by Islamic teachings. This binary positioning of these notions within Turkey subsequently delineated the possibility of perceived compatibility of the two, thus a distinctly Turkish ideological opposition was embedded in the national imagination. Consequently, during the Tanzimat Westernization era (Arsal, 2000, pp. 74, 123) and in particular post-1922, the bulk of Turkish mass media has demonstrated tendency to portray all that is related to religion (and especially Islam) in a negative light (Akıner and Mencet, 2016, p. 191). Therefore, where such critique of this nature would have typically historically emerged via the Western Orientalist lens, it was now being produced by Turkish sources themselves.

The arrival of Western-style humour[3] in Ottoman lands arose during the time of Sultan Abdulhamid II (1842–1918) and depicted the ruler as 'aggressive', 'oppressive' and 'backward'. This critique of the nation's ruler led to the emergence of the period of 'Union and Progress'. It was characterized by the rise of a new wave of dissidents responding to the relatively novel internal and external circumstances associated with Neo-Imperialism, the rise of nationalism, and the suggested autocracy of Sultan Abdulhamid (Zürcher, 2013). Against this backdrop the Turkish humour industry was seen to be at its most 'fertile' period, amassing significant satirical imagery used to mock the ruler and faith. Following the establishment of the second constitutional period under the rule of Sultan Abdulhamid II, almost 40 satirical newspapers and magazines were published (Demir, 2016, p. 16), these include *Diyojen* established by Teodor Kasap, who was explicit in his adoption of Western-style humour (Demir, 2016, p. 16). Following the publication of *Diyojen*, Kasap launched newspapers such as *Çıngıraklı Tatar*, *Hayal* and *İstikbal*, thus cementing his centrality position in

Turkish satirical press (Demir, 2016, p. 16). Subsequent to Sultan Abdulhamid II's rule, humour and satire became a routine means of applying political pressure and was used by not only the opposition but also by the state as an effective means of propaganda (Akıner and Mencet, 2016, pp. 174–175).

During the Turkish Republican period, satirical humour has distinctly been influenced by typically Western value systems and, more often than not, its central tenants are of secular–nationalist inclination. Politically speaking, this influence was primarily derived from the Union and Progress Committee and subsequently the CHP (Republican People's Party) paradigms in the first instance. In sum, the satirical press represented the glossy campaign face of the Kemalist Turkish revolution. Historians, such as Demir (2016), allege republican humour dismissed the traditional, or the non-scientific, replacing it with a colourful and rich sense of humour. As Demir states:

> The Republican culture represented emancipation of the social space from the perceived narrow and obsolete context of the Middle Ages and an opening-up to the Western culture in scientific sense, and it is precisely this radical transformation [that] determined the basic structure of the Republican humour.
>
> (Demir, 2016, pp. 17–18)

Satirical magazines continued in much the same vein (i.e. demonstrating clear support for the governing powers) until the 1940s when *Markopaşa* was published. Its emergence paved the way for the construction of humour as an element of entertainment and eroticism rather than simple satire. On the whole, Westernization was adopted as the indisputable national truth of the day by satirical magazines. In short, it became increasingly apparent that '… anyone who was against Westernization and nationalism were illustrated as a figure in gallows' (Demir, 2016, p. 18), thus, demonstrating their ill-fated position, while also clearly marking the position of satirical publications in the ever-increasing and, arguably, oversimplified binaries emerging post-revolution Turkey.

More specifically, beyond the East/West and modernity/archaism general oppositional construction that was made ever-more entrenched, negative depictions of Islam and Muslims have been a constant feature within the most widely read Turkish humorous magazines. Muslims are depicted through the use of clichés as being aggressive, unsightly and fearsome, and are often subject to mockery along political and normative lines. Taking into account the historical roots of these images in the West, it is understood that these representations in Turkey do not differ significantly from the negative representations of the Muslims and Turks in Medieval Europe. In this regard, the Turkish satirical press has become 'auto-Orientalist', in that it applies Orientalist ideologies from within to a traditionally Muslim society.

Along gendered line, within the Turkish satirical press, Muslim women are depicted as veiled and voiceless. The drawing of women is almost the same; veiled and often not speaking, thus 'de-humanized'. On other occasions Muslim women are reduced to burdensome animals or even insects. Often, Muslims are portrayed as other worldly figure, such as being represented by a four-headed snake impairing the country, sometimes as a tortoise, mosquito or even as a microbe seen on a microscope. On other occasions Islam and Muslims are represented as animals oppressing humans. In short, the imagery used within the satirical press derives from ideological selection and the argued intentional negative portrayal of Islam (Akıner and Mencet, 2016, p. 187).

Penguen and Islamophobia

Having established the general trajectory and tendency within the Turkish satirical press towards the use of Islamophobic and auto-Orientalist imagery, the following section of this chapter pays specific attention to the use of auto-Orientalist visuals in the Turkish magazine *Penguen.* Generally speaking, *Penguen* is noted for being critical of both socio-political issues, and also the religious. For example, its regular column 'Compulsory Religious Education', based on an imagined grandfather's answers to incoming reader questions, uses religious symbols such as mosques, rosaries, beards and headscarves, to mock Islamic practices in Turkey and thus provokes offence among sections of the Turkish community (Okutan, 2013, pp. 20–21). The magazine *Penguen* has implicitly embedded the 'us versus them' dichotomy on the axis of 'West' versus 'East'. In addition, we argue that the publication has adopted auto-Orientalist tendencies manifest in its use of Islamophobic exaggerations and oversimplified binary portrayals and, via the use of a thematic approach, we discuss these in further detail in the sections below.

Violence, intolerance and barbarism

In its use of satirical imagery, *Penguen* routinely draws on and enforces the Islamophobic narrative of Islam and Muslims as prone to violence. We see this Islamophobic narrative as being historically rooted in Western constructions of the Muslim world and Islamic faith.

In its use of satirical imagery, Penguen routinely draws on and enforces the Islamophobic narrative of Islam and Muslims as prone to violence. We see this Islamophobic narrative as being historically rooted in Western constructions of the Muslim world and Islamic faith. An example of the portrayal of Islam and Muslims as being carriers of violence within Penguen's imagery is depicted in the cartoon published in 2011.[4] It demonstrates a crowd is gathered in front of the Hagia Sophia. The accompanying text reads 'those who wish to pray in the church gathered in Kartal and Yenikapı ...'[5] The image and its text problematize the widely held Turkish notions surrounding the position of Istanbul in the national current and historical imagination, rather Istanbul is constructed as symbolic in the historical and contemporary resistance to the spread of Islam (İnalcık, 1995, p. 243).

Commissioned by Emperor Justinian in 532 AD and intended to be used as a Christian Church, *Hagia Sophia* has become known as one of the greatest architectural masterpieces of its time. *Hagia Sophia* as it stands today was built on the site of two earlier churches that bore the same name. Serving as the Papal seat of Constantinople and also the throne of the Byzantine Empire, the building functioned as the most decorated Christian basilica for nearly 900 years. It remained a Christian place of worship until 1453 when the Ottoman Empire gained control of the then-named Constantinople. Sultan Mehmed II, leader of the Ottoman Empire, quickly recognized *Hagia Sophia's* imperial prestige and monumental magnificence and had the building converted to a mosque, while retaining the same name, albeit with a new Turkish style spelling, *Ayasofya*. The building functioned as a mosque (or masjid) up until the end of the First World War; after which Mustafa Kemal Ataturk was elected President of the Republic of Turkey in 1923, when he commissioned the conversion of *Hagia Sophia* from a mosque into a museum (Avdoulos, 2015, p. 182). This brief historical description of *Hagia Sophia* highlights its sensitive and symbolic position over time.

Returning to the image published in *Penguen*, it draws on these complexities symbolized within *Hagia Sophia* to recall the historical Islamic conquest of the building (and thus alluding to the past Christian/'Western' heritage of the area) and also touches upon the central position of Istanbul within the Islamic tradition and Prophetic *hadith*.[6]

The text on the cartoon also reads 'apparently, the foreign-force Ka'bah imam has been followed by tens of thousands. The castle in his hometown from the Ottoman Empire was destroyed but he didn't utter a word ...'. This excerpt from within the satirical image enforces stereotypes and essentializations related to Islam and especially notions of Jihad (or holy struggle). Here we see a reproduction of a historically rooted Orientalist tropes that Muslims, due to Islam and specifically Jihad, are inherently violent and warmongering (Köse, 2013, p. 331). According to Esposito (2002), throughout history (as in other faiths), sacred scripture has been used and abused, interpreted and misinterpreted, to justify resistance and liberation struggles, extremism and terrorism, holy and unholy wars. Thus, such notions are not specific to Islam and Muslims; rather they represent power-seeking behaviours across nations, peoples and times. Nonetheless, this essentialization of Muslims and Islam contributes to the overall Islamophobic and auto-Orientalist tropes within *Penguen* and by extension subsections of Turkish society.

Furthermore, and perhaps in an attempt to emphasize a Turkish heritage that is more closely aligned with an imagined Judeo-Christian Europe, Islam and its clerics are constructed as outsiders to the nation. This constructed alterity of Islam goes somewhat towards explaining both the Islamophobic and auto-Orientalist tendencies of the both the image and the magazine more generally.

Within its Islamophobic imagery, *Penguen* also depicts Islam and Muslims in Turkey as intolerant, thus they are the source of troubles within the national context, and therefore consequently worth of critique. This Islamophobic narrative too finds its roots in Orientalist historical constructions of Muslims.

The example image above illustrative of the reproduction of this narrative in *Penguen* reads: 'In a debate which began with sahur (the pre-dawn meal consumed during Ramadan) in Malatya, an Alevi family's house was stoned and barns were burned-down.... What are we burning next?' In terms of context, we see that the image above refers to previous Alevi–Sunni tensions in Ramadan, whereby the houses and stables belonging to the Alevis were set on fire. It indicates a weak tradition of living together and tolerance of the 'other', which occasionally turns into tension and conflicts. These tensions are heavily satirized and allege that the problems experienced stem from the Sunni insistence on Ramadan drumming (an Ottoman tradition that typically accompanies the *sahur* period in Turkey and other Arabic speaking Muslim countries and is intended to inform the religious that it is time to eat and then begin the fast), along with their intolerance that eventually results in the burning of Alevi property.

Within the cartoon, and reminiscent of a colonialist-style divide and conquer-type analogy, Alevism is constructed in opposition to Sunni Islam, with the former being shown as reasonable and espousing Western-style values and the latter as symbolic of the alleged ills of Islam – regulatory, dogmatic, intolerant and violent. Theological and transcendental dimensions of Alevism have been overlooked while the aforementioned fashionable concepts have been brought to the fore. To put it another way, a rich religious and cultural heritage conveyed by verbal culture through centuries has been outshone by a few concepts. Of the expansive Alevi Bektashi tradition, only practices that have survived the fashion concepts have been transferred as Alevism to new generations. As a result, Alevism has been almost presented as a modern, scientific, positivist religion, and philosophical pantheism and Sufi idea of *wahdat-i vucud* meaning the unity of existence anthropomorphism has been evolved to anthropomorphism in the hands of ideologists (Aktürk, 2016, p. 65). In sum, Orientalist and colonial divisive rhetoric that would have typically historically been applied from a Western standpoint emanates from within the nation.

Gendered auto-Orientalism – Muslim women's dress

Within the wealth of literature pertaining to Islamophobia in the traditionally Western world, it is commonly accepted that the bulk of narrative, political legislation and violent Islamophobic attacks affect Muslim women, and in particular visibly Muslim women.[7] Consequently, the gendered nature of Islamophobia coming from the typically Muslim world is often comparatively far less considered. Notwithstanding, in Turkey Muslim women's dress has been under scrutiny since the 1923 Constitutional reforms (see McGoldrick, 2006 for further details, especially those pertaining to the Şahin versus Turkey case).

Against this national position, perhaps unsurprisingly, *Penguen* also uses satirical imagery featuring visibly Muslim women. These women are often portrayed as being subject to oppression and as holding an inferior position in Turkish society, and furthermore the images make light of this position. Examination of the issues of the *Penguen* published between 6 September 2012 and 27 December 2012 show that headscarf-wearing women, whether they are central or complementary figures within the illustration, often represent middle-aged or elderly figures with lower socio-economic status and are portrayed as individuals with lower levels of education. These women are essentializsed and often cast in stereotypical roles, such as that of housewife (apparent in the depiction of them carrying household objects). Furthermore, this role is one that exists in relation to her husband, rather than as an independent woman, thus further emphasizing her presumed inferiority. With regards to attire, these women are shown as long-skirt and jacket wearing and therefore dowdy and not as desirable women.

For example, on 8 March 2011, coincidently – the day of International Women's Day celebrations, the front cover of *Penguen*[8] shows a lady in a headscarf, waistcoat cardigan, long skirt and slippers, with a speech bubble caption that reads 'I don't know how to celebrate, my lord knows how to celebrate'. The visual signifiers and text implies Muslim women's dowdiness, outdatedness and stupidity. The above image, along with its accompanying text, recalls the false dichotomy of the non-fashion savvy (and therefore unattractive) visibly Muslim woman versus the modern Turkish woman. Her position points towards the internal Turkish struggle between the perceived Islamic past of the nation and her journey to modernity.

In his work *The History of the Banal (Histoire des choses banales. Naissance de la Société de consommation, XVIIIe-XIXe siècle*, Daniel Roche (1997), says 'Clothes, beyond being material culture items, bring together the values of the social imagination and norms of the real world. This is the battleground of the conflict between custom and change'. In the image described above, and in particular its use of reductionist oversimplifications, we see the way in which, in contemporary Turkish satirical culture, Muslim women's bodies and their dress continue to constitute an ideological battleground.

While the nature of the image above can be argued to represent the internal Turkish ideological struggle and difficulties in reconciling its own Islamic and Western identities, the imagery also draws on stereotypical tropes pertaining to Muslim women in the Western Islamophobic imagination; namely those that imply that covered visibly Muslim women are controlled (be it by their faith or Islamic scripture), backward, poor, sexually limited and uneducated. Once such a category has been put forth, it does not take much pain to position a category of Western women who are educated, modern, arbiter on their own body and sexuality, and free to make their own decisions (Balcı, 2017, pp. 80–81). In short, given the analysis proposed above, we argue that the image described above represents a reproduction of Western Oriental-inspired Islamophobic constructions of Muslim women and therefore the image taken from *Penguen* would not seem out of place on the cover of *Charlie Hebdo* or other magazines in a similar vein.

Further to the construction of Muslim women as oppressed and backward, *Penguen* also uses satirical imagery to portray Muslim women as unsavoury characters.[9] For example the Muslim woman pictured is shown to be a fortune teller – a role that is linked to anti-Gypsyism and generally negatively perceived in past and Turkish society (Bars, 2014, p. 135). This perception extends to the Western context where fortune tellers are seen as the opposite of the privileged bourgeois class (Özgenç, 2014, p. 21). Interestingly, the construction also recalls current dominant Islamophobic narratives present in Eastern Europe, such as the Czech Republic (Čada and Frantová, 2017), thus there is an apparent amalgamation of prejudiced ideas and Islamophobia in Turkey and beyond and, as such *Penguen*'s cartoons, may equally be found in the typically Western World.

Comparisons and conclusions

To summarize and conclude, we identified significant convergences in the nature of Islamophobia rhetoric employed in both the French satirical magazine, *Charlie Hebdo* and the Turkish magazine, *Penguen*. These similarities in Islamophobic narrative include the framing of Islam as backward and contrary to progressive, liberal Western values, Muslim males as aggressive and sexually perverse, and Muslim females as either submissive or carriers of demographic threat. In both cases, these typical Islamophobic narratives are significantly informed by Orientalist ideas. In short, both magazines construct Muslims and Islam as being diametrically opposed to the hegemonic, and often Westernized, culture.

However, in the Turkish case, *Penguen* draws on both Western Islamophobic narratives in addition to its own historical and sectarian conflicts (such as the alleged Sunni–Alevi tensions). This multifaceted influence on the portrayal of Islamophobic satirical imagery in the country gives rise to an interesting and perhaps unique set of competing variables shaping the nature of Turkish Islamophobia. Arguably, the multi-layered nature of Islamophobic imagery apparent in *Penguen* relates to the internal Turkish national tensions between its Islamic past and, as perceived by some, its Western-facing future.

Most notably, we described Islamophobic content published in the Turkish magazine *Penguen* as being auto-Orientalist, thus ideologically speaking it was Orientalist in its basis, yet rather than these Orientalist and Islamophobic nations being applied by a traditional colonial or Western powers, the ideas are employed from within predominantly Muslim nations. Thus, the Orientalist lens is shifted from solely the Western gaze and adopted by the Orient itself.

Having reviewed the case of *Penguen*, we postulate that the roots of Turkish auto-Orientalism can, in part, be located in the 1923 revolution of the nation and in particular the move towards Western secularism by the country's elite.

We argue that while the nature of Islamophobia apparent in *Charlie Hebdo* may not be novel or even unexpected, in the Turkish case our chapter not only sheds light on modes of Islamophobia in Muslim majority Turkey, but also problematizes assumed Eurocentric discourse of Islamophobia to underline that anti-Muslim tropes and their deployment is not limited to the traditional West, rather, it increasingly permeates previously considered geographical and ideological fault lines, thus calling into question the need for further evaluation of Islamophobia beyond the West.

Notes

1 For example, see *Charlie Hebdo* 1099, p. 1 (2013), 1163, p. 1 (2014), 1164, p. 1 (2014) among many others.
2 Here auto-Orientalism is used to refer to Orientalist tropes applied by those in historically Orientalized positions.
3 In contemporary Western culture, humour has not always been viewed so positively. Indeed, the earliest theories of laughter, dating to Aristotle and Plato, and continuing in some form to the present day (e.g. Gruner, 1997), view it as resulting from a sense of superiority derived from ridiculing others for their stupidity, weakness or ugliness. Such a view does not seem to hold much promise for the inclusion of humour as a component of positive psychology (Martin, 2007, pp. 5–6).
4 *Penguen*, Year 2011, 5, p. 10.
5 Emphasis added.
6 Reported sayings or teaching of the Prophet Mohammad (peace be upon him).
7 For example, see the annually published European Islamophobia Report (Enes Bayraklı and Farid Hafez) www.islamophobiaeurope.com for examples from across Europe, SETA, 2016. Also *Forgotten Women: The Impact of Islamophobia on Muslim Women*. Brussels: ENAR, European Network Against Racism.
8 *Penguen*, Year 2014, 12.
9 *Penguen*, Year 2012, 18.

Bibliography

Akıner, N. and Mencet, M. (2016). 'Türkiye'de İslamofobi: Mizah Dergilerinde İslam' ın Temsili, *Akademik İncelemer Dergisi*, 11(2).

Aktürk, H. (2016). 'Alevilik Araştırmalarında Self Oryantalist Tutum', *Ekev Akademi Dergisi*, 19(62).

Arsal, O. (2000). *Modern Osmanlı resminin sosyolojisi (1839–1924)*. (Çev. T. Birkan). İstanbul: Yapı Kredi Yayınları.

Avdulos, E. (2015). 'İstanbul's Hagia's Sophia: Challenges of Managing Sacred Places'. *Personas Y Comunidades*, Alicia Mena (Ed.), Universidad Complutence de Madrid, pp. 180–203.

Balcı, A. (2017): 'Sömürgeci Feminizm: Ortadoğu'da "Kurtarılacak" Kadın Öznenin İnşası', Ortadoğu Ocak-Şubat 2017 Cilt: 9 Sayı: 78.

Bars, M. (2014). 'Türk Kahramanlık Destanlarında Kadın Tipleri', *İnternational Journal of Languages, Education and Teaching*, 3.

Bonde, B. (2007). 'How 12 Cartoons of the Prophet Mohammed Were Brought to Trigger an International Conflict'. *Nordicom Review*, 28(1).

Čada, K. and Frantová, V. (2017). 'Burkinis and Slippery Slope Narratives: Islamophobia in the Czech Republic'. *Counter-Islamophobia Kit Blog* [online], date of access 3 August 2017.

CCIF (2014). *Annual Report 2014*. Paris: Collectif Contre L'Islamophobie.

Chazan, D. (2018). 'Three Years After the Charlie Hebdo Terro Attack The Satirical Magazine Struggles with £1.3 Billion Security Bill', *Telegraph*, 6 January 2018.

Demir, S. (2016). *Türkiye'de Mizah Derriere: Kültürel Hegemonya ve Muhalefet*. Istanbul: SETA Yayınları.

Esposito, J. (2002). *Unholy War: Terror in the Name of Islam and What Everyone Needs to Know about Islam*. Oxford: Oxford University Press.

Fassin, D. (2015). 'In the Name of the Republic: Untimely Mediations on the Aftermath of the Charlie Hebdo Attack'. *Anthropology Today*, 31(2).

Gruner, C. R. (1997). *The Game of Humor: A Comprehensive Theory of Why We Laugh.* New Brunswick, NJ: Transaction.

İnalcık, H (1995). 'İstanul: Bir İslam Şehri'. *İslam Tetkikleri Dergisi*, 9(2).

Kar, İ. (1999). *Karikatür Sanatı*. Ankara: TC Kültür Bakanlığı Yayınları.

Klug, B. (2016). 'In the Heat of the Moment: Bringing "Je suis Charlie" into Focus'. *French Cultural Studies*, 27.

Köse, S. (2013). 'Cihadın Şiddetle Kurulan Bağlantısının Tutarsızlığı Üzerine'. *Uluslararası Dini Araştırmalar ve Küresel Barış Sempozyumu.*

Kublitz, A. (2010). 'The Cartoon Controversy: Creating Muslims in a Danish Setting'. *Social Analysis*, 54(3).

Martin, R. (2007). *The Psychology of Humor*. Burlington: Elsevier.

McGoldrick, D. (2006). *Human Rights and Religion: The Islamic Headscarf Debate in Europe*. Oxford: Hart Publishing.

Okutan, B. (2013). 'Karikatürlerde Başörtüiü Figürlerin Göstergebilşmsel Analizi: Penguen Dergisi Örneği', *İstanbul Üniversitesi İlahiyat Fakültesi Dergisi*, 29(9–38).

Özgenç, N. (2014). 'Sanatın Ciddiyeti Üzerine: 17. Yüzyıl Hollanda Resim Sanatında Gülme Eylemi'. *Yedi: Journal of Art, Design & Science*, 11.

Palacios, M. (1919). *La escatologia musulmana en la Divina Comedia*. Madrid: Real Academia Espanola.

Résolution du Parlement Européen (2006). www.europarl.europa.eu/sides/getDoc.do?pubRef=-//EP//TEXT+TA+P6-TA-2006-0418+0+DOC+XML+V0//FR, date of access 11 October 2018.

Roche, D. (1997). *Histoire des choses banales. Naissance de la consommation, XVIIe-XIXe siècles*, Paris: Fayard.

Said, E. (1978). *Orientalism*. London: Routledge.

SETA (2016). *Forgotten Women: The Impact of Islamophobia on Muslim Women*. Brussels: ENAR, European Network against Racism.

Todd, E. (2015). *Who is Charlie? Xenophobia and the New Middle Class*. Cambridge: Polity Press.

Yardımcı, İ. (2010). 'Mizah Kavramı ve Sanattaki Yeri'. *Uşak Üniversitesi Sosyal Bilimler Dergisi*, 3(2).

Zürcher, E. (2013). 'Askere Alımlarda ve Askeri İstihdamda Dünyadaki Değişiklikleri Anlamak', in Erik Zürcher (Ed). *Fighting for a Living: A Comparative History of Military Labour 1500–2000*, translated by Dilek Şendil as *Askerlik "İşi" Askerî İşgücünün Karşılaştırmalı Tarihi (1500–2000)*, İletişim yayınları, 11–40.

7 Paradoxical Islamophobia and post-colonial cultural nationalism in post-revolutionary Egypt

May Kosba

Introduction

Between European colonial racial constructs of a civilized whiteness and an inferior blackness, the Egyptian identity has long occupied a *liminal* status. This liminality is reflected both in an undiagnosed 'double-consciousness' (Du Bois, 1903, p. 4) of the proximity of the Egyptian race to whiteness, and in the liminal role that Islam played during European colonialism. That liminal space which both Egyptians and Muslims have occupied in their relationship with the West has been key in serving Western colonial ideology and practice in both colonial and 'post-colonial' epochs. Drawing on different histories of relations between Islam and the West during the colonial period, we will find two conflicting narratives. The first narrative posits Islam as a *civilizing* ideology or religion. The second narrative casts Muslims as savages. The first narrative often operates when Muslims are contrasted with pagans, and people of African descent. The second is when Muslims are compared to Western European Christians. To what degree the Muslim subject is civilized is a matter dependent on their proximity to whiteness. This notion of a Muslim civility and peacefulness was never fixed; rather, it varied from one context to another.

In this chapter, I use the anthropological concept of *liminality* to help understand the rise of Western Islamophobia in a Muslim majority country like Egypt. Applying GhaneaBassiri's conceptualization of liminality in the Egyptian context might help us understand how colonial reconfiguration of Egyptian identity has impacted contemporary Egyptian self-identification. While determining whether Egypt's future identity should be secular or Islamic remains a vehemently contested issue, liminality may offer a deeper understanding of how colonialism has contributed to its complexity.

Framing Egyptian liminality

Liminality of African Muslims in the New World

Liminality is an anthropological term derived from the Latin *līmen*, meaning 'threshold', first coined by the French folklorist and ethnologist Arnold van

Gennep (1909/1960), referring to 'rites of passage' as people transition from one stage to another (p. 21). Anthropologist Victor Turner (1969) later expanded on the term and defined 'liminal entities' as being 'neither here nor there; they are betwixt and between the positions assigned and arrayed by law, custom, convention, and ceremonial' (p. 95). The term was further developed by historian Kambiz GhaneaBassiri (2010) in understanding the status of African Muslim slaves in antebellum America as opposed to their non-Muslim counterparts, and it is this framing of liminality that is particularly relevant in the Egyptian context.

Liminality of African Muslims in antebellum America, as described in GhaneaBassiri's (2010) narrative, was a racial and religious construction of the enslaved peoples by Protestant Anglo-Americans who treated them as 'semi-civilized' peoples (p. 30). According to GhaneaBassiri, colonial settlers in the New World sought to 'de-negrofy' and 'de-Islamize' African Muslim slaves, who oscillated between a 'semi-civilized' and a 'semi-savage' status. *De-negrofication* of African Muslims is the first of two steps, and it means dissociating black African individuals in America from 'Negroid attributes and stereotypes' (GhaneaBassiri, 2010, p. 19). *De-Islamization*, on the other hand, is dissociating Muslim individuals from 'negative stereotypes of Islam', which often involved converting Muslims to Christianity (GhaneaBassiri, 2010, p. 27).

GhaneaBassiri presents de-negrofication and de-Islamization as two manifestations of liminality of African Muslims in a colonial setting, being stripped of their blackness and creed in their previous condition, forced to pass through the threshold, only to become liminal figures. This threshold becomes their permanent condition. The state of liminality that African Muslims occupy is in the middle of two fixed stages or worlds – the uncivilized and civilized stages. Forcing African Muslims to reside in the semi-civilized stage, the threshold, means they cannot retrieve their pre-liminal stage which was uncivilized, nor can they pass through the threshold to their post-liminal stage to become civilized. They are destined to become permanently liminal. They are not meant to be equalized.

In the following section I draw upon GhaneaBassiri's concept of liminality while discussing the liminality of the Egyptian subject to draw parallels between African Muslims in the New World and Egyptians under an overarching European colonial framework and a waning Ottoman sub-colonial rule.

De-Africanization of Egyptians

Liminality of the African Muslim racial and ethnic identity is based on a racial construction that transpired during the sixteenth century transatlantic slave trade in the Americas. Liminal, then, meant that enslaved African Muslims or Arabs who were brought into America, often literate, were treated as 'not-quite-black, not-quite-white' people (GhaneaBassiri, 2010, p. 380). They were semi-civilized. Egyptians, similarly, have historically occupied a liminal status in Western consciousness, and constructed in Western academia as Caucasian peoples. During

British colonial rule, de-negrofying or de-Africanizing, and de-Islamizing Egyptians were key components of Western European colonial ideology.

Colonialism in Egypt existed as a form of 'double colonization' (Young, 1995, p. 162), with colonization by both the British and the Turks. Being occupied, historically, by two rival, hegemonic colonial powers contributed to shaping multiple layers of racism to which Egyptians have lived as the subaltern. For example, the doors for Western whitewashing or whitening of Egyptian history and civilization were flung open by Muhammad Ali Pasha, the Ottoman ruler of Egypt, who set the precedent, adopted by his offspring, of decentring Egyptian culture and replacing it with European cultural transplants in order to modernize Egypt. In *The Great Social Laboratory*, Omnia El-Shakry (2007) explains that Egyptian state institutions were complicit in their collaboration with Western Orientalist institutions, scientists and intellectuals who 'desired to represent Egypt on a Western stage to a Western audience' (pp. 23–24).

De-negrofying or de-Africanizing Egyptians, as colonized peoples, meant cutting ties between them and their African roots or affiliations, leading to Egyptians seeking whiteness on European terms. Examples of this 'whitening' of Egypt abound in Western academia, particularly American academia in the nineteenth and twentieth centuries. For example, Egyptologist George Robbins Gliddon wrote in a letter to Samuel Morton in 1841 about 'the Caucasian basis of Egyptian civilization' (Young, 1995, p. 120). Gliddon wrote about his 'hostile' position towards an idea that assigns African roots to Egyptians, stating that they 'never were African, still less Negroes' (Young, 1995, p. 120). In *Colonial Desire*, Young (1995) argues that Egyptologists like Josiah Nott, Gliddon and Morton used Egyptian skulls to prove their theory about Egyptians as Caucasians, and to justify slavery in 'American society through a theory of a permanent natural apartheid' (p. 121). Ancient Egyptians are dissociated from blackness to deny and erase any contribution of the black race to civilization. These Egyptologists argued that ancient Egyptian civilization must by default be constructed as Caucasian, to emphasize white supremacy. Scientists were more concerned with ancient Egyptians than modern Egyptians, for the latter's presence, they thought, was an unfortunate degeneration of the Caucasian or Aryan race. Nott (1844) argued that it is the adulteration of Egyptian blood that will prevent Egypt from ever rising again, unless the 'present races are exterminated, and the Caucasian substituted' (p. 16).

De-Islamization of Egyptians

De-Islamization, as mentioned above, denotes dissociating Muslims from Islam. GhaneaBassiri presents this as a colonial practice used to force African Muslims to leave their faith, convert to Christianity, promote it and join the slave trade across the Atlantic. In the Egyptian context, even though Islam was deemed inferior to (Western) Christianity, Muslims were not coerced into conversion. The mission of the English statesman in Egypt did not involve proselytization.

During the early phases of the British occupation of Egypt in 1882, the British colonial administrator Evelyn Baring, 1st Earl of Cromer, was a key figure, who, as Egyptian historian Leila Ahmed (2011) describes, ruled as Egypt's 'uncrowned king' (p. 29). De-Islamization in the Egyptian context can be traced through his account in *Modern Egypt* of 'Europeanized Egyptians' who 'deserve all the encouragement and support which can be given to them' (Cromer, 1908, p. 180). Europeanized Egyptians are young Egyptian generations who grew up under Anglo-Saxon, Christian colonial rule, 'de-moslemized' which means they have become less Muslim, or secularized Muslims. Cromer (1908) called Europeanized Muslims 'agnostics', which today could pass as secular (p. 229). In *Modern Egypt*, Cromer found hope in young Egyptians who will emerge as a new race, Europeanized. They are not Europeans' equals, yet superior to their fellow Egyptian compatriots. Cromer (1908) defines Europeanized Egyptians as follows:

> If ... the Government and society of Egypt were farther advanced on the road to civilisation, the Europeanised Egyptian would probably be something different from what he actually is; he would have become in spirit, though not necessarily in sentiment, less Egyptian and more thoroughly European. But inasmuch as Egyptian society is in a state of flux, the natural result has been to produce a class of individuals many of whom are, at the same time, de-moslemised Moslems and invertebrate Europeans.
>
> (p. 228)

De-Islamizing or de-Moslemizing is a common thread detected between African Muslim slaves in the New World, and Egyptian Muslims under the British occupation. It lays a historical foundation of contemporary Islamophobia. In the following section, I will discuss the scope of Islamophobia in Egypt within an overarching Western Islamophobia.

The scope of Islamophobia in Egypt

Islamophobia is a Western term, coined to describe hate and fear of Muslims. The hate is based on perceiving Islam as a religion that inspires violence, and thus Muslims are viewed as inherently violent. Although Islamophobia has become a prevalent term to describe Western irrational and 'rational' (Gibbons-Neff, 2016) fear of Islam and Muslims, it was not a product of the 9/11 attacks. Western Islamophobia has 'deep historical roots' (Mastnak, 2010, p. 46). Esposito and Kalin (2011) trace Islamophobia's contemporary resurgence, describing it as

> triggered by the significant influx of Muslims in the West in the late 20th century, the Iranian revolution, hijackings, hostage-taking and acts of terrorism in the 1980s and 1990s, attacks at the World Trade Centre and Pentagon on 9/11 and subsequent terrorist attacks in Europe.
>
> (p. xxii)

Esposito, and Gottschalk and Greenberg (2008) talk about historical rivalry between a Muslim Middle East and Christian Europe over 'economic resources, political power, and religious sites' (p. 4), resulting in the portrayal of Islam and Arabs as threatening and despotic, evoking suspicion.

The term Islamophobia is often defined as 'a social anxiety toward Islam and Muslim cultures', according to Gottschalk and Greenberg (2008, p. 5), or 'a rejection of Islam, Muslim groups and Muslim individuals on the basis of prejudice and stereotypes. It may have emotional, cognitive, evaluative, as well as action-oriented elements (e.g. discrimination, violence)', according to Stolz (2005, p. 548). Islamophobia has also become a 'form of racism' aimed at a group of people on the basis of their 'race ... ethnicity, language, culture and religion all at the same time' (Kalin, 2011, p. 11). Hence Islamophobia is an irrational or rational fear of Islam and Muslims, encompassing hate, suspicion, discrimination and old forms of biological racism deeming the non-white other as inferior.

Importantly, fear and animosity towards Islam and Muslims in the West is 'intertwined with modernity, colonialism, and globalization' (Maira, 2011, p. 109). At its historical core, it can be argued that Islamophobia emerged with the Crusades where the 'construction of the Muslim enemy was an essential moment in the articulation of the self-awareness of the *res publica christiana* [Christendom]' (Mastnak, 2010, p. 33). Islam and Muslims were constructed as

> emblematic of 'other' peoples, cultures, and civilizations in opposition to Western civilization, Christianity, and also later Judaism in the context of the European Inquisition, the Crusades, and sectarian wars and also in relation to Western capitalism and New World settler colonialism.
>
> (Maira, 2011, p. 110)

Islamophobia thrived during the Western colonization of Africa, the Middle East and Asia.

Orientalism and Islamophobia are not identical, but strongly related; the former concept 'paved the way' (Sheehi, 2010, p. 38) for the latter. Edward Said (1985) first used the term Islamophobia to describe how 'hostility to Islam in the modern Christian West has historically gone hand in hand with, has stemmed from the same source, has been nourished at the same stream as anti-Semitism' embedded in Western Orientalist discourses (p. 99). Contemporary Islamophobia is a product of historical European colonial and Orientalist thought, which posits Muslims as a backward, intolerant and violent 'other' threatening European values. The 'terrorist' label that singles out Muslim extremists is in the same spirit as 'war savages', which is how Muslims were described by Cromer (1908) to show that Islam is an inherently violent religion.

As we look into the Egyptian context and consider the paradox of how Islamophobia can exist in an overwhelmingly Muslim majority country, it is imperative to look at how colonial and Orientalist practices can be internalized by the colonized. European colonial figures like Cromer promised that post-colonial generations will become *Europeanized* and *civilized*, and that Muslims would be *de-Islamized*. The longstanding Western European animosity towards Islam and Muslims manifests itself in many ways in contemporary political and historical conjunctures. In Western contexts, contemporary Islamophobia exists as both institutional and social racism against the Muslim community. Institutional racism occurs when Muslims are viewed as a threat to national security and the Western way of living by Western governments and institutions. Hence a vast array of policies are in place to limit the scope of the Muslim threat to the West through surveillance programmes, Countering Violent Extremism (CVE), the global war on terror, using terrorists who affiliate themselves with Islam as a pretext to police Muslims and reform Islamic theology, and passing laws banning conspicuous signs of religiosity in some European countries such as France, Belgium and Denmark. Beyond governments, both conservative and liberal media often provide platforms for those with antagonistic views towards Islam. As for social racism, it manifests itself in verbal and physical attacks against Muslims and those perceived to be Muslims, often targeting *hijabi* women and Sikh men, bombing mosques, and bullying Muslim kids in schools.

When contextualizing Western Islamophobia in Egypt, how do we measure a phenomenon with such varied manifestations? Political scientist Erik Bleich (2011) presents two approaches for measuring Islamophobia: it can be measured quantitatively through surveys, focus groups, interviews and questionnaires, or it can be measured 'by examining unsolicited statements proffered by politicians, civil servants, public figures, religious leaders, journalists, bloggers, and others whose words are recorded for posterity' (p. 1590). This research focuses on the latter methodology, a *narrative analysis*, depending on statements and official positions from Egyptian media, institutions, political and religious leaders, and other public figures. In the following section, I will show how the narratives of the global war on terror are mirrored in post-revolutionary Egypt, particularly around the otherization and targeting of specific groups, manifesting as a paradoxical Islamophobia.

Manifestations of Islamophobia in Egypt

Egypt's war on terror in the global context: Islam between binary discourses

Since 9/11, Western governments, including those of the United States and the United Kingdom, have produced narratives and conducted policies negatively affecting Muslims in the name of the global war on terror. Systematic dehumanization and targeting of an entire community in Western countries, confusing regular Muslim citizens with militant religious extremists through laws and surveillance programs, are all hegemonic practices which come from historically perverted misconceptions about Islam that dictated and informed colonial powers, and created 'Islam and the West' as two binary ideologies, contentious civilizations with incompatible sets of values. In response to the 9/11 attacks, Western liberal democracies adopted language that centred a Muslim threat facing the civilized world, characterizing terrorists' ideologies as backward and uncivilized, along with the countries that harbour them. Linguist Paul Chilton (2004) asserts that 'politics is very largely the use of language' (p. 14). Similarly, Butt, Lukin and Matthiessen (2004) state that 'the very use of language is ideological' (p. 288). They argue that 'the use of language necessitates choices between different modes of meaning' (Butt *et al.*, 2004, p. 288). It is language that can become a 'fearsome resource' that is used to not only 'shape reality, but … to also defend that reality, against anyone whose alternative values might threaten ours', according to Hasan (1996, p. 34).

This was the kind of language espoused by some Western leaders in public speeches, mobilizing binary narratives, constructing binary identities and positing the language of 'us' versus 'them'. Tony Blair's (2001) 'good' versus 'evil' narrative, following the attacks, where the good is associated with Britain and friends, while evil is a distant other threatening the Western 'free and democratic world' mirrors that of George W. Bush's, where the us and them is clearly pronounced in his 9/11 speech. 'America and our friends and allies join with all those who want peace and security in the world, and we stand together to win the war against terrorism', says Bush (2001a). Bush's statement constructs a hierarchy of 'otherization' through which the United States is positioned on top of the pyramid of human civilization as the ultimate leader of the free world; second comes Britain, America's truest friend (Bush, 2001b), followed by the civilized world, mainly referring to European countries who are America's 'friends'; then allies, who are the 'good' Muslims, 'good' Arabs, and others who choose to join the fight complying with Bush's statement as he famously warned, 'either you are with us or you are with the terrorists' (Bush, 2001a). The terrorists come last, representing evil.

Apart from that, Bush sought to make specific distinctions between terrorists with an extreme Islamic ideology, and mainstream 'peaceful' Muslims. Mahmood Mamdani (2004) conceptualizes the formation of Muslim political identity post 9/11, saying, 'after an unguarded reference to pursuing a "crusade", President Bush moved to distinguish between "good Muslims" and "bad Muslims"' (p. 15). Mamdani (2004) argues that while Bush assured Americans it was 'bad Muslims' who were clearly responsible for the 9/11 attacks, he also 'seemed to assure Americans that "good Muslims" were anxious to clear their names and consciences of this horrible crime and would undoubtedly support "us" in a war against "them"' (p. 15). Furthermore, Mamdani (2004) highlights the core of Bush's message saying,

> but this could not hide the central message of such discourse: unless proved to be 'good', every Muslim was presumed to be 'bad'. All Muslims were now under obligation to prove their credentials by joining in a war against 'bad Muslims'.

> (p. 15)

The contemporary good Muslim–bad Muslim trope initiated by the Bush administration, continuing through Barack Obama's administration and thriving under Donald Trump's administration, provided a convenient excuse for authoritarian regimes to use similar rhetoric to torture and detain their political opponents, deemed as 'bad' Muslims. Egypt's war on al-Ikhwan is a prime example.

In July 2013, after widespread popular protests, General Abdel Fattah el-Sisi forcibly ended Islamist Mohamed Morsi's short presidency, ultimately taking over as President of Egypt. El-Sisi's ascendance was followed by an uptick in deadly terrorist attacks on civilians by ISIS-affiliated terrorist groups based in Sinai, primarily targeting Coptic Christian citizens, police stations and security officers. This has led to a full-scale war on terror in Egypt, with the Egyptian military fighting the terrorist groups in Sinai, and the government and other institutions engaging in Bush-like rhetoric and implementing policies with strong parallels to those of the Western-led global war on terror.

For example, similar to Bush's (2001a) 'either you are with us or you are with the terrorists', el-Sisi warned, 'if the Egyptian state falls you don't know what will happen to the Arab World and to Europe at large' ('Sisi in press conference with Hollande', 2016). Despite its subtlety, el-Sisi's statement stands as a warning to the international community, particularly Europe: should Egypt fail in its fight against terrorism due to lack of international support, it will lead to the collapse of the country and the ensuing collapse of both the Arab world and Europe. El-Sisi's warning resembles Bush's rhetoric – and as Bush demanded allegiance to the United States by casting the nation as the most powerful Western democracy in the world, the only way through which Egypt could claim ownership of and obtain allegiance for its 'war on terror' is by similarly reminding Westerners of the indispensable role that Egypt has long played historically in restoring peace and stability in the region.

El-Sisi, his government and the military were quick to tie the terrorism by ISIS-affiliated groups to the ousted Ikhwan, casting them as terrorists despite their long-standing denunciations of violence and their pursuit of 'ideological moderation' (Hamid, 2014, pp. 30–38). When the Egyptian military declared al-Ikhwan a terrorist organization, the media rallied to delegitimize and otherize al-Ikhwan and their supporters. The military in general, and the character of el-Sisi in particular, were glorified, the former being viewed as the country's most loyal and unpoliticized institution, and the latter for representing this honourable institution and his bravery to take on the alleged terrorist organization to save the nation. Patriotic songs swept television and radio to show support for the military. Meanwhile, media outlets waged a war against political activists associated with the original 25 January revolution, calling them spies, traitors, *agendat agnabeya* (agents of foreign countries) and al-Ikhwan sympathizers, regardless of their secular political orientation. For example, the 6 April movement, one of the central players during the 25 January revolution, was outlawed by a court order and accused of 'espionage and tainting the state's image' (Kholaif, 2014).

Associating terrorism with Islamist extremist groups long preceded the 9/11 attacks. Islamist militant groups who adopted violence as a means to reform the political system and Islamize Egyptian society have been known as terrorists since the early days of al-Ikhwan. Their use of violence is what rendered them terrorists in the eyes of Egyptian society. The use of violence involved assassinating key figures in the government to express political grievances and animosity towards both a secular government and colonialism, which were viewed by al-Ikhwan as complicit in causing the moral corruption of the Egyptian society. In December 1948, al-Ikhwan were found guilty of the assassination of King Farouk's Prime Minister Nuqrashi Pasha who 'disbanded the organization and arrested some of the key leaders of the Brotherhood except Al-Banna' (Dede, 2009, p. 263). Many political assassinations followed, which increased the fear, distrust and hate towards al-Ikhwan as an Islamist group with political greed. This, perhaps, marks the beginning of an *Ikhwanophobia* in Egypt. Decades later, the 1990s witnessed a major surge in mass arrests of al-Ikhwan members under Hosni Mubarak's rule (Campagna, 1996, pp. 298–299), for fear of 'losing control' (Hamid, 2014, p. 89) to al-Ikhwan in the parliamentary elections of 1995. Al-Ikhwan have tried to dissociate themselves from violence multiple times. In the 1970s, al-Ikhwan first denounced violence (Albrecht, 2013, p. 98), followed by a more formal testimony of rejection and disavowal of violence and terrorism in 1994, reaffirmed in 2006 ('Our testimony', 2006). Since then, al-Ikhwan have denounced violence a number of times, especially after major violent attacks in Egypt and beyond. Nevertheless, governments of Egypt have routinely associated them with the terrorist moniker.

The 'otherization' of Muslims and Islam as internalized and perpetuated by post-colonial generations in Egypt, disenfranchizing and targeting Islamists – mainly mainstream Ikhwan members – can be traced back to the four anti-Islamist Egyptian regimes of Gamal Abdel Nasser, Anwar Sadat, Mubarak and el-Sisi. Despite anti-Ikhwan repression in prior regimes, the current Egyptian state has expanded the reach and ferocity of this repression, hoping to wipe out the very existence of the group and everything it stands for. Following a string of terrorist attacks, and more significantly the assassination of Prosecutor General Hisham Barakat in 2015, el-Sisi vowed to 'amend the law … to implement justice as soon as possible' (Kingsley, 2015). Through the Egyptian Revolutionary Council, al-Ikhwan condemned Barakat's assassination and once again disavowed 'all acts of terrorism' ('ERC condemns assassination of public prosecutor Hisham Barakat', 2015). Nevertheless, a new counterterrorism law was approved by the cabinet and signed by the President (El-Sadany, 2015).

Egyptian counterterrorism laws define terrorism using

> ambiguous language to describe intentions and conflates acts with intentions. The reason for this is to broaden the list of intentions to include normal criminal acts such as 'damaging public or private property' as well as vaguely worded acts such as 'obstructing public authorities' activities'.
>
> (Yehia, 2014)

Previous counterterrorism laws were similarly broad. In 1992, an anti-terrorism law, Law 97/1992, was passed, 'granting authorities extensive powers to detain political opponents ... The main pretext was the gathering extremist insurgency in Upper Egypt, but the definition of 'terrorism' became so broad as to include nearly anything the regime saw as a threat to its power' (Hamid, 2014, p. 90). This is illustrative of how old and new anti-terrorism laws are not only protocols by which anti-Ikhwan strategies emerge, but are also used in a wide repressive campaign targeting political activists, journalists, human rights advocates and lawyers, civil rights leaders, young people, university students and NGOs.

The state had three objectives in carrying out the war on terror: it is used to legitimize the toppling of the Islamist president and convince the international community to acknowledge the new regime based on a shared cause, that Egypt is fighting the same enemy: 'radical Islamists'; carrying out an effective theoretical, practical, moral and political elimination of political Islam, particularly al-Ikhwan; and lastly, but most importantly, *de-revolutionizing* Egypt. After decades of perpetual turmoil, it was the 25 January revolutionary uprising that gave al-Ikhwan the opportunity to achieve power.

Egypt's contemporary 'war on terror' is a continuation of a longstanding anti-Islamist legacy by previous repressive regimes prior to el-Sisi, bringing together elements of Western Orientalist thought and contemporary right-wing anti-Muslim ideology. Western Islamophobic rhetoric and practices have been internalized and propagated by the Egyptian ruling class, popular media, political elites and religious leaders. This leads us to a series of questions: if we were to track the roots of the global war on terror, where would it begin? Does it begin with Egypt's historical repression against Islamists and their ideology and symbols – specifically, leaders and members of al-Ikhwan? Does it begin with Arab secular dictatorships struggling with questions of identity, democracy, modernity, governance and economic dependency on the West, while controlling Islamism? Or does it begin with the aftermath of the 9/11 attacks? If Egypt is waging a war on militants with Islamist ideologies, why are 25 January revolutionary activists and dissidents targeted, detained and tried for allegedly joining terrorist groups? Has the global war on terror transformed from a specific set of policies and actions into an ideology with worldwide adherents?

It is conceivable that the longstanding conflict between secularism and political Islamism may have created a precedent of anti-Muslim rhetoric, and the global war on terror may have capitalized on a longstanding contention between Arab dictatorships and Islamists. Consequently, secularism became a prerequisite for modernity, a continuation of Western colonial theory put into practice to modernize the world. This invites the question of Islam's compatibility with modernity, and whether the 'war on terror' demonstrates a clash of civilizations, as discussed and argued by a considerable number of scholars. For example, Mamdani offers two distinctive features of both Bernard Lewis's and Samuel Huntington's accounts of Islam. First, 'Huntington cast Islam in the role of an enemy civilization. From this point of view, Muslims could be only bad' (Mamdani, 2004, p. 21). Second, it was Lewis, 'who provides the intellectual support for the notion that there are "good" as opposed to "bad" Muslims, an idea that has become the driving force of American foreign policy' (Mamdani, 2004, p. 23).

Thus, according to Mamdani, one could argue that the war on terror is but a practice that falls under the modern Western theory of a clash of civilizations. For example, Bush's earlier response to the attack by waging a Huntington-style anti-Muslim 'crusade' was eventually reduced to a 'Lewis-style caution against taking on an entire civilization' (Mamdani, 2004, p. 24). The theory, language, and practices in place dictate that 'Islam must be quarantined and the devil exorcized from it by a Muslim civil war' (Mamdani, 2004, p. 24).

Obama's distancing from Bush's take on the Muslim world could be interpreted through the former's loud and clear rejection of a Huntingtonian clash of civilization between Islam and the West. In almost every speech pertaining to Islam and Muslims, Obama (2014) reiterates, 'we reject any suggestion of a clash of civilization' (p. 4). Despite an alleged distancing in both approach and narrative, considering Mamdani's analysis, Obama may reject a Huntington-style clash of civilizations, but his approach appears to be embedded in a Lewis-oriented rational recognition of the good, the bad and the ugly about Islam and Muslims, and how the West can operate accordingly. Even though Obama rejects a binary conflict between the West and Islam, his narrative and legacy are vehemently embedded in classic European colonial notions of Islam and Muslims and reproduces an 'us' and 'them' narrative. The war on terror-inspired 'good' Muslim, 'bad' Muslim dichotomy seems to have infiltrated Egyptian consciousness. The palpable violence in Egypt could also mean that by joining the global fight, the country is exterminating its own 'bad' Muslims.

Construction of binary Muslim identities in Egypt and the United States

Bush's global war on terror intensified the narrative of the 'good' versus 'bad' Muslim in the West. 'Good' has become a synonym for 'moderate' or 'non-traditional' Muslim which oftentimes implies that the only acceptable type of Muslim is a non-practicing Muslim. The National Security Research Division of the RAND Corporation issued an alarming report in 2003 entitled, 'Civil Democratic Islam: Partners, Resources and Strategies' (Benard, 2003), arguing that even though Islamic militant groups are a serious problem, the larger threat to the United States comes from 'traditionalists': those who adhere to the orthodox Islamic tradition. Meanwhile, one of the objectives of the CIA's counterterror strategy is 'waging a war of ideas' to delegitimize terrorism, through supporting 'moderate and modern governments, especially in the Muslim world' (Central Intelligence Agency, 2003). This narrative infiltrates peoples' consciousness, and transports Western moral panics to vulnerable societies who are engaged in a perpetual fight for the preservation of identity, as in Egypt.

The question of Egyptian identity has long been a contested issue. More recently, the tension has been fuelled by Islamists' rise to the political arena, with Islamization of Egyptian society as their objective. The fight for identity has since been a binary one, where all sides, whether Islamist or secular, take a 'your Islam versus my Islam' (Ismail, 1998, p. 215) position. The state and its

Islamic establishment allies align to affirm their vision of Egyptian identity. As Ismail (1998) writes, the 'state uses dialogue and repression', while the religious establishment assumes the role of 'defenders or guardians of *al-Shabab al-Salih* (the good youth)' (p. 215). For years, there has been a 'state of balanced tension' (Ismail, 1998, p. 215) that describes the relationship between Islamists and the establishment. Since the revolution, the rivalry between establishment Islam and political Islamism has flared. Islamic institutions such as al-Azhar declare themselves as vanguards of 'moderate' Islam, and thus 'the field of struggle is defined in terms of a contradiction between a correct understanding of Islam and a mistaken and misguided one' (Ismail, 1998, p. 215). This invites a puritanical conflict over Islamic 'orthodoxy' and 'authenticity'. Hence, the struggle between 'orthodox' and 'heterodox' versions of Islam surged in the aftermath of the downfall of al-Ikhwan.

Egypt is a Sunni Muslim majority country where Muslims take pride in adopting a 'moderate' version of Islam. Being a 'moderate' Muslim in the Egyptian context is by no means a Western imposition; it primarily draws from the Islamic tradition itself. In the Qur'anic text (2:143), believers are encouraged to live a justly balanced way of life, '*wa kadzalika ja'lnakum ummatan wasatan*' ('Thus have we made of you an *Ummah* [community] justly balanced', as translated by A. Yusuf Ali). The word *wasat* in Arabic is defined as the centre, the middle way, or a justly balanced way of life by seeking moderation and avoiding the extremes; it also 'implies a touch of the literal meaning of intermediacy' (Ali, 1992, p. 58). This refers to the intermediate position of Arabia, geographically, in the Old World, as later Islam spread out to the East, West, North and South. The most commonly used theological exegeses of the word is living in moderation and avoiding extremes. Thus, aspiring to practice Islam in moderation is in fact a form of '*ibadah*' (worship). From al-Azhar's perspective, political Islamist ideology is a deviation from these fundamentals, and thus an extreme understanding of the tradition, alien to al-Azhar's brand of 'moderate Islam'. Meanwhile, on the other end of the spectrum, the Western secular obsession with reforming Islam and defining what a 'moderate' Muslim looks like has infiltrated the Egyptian consciousness through the rhetoric produced by the government, media and Egyptian intellectuals.

El-Sisi's call to reform Islam and parallels to Western Islamophobia

In a 2015 televised conference with top religious leaders during the annual *Mawlid al-Nabi* celebration of the birth of the Prophet, el-Sisi controversially called for reforming Islam. He addressed the imams of al-Azhar, saying, 'We should closely examine the situation in which we are. It does not make sense that the thought we sanctify pushes this entire nation to become a source of apprehension, danger, murder and destruction in the entire world' (Fayed, 2015).

El-Sisi claimed that the need for a religious revolution was an answer to a stunning question: 'Is it possible that 1.6 billion [Muslims] should want to kill the rest of the world's inhabitants – that is 7 billion – so that they themselves may live?' (Fayed, 2015). Two key problematic categorizations and claims occur in el-Sisi's statement: first, who is el-Sisi referring to by the 'world'? Is the 'world', in his context, synonymous with the West, or is it the world at large? Second, if el-Sisi's war of words and actions mainly targets Islamists with an extreme Islamic slant, why did he lump the entire Muslim population as antagonistic to the non-Muslim world with their absolute entirety? El-Sisi's positioning of a 'bad Islam' against the world is analogous to classic Orientalist and Islamophobic narratives, which designate Islam and the West as adversaries. The generalizations drawn in his speech about the Muslim community at large, casting it as an enemy of the entire world, collapses and conflates mainstream Muslims with Islamists and terrorists, overlooks the Muslim community's diversity and multiculturalism, dismisses political, social, economic and historical grievances from which violence and radicalization emanate, and more importantly, the way with which he contextualized the threat Islam mounts to the West aligns with anti-Muslim Western narratives which portray Islam as a perpetual adversary of Western values and identity.

While el-Sisi's call for religious reformation had a divisive reaction among Egyptians and Muslims, it found a warm welcome among right-wing Republicans in the United States. To give an example, conservative columnist George Will (2015) recommended that the Nobel Peace Prize committee should consider el-Sisi, to reward him for his bravery. In another televised interview between Ann Coulter and Megyn Kelly on Fox News, both hailed el-Sisi for 'having the nerve to stand up there and speak to a bunch of imams' (Coulter, 2015). Coulter (2015) described el-Sisi as the 'good guy' who is brave enough to take on al-Ikhwan. Coulter's statement feeds into the good and bad Muslim binary. The 'good' Muslim is the one who speaks *our* language and internalizes labels *we* assign to subaltern groups. Coulter celebrates the exporting of Western moral panics to non-Western territories. The war on terror verbiage, rhetoric, and actions epitomize Egypt's internalization of Western colonialist and Orientalist 'othering' that constitutes stripping the 'other' of their identity.

On the policy front, the Egyptian government has taken extreme measures against free religious expression in the name of fighting terror. In a series of moves, approximately 20,000 mosques were shut down across Egypt in 2018, cameras were installed in mosques to monitor preachers, and a hotline service was created for 'complaints about 'immoderate discourse from citizens' (Wirtschafter and El Tohamy, 2018). Additionally, 'unregistered' preachers were banned from preaching and standardized government-drafted sermons were introduced ('Reforming Islam in Egypt', 2017). From banning minarets in Switzerland in 2009 (Cumming-Bruce and Erlanger, 2009) to closing seven mosques in Austria in 2018 (Eddy, 2018), it is hard to argue whether Egypt is leading or following the West by banning some mosques and surveilling others.

In the following section, I will highlight instances in post-revolutionary Egypt where the *hijab*, despite being worn by a majority of Egyptian women, is cast as unmodern and uncivilized by 'secular' Egyptian intellectuals following el-Sisi's call for religious reformation. I will showcase different narratives provided by secular elite and media personnel on television and in news-papers, whose rhetoric demonstrates a deep internalization of Western Orien-talism and Islamophobia.

Secular responses: anti-hijab narratives

Complying with the President's call, different 'secular' intellectuals and religious figures took different stances that expressed the essence of el-Sisi's call for reforma-tion, while pushing their own personal agendas. Responses included voices calling for religious reform, and others criticizing fundamental aspects of the faith. Some 'secular' responses reminisce about women's dress code prior to Egypt's Islamic awakening (Mahmood, 2005) in the 1970s, seeking to launch a second wave of unveiling, in commemoration and in continuation of Hoda Shaarawy's 'casting off the veil' initiative (Choubachy, 2015). Writer Cherif Choubachy initiated a call upon women to take to Tahrir Square and take off their veils, claiming, 'Ninety-nine percent of Egypt's prostitutes are veiled', and encouraging or demanding women who wear the veil out of fear of their male guardian to 'take it off' ('Writer calls for taking hijabs off', 2015). Former Minister of Culture Gaber Asfour showed that alarming remarks about the hijab could come from the top levels of government. In 2014, appearing in a televised interview, Asfour reminisced of his college years in the 1960s when Egyptian women did not wear the hijab, describing them as a 'model of progress and open-mindedness' (Samir, 2014).

These growing anti-hijab instances build on similar instances preceding el-Sisi's religious revolution. Until 2012, Egypt's first ladies have always been unveiled, with Jihan al-Sadat and Suzanne Mubarak also being half-British. However, in the first presidential election after the 25 January revolution, Egyp-tians found themselves faced with the prospect of a veiled First Lady for the first time. Naglaa Ali Mahmoud, the wife of Mohamed Morsi, was not only veiled but wore the traditional hijab that drapes over her body to her waist, popular in rural and conservative parts of the country. Her dress is more representative of Egyptian women than any of her predecessors, yet she was pilloried by the media and other elites for the way she looked.

In one popular example, *al-Shorouk*, one of the most popular private news-papers in Egypt, compared Mahmoud to her predecessor Suzanne Mubarak and to Intessar Amer the wife of el-Sisi (Hamed, 2014). While referring to Amer and Mubarak as First Ladies, the article referred to Mahmoud as '*Khademat Misr al-Oula*', Egypt's First Servant. Even though the article highlighted that she pre-ferred to be called the first servant rather than the first lady because she was at the service of her country, the title of the post had an unmistakable play on words, as the word *khadima* also means a 'house servant' (Hamed, 2014).

In the West, Orientalism and Islamophobia have often manifested themselves through the lens of women. Muslim women are viewed as oppressed and in need of saving. It is a common trope in the West that the only reason Muslim women wear hijabs or *niqabs* is because they are afraid of some man, whether their father, brother or husband. Hijab, in the West, is said to be a 'symbol of the oppression of a sex' (Winter, 2009, p. 150). Recently similar language has been expressed from within Egypt, a Muslim majority country where the vast majority of women in fact wear some form of veil. Egyptian secularists' expression of pursuing (Western) modernity aligns with Western rhetoric, which oftentimes targets, scrutinizes, and disenfranchizes Western Muslim communities in their entirety.

Paradoxically, while Egypt is an Islamic country where the people celebrate the outward display of religion, from the loudspeakers of mosques to beards, veils and bumper stickers, the Egyptian media is relentless in its pursuit of a nostalgic Egyptian version of *secularity*. The West's obsession with the hijab, spearheaded by France's stringent laws, has filled the Egyptian collective psyche, making it acceptable to criticize hijab and other forms of conspicuous signs of religiosity. From a Western perspective, 'objections to the *burka* or the *niqab*, to Islamic enclaves and the intrusion of other ways of life, are objections to difference, to the alien, to the erosion of a familiar way of life' (Norton, 2013, p. 90). One can only wonder how the courageous role of Egyptian women in the 25 January revolution that 'challenged this picture of Muslim women as victims' (Norton, 2013, p. 68) in the West is being diluted to a discussion on what should Egyptian Muslim women wear? Egyptian women's contribution to the revolution placed Muslim women as 'leading revolutions' instead of 'silent victims of Muslim misogyny' (Norton, 2013, p. 69). Why is 'secular' misogyny leading the objectification of Egyptian Muslim women's bodies? To what extent is the hijab or the niqab alien to the Egyptian society? What danger does the hijab constitute to the Egyptians' familiar way of life?

Conclusion

In this chapter I argue that the Egyptian war on terror, which on one hand includes fighting ISIS-affiliated terrorists but on the other hand includes taking repressive measures against mainstream al-Ikhwan supporters and sympathizers as well as, more broadly, 25 January revolutionaries and secular activists, employs a fearmongering narrative familiar in the West. This narrative often takes on anti-Muslim language, policies and actions, mirroring the global war on terror, taking the form of Western-style Islamophobia. The relationship between the Egyptian and Western production of Islamophobic rhetoric and actions is complex, easily circulating from one context to the other, and embedded in a deep history of Orientalism and colonialism. In both cases, entire communities are painted with a broad brush, disrupting lives in both Egypt and the West, and isolating Islam and Muslims as people particularly worthy of suspicion and policing.

Bibliography

Ahmed, L. (2011). *A quiet revolution: The veil's resurgence, from the Middle East to America.* New Haven, CT: Yale University Press.

Albrecht, H. (2013). *Raging against the machine: Political opposition under authoritarianism in Egypt.* Syracuse, NY: Syracuse University Press.

Ali, A. Y. (1992). *The meaning of the Holy Qur'an.* Brentwood, MD: Amana.

Benard, C. (2003). *Civil democratic Islam: Partners, resources and strategies.* Santa Monica, CA: RAND Corporation. Retrieved from www.rand.org/content/dam/rand/pubs/monograph_reports/2005/MR1716.pdf, date of access: 12 July 2018.

Blair, T. (2001, 11 September). *Prime Minister Tony Blair statement in response to terrorist attacks in the United States.* Retrieved from http://webarchive.nationalarchives.gov.uk/20050513232058/www.pm.gov.uk/output/Page1596.asp, date of access: 12 July 2018.

Bleich, E. (2011). What is Islamophobia and how much is there? Theorizing and measuring an emerging comparative concept. *American Behavioral Scientist*, 55(12).

Bush, G. W. (2001a, 11 September). Address to the nation on the terrorist attacks. *Weekly Compilation of Presidential Documents*, 37.

Bush, G. W. (2001b, 20 September). Address to the nation by the President of the United States. *Congressional Record*, 147(123).

Butt, D. G., Lukin, A. and Matthiessen, C. M. I. M. (2004). Grammar – the first covert operation of war. *Discourse and Society*, 15(2–3).

Campagna, J. (1996). From accommodation to confrontation: The Muslim Brotherhood in the Mubarak years. *Journal of International Affairs*, 50(1).

Central Intelligence Agency (2003, February). *National strategy for combating terrorism.* Retrieved from www.cia.gov/news-information/cia-the-war-on-terrorism/Counter_Terrorism_Strategy.pdf, date of access: 12 July 2018.

Chilton, P. A. (2004). *Analysing political discourse: Theory and practice.* London: Routledge.

Choubachy, C. [Cherif]. (2015, 21 February). Nada' 'ajil ila nisaa' masr [Facebook status update]. Retrieved from www.facebook.com/cherif.choubachy/posts/10152911670245668, date of access: 12 July 2018.

Coulter, A. (2015, 11 January). Interview by M. Kelly. *The Kelly File* [Television broadcast]. New York: Fox News. Retrieved from http://nation.foxnews.com/2015/01/11/can-we-fight-radical-islam-while-being-politically-correct, date of access: 12 July 2018.

Cromer, E. B. (1908). *Modern Egypt, by the Earl of Cromer* (Vol. 2). New York: Macmillan.

Cumming-Bruce, N. and Erlanger, S. (2009, 29 November). Swiss ban building of minarets on mosques. *New York Times.* Retrieved from www.nytimes.com/2009/11/30/world/europe/30swiss.html, date of access: 12 July 2018.

Dede, A. Y. (2009). *Islamism, state control over religion and social identity: Turkey and Egypt* (Doctoral dissertation). Retrieved from https://scholarworks.wmich.edu/cgi/viewcontent.cgi?article=1763&context=dissertations, date of access: 12 July 2018.

Du Bois, W. E. B. (1903). *The souls of Black folk.* Chicago: A.C. McClurg.

Eddy, M. (2018, 8 June). Austria closes 7 mosques and seeks to expel imams paid by Turkey. *New York Times.* Retrieved from www.nytimes.com/2018/06/08/world/europe/austria-islam-mosques-turkey.html, date of access: 12 July 2018.

El-Sadany, M. (2015, 6 July). Yet another terrorism law. *The Tahrir Institute for Middle East Policy.* Retrieved from http://timep.org/commentary/yet-another-terrorism-law/, date of access: 12 July 2018.

El-Shakry, O. (2007). *The great social laboratory: Subjects of knowledge in colonial and postcolonial Egypt.* Stanford, CA: Stanford University Press.

ERC condemns assassination of public prosecutor Hisham Barakat (2015, 20 June). *Ikhwanweb.* Retrieved from www.ikhwanweb.com/article.php?id=32197, date of access: 12 July 2018.

Esposito, J. and Kalin, I. (Eds) (2011). *Islamophobia: The challenge of pluralism in the 21st century.* Oxford, UK: Oxford University Press.

Fayed, H. (2015, 2 January). Al-Azhar responds to Sisi's call for 'religious revolution'. *The Cairo Post.* Retrieved from http://thecairopost.youm7.com/news/132144/news/al-azhar-responds-to-sisis-call-for-religious-revolution, date of access: 12 July 2018.

GhaneaBassiri, K. (2010). *A history of Islam in America: From the New World to the New World Order.* Cambridge, UK: Cambridge University Press.

Gibbons-Neff, T. (2016, 18 November). 'Fear of Muslims is rational': What Trump's new national security adviser has said online. *Washington Post.* Retrieved from www.washingtonpost.com/news/checkpoint/wp/2016/11/18/trumps-new-national-security-adviser-has-said-some-incendiary-things-on-the-internet, date of access: 12 July 2018.

Gottschalk, P. and Greenberg, G. (2008). *Islamophobia: Making Muslims the enemy.* Lanham, MD: Rowman & Littlefield.

Hamed, Z. (2014, 8 June). Bil sowar: ta'raf 'ala abraz al-forooq bayn zawjat Mubarak wa Morsi wa el-Sisi [In pictures: Know the main differences between the wives of Mubarak, Morsi and el-Sisi]. *Al-Shorouk.* Retrieved from www.shorouknews.com/mobile/news/view.aspx?cdate=08062014&id=4b3fa635-fcda-4975-b383-680d0c1234a3, date of access: 12 July 2018.

Hamid, S. (2014). *Temptations of power: Islamists and illiberal democracy in a new Middle East.* Oxford, UK: Oxford University Press.

Hasan, R. (1996). What kind of resource is language? In C. Cloran, D. Butt and G. Williams (Eds), *Ways of Saying, Ways of Meaning: Selected Papers of Ruqaiya Hasan* (pp. 13–36). London: Cassell.

Ismail, S. (1998, May). Confronting the other: Identity, culture, politics and conservative Islamism in Egypt. *International Journal of Middle East Studies,* 30(2).

Kalin, I. (2011). Islamophobia and the limits of multiculturalism. In J. Esposito and I. Kalin (Eds), *Islamophobia: The challenge of pluralism in the 21st century* (pp. 3–20). Oxford, UK: Oxford University Press.

Kholaif, D. (2014, 28 April). Egypt outlaws anti-Mubarak April 6 Movement. *Al Jazeera.* Retrieved from www.aljazeera.com/news/middleeast/2014/04/egypt-outlaws-anti-mubarak-april-6-movement-20144281135421761.html, date of access: 12 July 2018.

Kingsley, P. (2015, 30 June). Egyptian President 'to change law to allow faster executions'. *Guardian.* Retrieved from www.theguardian.com/world/2015/jun/30/egyptian-president-al-sisi-change-law-faster-executions-death-penalty, date of access: 12 July 2018.

Mahmood, S. (2005). *Politics of piety: The Islamic revival and the feminist subject.* Princeton, NJ: Princeton University Press.

Maira, S. (2011). Islamophobia and the war on terror: Youth, citizenship, and dissent. In J. Esposito and I. Kalin (Eds), *Islamophobia: The challenge of pluralism in the 21st century* (pp. 109–126). Oxford, UK: Oxford University Press.

Mamdani, M. (2004). *Good Muslim, bad Muslim: America, the Cold War, and the roots of terror.* New York: Three Leaves Press.

Mastnak, T. (2010). Western hostility toward Muslims: A history of the present. In A. Shryock (Ed.), *Islamophobia/Islamophilia: Beyond the politics of enemy and friend* (pp. 29–52). Indianapolis, IN: Indiana University Press.

Norton, A. (2013). *On the Muslim Question.* Princeton, NJ: Princeton University Press.

Nott, J. C. (1844). *Two lectures on the natural history of the Caucasian and Negro races.* Mobile, AL: Dade and Thompson.

Obama, B. (2014, 24 September). Remarks to the United Nations General Assembly in New York City. *Daily Compilation of Presidential Documents.* Retrieved from www.gpo.gov/fdsys/pkg/DCPD-201400699/pdf/DCPD-201400699.pdf, date of access: 12 July 2018.

Our testimony, issued in 1994 (2006, 30 May). *Ikhwanweb*. Retrieved from www. ikhwanweb.com/article.php?id=4185, date of access: 12 July 2018.

Reforming Islam in Egypt: Egypt's clerics are resisting the president's call to renew Islam (2017, 18 February). *The Economist*. Retrieved from www.economist.com/middle-east-and-africa/2017/02/18/reforming-islam-in-egypt, date of access: 12 July 2018.

Said, E. (1985). Orientalism reconsidered. *Cultural Critique*, 1(Autumn).

Samir, A. (2014, 6 October). Culture Minister under fire for perceived anti-veil statements. *The Cairo Post*. Retrieved from http://thecairopost.com/news/126519/news/culture-minister-under-fire-for-perceived-anti-veil-statements, date of access: 12 July 2018.

Sheehi, S. (2010). *Islamophobia: The ideological campaign against Muslims*. Atlanta: Clarity Press.

Sisi in press conference with Hollande: We're confronting the forces of evil (17 April 2016). *Mada Masr*. Retrieved from www.madamasr.com/news/sisi-press-conference-hollande-were-confronting-forces-evil, date of access: 12 July 2018.

Stolz, J. (2005). Explaining Islamophobia: A test of four theories based on the case of a Swiss city. *Swiss Journal of Sociology*, 31(3).

Turner, V. (1969). *The ritual process: Structure and anti-structure*. New York: Aldine de Gruyter.

van Gennep, A. (1960). *Rites of passage*. (M. B. Vizedom and G. L. Caffee, Trans.). London: Routledge. (Original work published 1909).

Will, G. (2015, 11 January). *Fox News Sunday* [Television broadcast]. Washington, DC: Fox News. Retrieved from www.youtube.com/watch?v=qAlXO9irJB4, date of access: 12 July 2018.

Winter, B. (2009). *Hijab and the republic: Uncovering the French headscarf debate*. Syracuse, NY: Syracuse University Press.

Wirtschafter, J. and El Tohamy, A. (2018, 25 May). Fearing extremist violence, Egypt silences 20,000 storefront mosques. *Religious News Service*. Retrieved from https://religionnews.com/2018/05/25/fearing-extremist-violence-egypt-silences-20000-storefront-mosques/, date of access: 12 July 2018.

Writer calls for taking hijabs off (2015, 15 April). *Egypt Independent*. Retrieved from www.egyptindependent.com/news/writer-calls-taking-hijabs, date of access: 12 July 2018.

Yehia, D. (2013, 24 November). Egypt's anti-terrorism legislation. *Mada Masr*. Retrieved from www.madamasr.com/opinion/egypts-anti-terrorism-legislation, date of access: 12 July 2018.

Young, R. J. C. (1995). *Colonial desire: Hybridity in theory, culture and race*. London and New York: Routledge.

8 Old wine in new bottles

Secularism[1] and Islamophobia in Egypt

Deina Abdelkader

Introduction

Secularism was born in the Middle East in a time of conflict. Colonial occupation claimed that its mission of civilizing the natives would bring about a more liberal politically aware population in the occupied countries. Actually civilizing the occupied countries came under the banner of establishing governments that were akin to the governments of Western Europe. Secularism was taken as a precondition to governance and thus also as a justification for occupation by the two major powers pre-World War I: Great Britain and France.

Therefore, the birth of secularism in the region was tainted with its utilization to occupy the peoples of the region. Not only was secularism forced as a measure of modernization, but also religion's role in public discourse was shunned and forcefully subjected to play a secondary and private role. The religion's appeal to the populace, as will be examined in this chapter, never ceased, and the change from above to 'modernize' was never accepted except by the few.

The British and the French destabilized their colonies by reinforcing stereotypes that legitimized their occupation of those territories. The colonies started creating a rift between the religiously/traditionally educated population and the 'modern'/secular educated population.

For example, this is obvious in the case of Egypt where the Al-Azhar institution (one of the oldest higher educational institutions in the region) was put into competition with King Fou'ad University at the turn of the century (later on known as Cairo University). Private citizens, wealthy landowners, nationalists, the royal family and journalists founded Cairo University. The idea started as early as 1816 when the college of Engineering was founded. The University was seen as a threat by British occupation due to its potential breeding of opposition to colonial rule. Cairo University was created to rival Al-Azhar University and represent a more Western secular-inspired education than its equivalent Al-Azhar's focus on religion.

Egypt was not an exception in the advent of 'modernity' and educational reform. Reform had already started in the early 1800s in today's Turkey; in an effort to 'modernize', the Tanzimat were set in action as policies to aid the Ottomans to achieve this. The delineation was so obvious that Christian nationalists later started to advocate for balancing the wave of secularism by paying homage to the Islamic civilization as their own.[2]

Ussama Makdisi highlights the effects of missionaries in the early 1800s and how missionary activity was closely tied to educational change in the region in his *Faith Misplaced* (2010).

Makdisi's thorough research of the intentions of the missionaries is clearly stated throughout his book, however one of the letters sent by Daniel Bliss is very telling about the missionaries influence on education and how they viewed Islam:

> This College is for all conditions and classes of men without regard to color, nationality, race or religion. A man white, black, or yellow; Christian, Jew, Mohammedan or heathen, may enter and enjoy all the advantages of this institution for three, four or eight years; and go out believing in one God, in many Gods, or in no God. But, it will be impossible for anyone to continue with us long without knowing what we believe to be the truth and our reasons and our reasons for that belief.
>
> (Makdisi, 2010, p. 53)

Makdisi comments on the zeal of Bliss: 'Americans, he intimated, were determined to consolidate a leading position in the scientific enlightenment of the Arabs, and from this position they hoped to inspire a belief in a Protestant God' (Makdisi, p. 52).

As Albert Hourani documents in the Liberal Age there were two sources of nationalism in the Middle East region:

> One source was the liberal secularism of nineteenth century England and France, directly assimilated and accepted: first expressed in Arabic by Bustani and his school, and passed on by them to Lutfi al-Sayyid and the school of Egyptian nationalists which he created.
>
> (Hourani, 1983, p. 343)

The second source was Islamic reformism which was formulated by Muhammad 'Abduh and Rashid Rida: Islamic because it stood for a reassertion of the unique and perfect truth of Islam, but reformist in that it aimed at reviving what it conceived to be certain neglected elements in the Islamic tradition. But this revival took place under the stimulus of European liberal thought, and led to a gradual reinterpretation of Islamic concepts so as to make them equivalent to the guiding principles of European thought of the time: Ibn Khaldun's 'umran gradually turned into Guizot's 'civilization', the 'maslaha' of the Maliki jurists and Ibn Taymiya into the 'utility' of John Stuart Mill, the ijma' of Islamic jurisprudence into the public opinion of democratic theory, and those who bind and loose into members of parliament. The effect of this in what we have called the secularizing wing of 'Abduh's school, was to bring about a de facto separation of the sphere of civilization from that of religion and so to open another door to secular nationalism; but even in the other wing, that of Rida and the neo-Wahhabis, the distinction which they made between doctrine and worship, which were based on unchanging revelation, and the rules of social morality, which should be decided in the light of Maslaha, led in the same direction, even if it was still maintained or at least asserted that those rules should be derived from the general principles of Islamic ethics.

(Hourani, 1983, pp. 343–345)

The ideas propounded here by the late Hourani are Eurocentric and do not go into depth about the history of Islamic thought, especially Islamic jurisprudence. I will illustrate this later in this chapter when I address the transfer of ideas comparing Al-Shatibi and St. Thomas Aquinas's Public Welfare/Common Good.

First, Hourani's claim that the reformers were under the influence of Western European liberalism is a contentious statement because the history of writing on the subject of Maslaha, for example, dates back to the leaders of the four schools of Sunni Islam and the Ja'fari Shiite Muslims. The attempt to liken Maslaha to utility and Ijma' to Parliament is not because Muslim reformers were imitating Western liberal thought, it was because Western liberal thought has embedded Islamic concepts of social justice and the spirit of ruler-ship that were exchanged centuries before the advent of the enlightenment and industrialization. The exchange of knowledge and ideas was free and abundant so much so that the influence of Averroes is obvious and documented, on the most important juris-consult writing about Maslaha Al-Shatibi, as well as Maimonides and St. Thomas Aquinas. There was no monopoly as Hourani suggested on knowledge. Therefore when Hourani writes about the reformists bending Islamic concepts to suit Western liberal thought, he does not pay homage to the historical traditions that were handed over from one civilization to the other in pre-modern times. Owning this knowledge is important because it is vital to assert currently that Islam has its indigenous and unique contribution in the discourse on civilization and setting of ground rules for social justice, change, and governorship.

However, the late Hourani and others were and still are pre-occupied with Western civilization and what Hamid Dabashi refers to in his native tongue as: Gharb Zadeh in his *Theology of Discontent* (1993). This symbolizes the quintessential nature of the discourse: the inferiority complex that plagues the literature and policies from pre-colonial to current times on the region.

The British occupation in Egypt was very clear as to its mission:

To liberate the country from the 'principles' of the Mohammadan faith which [the European powers considered] antiquated, obsolete, and opposed to commonplace ideas of modern civilization.

(Maghraoui, 2006, p. 64)

As Maghraoui adequately notes in his *Liberalism without Democracy*:

As Egypt became more European than Oriental in the eyes of the Egyptian liberals, the adoption of the modern 'European principles of order, progress, and liberalism' took on an existential significance: the principles became the sacred symbols of the new national identity, which the Egyptian liberals laboriously attempted to fabricate and validate on the basis of 'scientific' studies and theories.

(Maghraoui, 2006, p. 65)

It is this essentialist and existential discourse that still affects liberals of contemporary Egypt as will be illustrated further in this chapter. A discourse that was impregnated from its very conception with the awkward alliance between colonizer and colonial subject that: 'legitimated and maintained the European imposed order of exclusion, hierarchy, and submission' (Maghraoui, 2006, p. 66). This alien identity that was imposed on the masses was clearly resisted by the religious nationalists namely the Muslim Brotherhood and its creation in 1928.

The Muslim Brothers perceptions and resistance to the new liberalists

The founding of the Brotherhood was based on two goals: one was nationalistic because of British occupation; the second was a reaction to the liberal attempts to derogate the popular attachment to the faith.

Hassan al-Banna's awareness of this rift gave him the opportunity to enlist public support directly. He was well aware that his message is a national–social message; al-Banna was the first to speak about social justice and religion outside of the confinement of a mosque. He gave his speeches at coffee shops, private homes and public arenas. The Muslim Brotherhood created a first in religious movements by going outside the traditional bound preaching (Mitchell, 1969).

The Muslim Brotherhood's view of the liberals was clearly expressed:

There were two kinds of Imperialism: 'external' (al-Isti'mar al-khariji), the brute force of the occupying foreign power, and 'internal' or 'domestic' (al-Isti'mar al-Dakhili), the forces which consciously or unconsciously – at best by indifference, at worst by 'treason' to the needs and the wills of the Muslim community – served the interests of that power. 'Domestic imperialism' spread dejection and moral defeat.

(Mitchell, 1969, p. 218)

This diverted Egyptians from their traditional faith to 'a dead pacifism, holy humiliation, and acceptance of the status quo' (Mitchell, 1969, p. 218).

The upper class therefore created a monopoly and the people ceased to voice their opinion on their perception of governance and egalitarianism. In Banna's view the struggles of the masses economically and politically were inseparable from religion and social justice. As an Azharite spoke:

European 'civilization' has developed in us a morbid mentality, a morbid taste and has made of us a morbid community that looks upon its own morbidity and decay as a thong of virtue and a sign of progress. Once corrupt, the greatest corruption is to regard one's own corruption as good and desirable.

(Mitchell, 1969, p. 224)

Qutb also emphasizes that: 'the enemies who are, the real hurdle to achieving social justice for the poor masses. Those enemies are classified as both indigenous and foreign. The indigenous include capitalists, journalists, dark-skinned Britishers- or Egyptians with white mentalities-politicians, and a good number of 'ulama' who sold out their religious allegiance for wretched worldly interests.

(Abu Rabi', 1996, p. 121)

Qutb realized at this early stage that society was split between the masses (al-Jamahir) and the 'coalition of regression'.[3] Qutb's views in the 1940s mirror Edward Said's main argument in *Orientalism* (1978). and the more recent contribution of Hamid Dabashi *Brown Skin, White Masks* (2011).

Thus the onslaught and dismemberment of the faith was felt and rejected by the Muslim Brotherhood and was part of their raison d'etre. The religious nationalists were born as a result of the violent attempt at removing religion forcefully from the public sphere because of the patronization of colonial powers and more dangerously 'al-Injileez al-Sumr' (the dark Britishers) as Qutb named them.

It is important to note here two elements in the Muslim Brotherhood discourse in the early stages, in order to reflect on their contemporary views/policies and their interactions with the liberalists: (1) the movement is not a traditional movement that is bent on living a glorious past (aka Salafists), it is rather a movement that is revolutionary/progressive because it was able to distract from its indigenous culture a formula to address social justice. It was also able to transcend the control of the state over religious institutions and stepped out of the conformity of institutionalization to reach out to the public; (2) aside from fighting the British occupier as a nationalist entity, the main interest, as expressed in many of Qutb's publications, was to seek social justice for the majority of Egyptians. Thus the Brotherhood was always historically a mouthpiece for the public that was in opposition to corruption and the abuse of power.[4]

The roots of Egyptian liberalism: Western liberalism and inevitability of secularism

In Foucault's *What is Enlightenment?* (1984) he discusses the tendency to confuse two concepts: the 'Enlightenment' and 'Humanism'. He explains that the Enlightenment is a well-defined 'set of events' that took place in Europe and stresses its historical specificity (Rabinow, 1984, p. 43). He defines 'humanism' as a set of 'conceptions of man borrowed from religion, science, or politics' (Rabinow, 1984, p. 44). Foucault concludes that:

I think that, just as we must free ourselves from the intellectual blackmail of being for or against Enlightenment we must escape from the historical and moral confusionism that mixes the theme of humanism with the question of the Enlightenment.

(Rabinow, 1984, p. 45)

Foucault's argument is relevant to the Islamist ideas mentioned because he clearly identifies the rigidity of the Enlightenment ideology and its followers. This rigidity lies at the crux of the liberalists' stress on secularism as a precondition to democracy and modernization. Actually, 'liberalism' in Egypt equates to secularization because although Western liberalism calls for a number of stipulations, Egyptian 'liberalism' is obsessive about 'secularization'. Therefore, the term liberalism will be used interchangeably with secularism in the Egyptian context.

The Enlightenment focuses on secularization as a prerequisite for modernity and democratization. Contemporary moderate Islamists are wary of the Enlightenment philosophy's dichotomy and intolerance of differences.

Not all Western theorists have thought that the 'Great Separation', as Mark Lilla refers to the faith/reason dichotomy in his 2007 book *The Stillborn God*, is necessary to the existence of democracy. Even Jean Jacques Rousseau – the father of the French and American revolutions – was radical in his belief that religion plays an important public role in democratic political life.

The Egyptian 'liberals' took those biases and applied them to their own societies. The separation of Church and State became part of their discourse and thus the tensions were born long before the revolution happened and long before a leader from the Muslim Brotherhood won the first free presidential elections.

Contemporary Egypt and antagonistic[5] 'liberalism': old wine in new bottles

Although Western liberalism is partially built on the acceptance and respect of others, the observance of pluralism and the protection of 'liberalism' in Egypt pre and post the 2011 revolution antagonistically rejects and refuses to co-exist with what it views as its main rival: Islamically oriented politics and parties. Quintessential liberalism is defined by the rejection of a privileged class, religion or national origin etc., however 'liberals' in Egypt have basically argued and acted on their assumption that they are the 'privileged' holders of the truth politically, socially and economically.

Historically speaking, the 'liberals' in Egypt have copied Orientalist criticisms of the 'Occident' and assumed that they are scientific truths with a capital T.[6] what distinguishes those 'secular–liberalists' was that they 'uncritically replicated European anti-Arabism and the debasement of the Arabo-Islamic culture' (Maghraoui, 2006, p. 67).

That is to say that the 'liberals' emphasized the same critiques of the other (the 'Orientalist'). They identified with the culture of the other to the demise of their own culture. They touted those critiques as 'scientific truths'. Their 'liberalism' was non-inclusive of the masses, which is still true today in the aftermath of the 2011 Egyptian revolution:

> The secular liberal reformers, who emphasized rationality and individualism, were paradoxically trapped in the cultural order of the Other and therefore could not provide an inclusive notion of national identity and an emancipating notion of political community.
>
> (Maghraoui, 2006, p. 68)

In the 1920s and 1930s, the 'liberals' of Egypt adopted wholeheartedly the discourse of the 'Orientalist' so much so that their writings included: 'overt racial and cultural discrimination' (Maghraoui, 2006, pp. 85–86). In evaluating the public discourse after the revolution, especially with the ascendance of Mohammed Morsi to power, social media expressed those biases, whether one observes the jokes on Facebook about how he and his wife look, or whether one refers to the dry humour of Bassem Yousef who became an icon of free speech under Morsi.

The language that was used was so derogatory that a television talk show host addressed it on her show on public television. Although the talk show host had opposing political views, she defended Mrs Morsi and said that one can critique her ideas if she speaks, but it is unfair to attack her based on her looks or her modest appearance; she said she looks like most middle-class women and that aiming those jokes at Mrs Morsi was a classic case of snobbery and classism (Majed, 2012).

Religious public discourse and public policy

Since the presidency of General Sisi, there has been a crackdown on the public display of religiosity including religious institutions and mosques:

> Two months ago worshippers at Al-Rahman, a small mosque in the Ain Shams district in eastern Cairo, turned up for prayers on Friday, the Muslim day of rest, to find the doors shut. From now on, they were told, they would have to go to one of the city's main mosques for the most important prayers of the week. Soon after, another restriction was added when a group that met for discussions about Islam was told to stop. Today the mosque is open for weekday prayer only.
>
> (*The Economist*, 2014)

> Human rights groups see good reason for all to be worried by the new restriction. 'This in effect kills the idea of religious freedom, since Egyptians can't opt for any religious practice not approved by the authorities.
>
> (*The Economist*, 2014)

Thus public policy towards the Islamic faith has been threatening since the advent of the new political regime in Egypt. Not only do people have restrictions in praying where they want, but also religious practice is controlled and monopolized by Al-Azhar, which in turn is controlled by the regime.

More recently the speech given by Sisi was also imbued with threats. In his speech, he indicated that the faith needs reform. Sisi's message created waves of discontent and fear:

> The religious discourse that should be idolized is one that is relevant to our time, to renew the faith every 100 years. I am talking here to the people of religion and the people who are responsible for this faith: It is impossible that the ideas that we adhere to are ideas that promote disturbance in the world, worry and killing. I do not mean the faith, but the ideas that are idolized for hundreds of years. Discarding those ideas has become very difficult, to the extent that those ideas are the enemy of the whole world. Is it possible for 1.6 billion to kill 7 billion it's impossible! I am saying this at al-Azhar, in front of the scholars of religion. I hold you responsible on the Day of Judgment about what I just said. It is impossible to feel the faith while one is enshrined in it; you have to (exit) the faith to judge it, and for one to be enlightened. You need to stop, we need a religious revolution.
>
> (Egyptian President Abdel Fattah el-Sisi's speech on
> New Year's Day, 2015)

Again, although opposition or commentary on Sisi's speech is non-existent, commentaries on social media express their fear and frustration. The perception of Sisi's speech is that policy wise there will be more restrictions on the public practice and public discourse about Islam. For him to refer to a religious revolution and to talk about renewal is reminiscent of the missionary and colonial discourse referred to previously. His call is also contradictory in spirit because Mr Sisi keeps repeating, 'I do not mean the faith', and meanwhile he is de facto addressing the religious scholars. Sisi also repeats several times that those scholars are responsible: how could he hold them responsible for what happened in Paris for example? Is he using the same discourse that is being used by Western countries to shame the 1.6 million Muslims for the actions of three or four Muslims?

Sisi's implied assumption that the 1.6 billion Muslims are out to fight the 7 billion is also indicative of Western Islamophobia because his speech has a lot more in common with people gathered at Dresden to request the ousting of Muslims from Germany, than with the majority of Muslims who are against violence. His call for renewing the faith and revolutionizing it was hailed by Western and Israeli media sources, but to his Muslim audience, it sounded threatening and repulsive. Recent historical facts and research show that when the public will to practice its faith is under attack, the followers of the faith become extreme. More importantly, as illustrated the leader of Egypt is repeating age-old colonial, Islamophobic arguments. His public discourse is accusatory of the whole faith and all of its followers: 'Is it possible for 1.6 billion to kill 7 billion it's impossible!'

Thus to add salt to injury, Sisi's speech transgresses identity politics in a country that is well renowned for its faith. Sisi's speech exemplifies the age – old problem with liberalism, basically taking on the Other's argument and adopting it as one's own, without adaptation or allowing public space for the masses and what they want.

Conclusion

In conclusion, the arguments used by the 'liberals' in the 1920s and 1930s have not changed in Egypt post-January 2011. The same tactics and opinions are held. The distance between the 'liberals' and the masses is quite vast. The revolt ('coup') carried out by the military supporters was replicated in many countries especially in Turkey's modern history.

> The Egyptian liberals held that in a culturally 'backward' society, the masses do not have the capacity to make meaningful choices, and therefore the exclusion of their voices needs no theoretical justification or political explanation. The kind of social and cultural 'emancipation' they preached is grounded in a self-evident cultural justification of political subordination. The masses became the object of an arbitrary and authoritative discourse telling them how to dress, how to eat, what to read, what to believe, how to cross the street, how to choose a conjugal partner, how to celebrate a birth, and how to mourn and bury the dead. In short, they were expected to renounce their cultural identities and moral values and assume an alien, 'superior' political identity, Except for the simplistic and phony racial theories on the inferiority of Arab culture and the superiority of Western civilization, the Egyptian reformers did not bother to offer the public compelling reasons to give up parts of their cultural identity in order to enjoy citizenship rights.
>
> (Maghraoui, 2006, p. 88)

It is the disconnect between the few and the masses that brought about the current political climate in Egypt. Democratic practice is founded on 'the people', when political actions and speeches go against the public will and ethos, the regime loses legitimacy and ceases to be democratic.

The 'liberals' in the 1920s and 1930s were shocked to see the reluctance of the masses in adopting their ways:

> The masses cannot adjust to the historic changes the country is undergoing. Complained the liberal reformers. Because of their inability to adjust, their allegiance to the new Egyptian nation could not be guaranteed. The masses were considered 'abnormal', 'socially ill' and in urgent need of containment, surveillance, and medical treatment. Egyptian society was viewed as a mixture of pathological groups to be treated, literally, by medical experts to 'normalize' their integration as abstract individual citizens into the newly defined political community.
>
> (Maghraoui, 2006, p. 90)

Those realizations noted by Maghraoui have continued to haunt Egyptian politics and act as constraints on the public will but they have come even further pronounced as a result of the 25 January revolution and the resultant free election of the Muslim Brotherhood-allied Freedom and Justice Party (FJP).

Oddly enough the liberals ignited the 25 January revolution; the Muslim Brotherhood were in a constant state of opposition before the revolution, however, when the public will gave birth to a different political view and the 'liberals' rushed to erase those choices.

The political–social divide has been addressed by popular media: A well-known pop-singer (Ali el-Haggar) released a song titled: 'They are a people, and we are a people'. The song vilifies the Muslim Brotherhood as 'terrorists' and glorifies the 'proper' citizens. As al-Effendi writes in an article published recently:

> There is indeed, a belief that the elite belong to a superior race and that the rest of the Egyptian people are up for slaughter as they increase in number. There is not a problem, therefore, if they are killed wholesale. There are still debates about the numbers of those who have been killed. Is it four thousand in total or one and a half thousand? In the end, it does not really matter.
>
> The conflict in Egypt is not simply a matter of disagreements between secularists and Islamists or between liberals and conservatives it is a dispute between Egypt's ordinary people, those who are rooted in its soil, and the elite who have been determining the way of things since the time of Muhammad Ali and his successors. These elites are the people who have hijacked the state and monopolized the nation's wealth for use as a weapon against the people so that they may know their 'place'.
>
> (Al-Effendi, 2015)

In conclusion, it is very dangerous to obliterate one side of the population, especially the majority from political participation and discourse. Social movement theories indicate that change can occur from above or from below. If one does a comparative study of the region, Egypt, in particular, has historically been resistant to change from above. Whether one takes Qasim Amin, Huda Shaarawi as feminists, or Nasserism as a national–socialist experiment, neither feminism from above nor socialist Nasserism gained traction as ideas that mobilized the masses.

In examining the history of the Muslim Brotherhood as a social movement, they gained traction as a movement and their ideas were popularized because they addressed the real needs of the people: free healthcare, free education, transportation, etc. Not only did the Brotherhood act as a state within a state providing those services, but also their reluctance to adopt Western liberalism wholesale brought their ideas and convictions closer to the people. The great divide between upper-class–liberal versus masses–religious is replicated in Turkey and Iran's modern history: whether we talk about Necmettin Erbakan and his struggles, as a precursor to Erdoğan, or Iran pre and post the 1979

Iranian revolution, both are proof that change from above and trying to shove 'secularism' down the throat of a religious population does not work. At the end of the day people hide their religious convictions until the system allows them to express those convictions freely.

The underscoring of social justice lies at the heart of this great divide, because as this chapter has illustrated, the divide between the elites' interest groups and the masses is complex. This divide is also based on the kind of education they received, the historical context of this education (i.e. power relations) and above all the ripples of colonization that are still felt until this day in the region.

Notes

1 This chapter will use liberalism and secularism interchangeably when referring to Egypt's 'liberals'. One of the chapter's arguments is that 'liberals' in Egypt reduce Western liberalism to one issue, which is secularism, i.e. tolerance, pluralism etc. are not pivotal in their self-definition of liberalism.

2 'Even for Arab nationalists who were Christians their nationalism implied a certain moral adherence to Islam, as a civilization if not as a religion' (Hourani, 1983, p. 343).

3 This coalition of regression that violates basic human rights and values without hesitation, is made up of the following forces: 1) oppressors-exploiters (tughat wa mustaghilun); 2) professional men of religion (rijal al-din al-muhtarifun); 3) mercenary writers (kutab murtaziqun); and 4) hired journalists (sahafiyun ma'jurin).

(Abu Rabi', 1986, p. 121)

4 As Maghraoui argues:

It would seem reasonable to consider the founding of the Muslim Brotherhood, by Sheikh Hassan al Banna in 1928, and the broad popular appeal the movement still commands today, as a principled rejection of politics that discriminate against local cultures. Yet much of the literature on what is called today 'political Islam', 'Islamic fundamentalism' or 'Islamic resurgence' continues to view movements like the Muslim Brotherhood in Egypt simply as a negative reaction against failed politics within Islamic discursive traditions- or even spiritual flourishing within Islam- is ethically denied and epistemologically censored.

(2006, p. 144)

5 The antagonistic quality that is added to 'liberalism' here expresses the inimical and oppositional stance liberals took against an ideological and socio-economic opponent; namely the Muslim Brotherhood. The antagonistic quality is also in reference to the disrespect and belittling of the majority of the masses ideas and beliefs. As former Vice President, Umar Suleiman said in a CNN interview in 2011: 'The Egyptians do not understand democracy', which oddly enough echo British colonial views of Egypt during its occupation.

6 Maghraoui lists those liberals:

This group included literary figures such as Taha Husayn, Muhammad Husayn Haykal, Abbas Mahmud al-Aqqad, and Tawfiq al-Hakim; social critics such as Fathi Zaghlul and Isma'il Mazhar; Christian Arab emigres, mainly publishers, such as Salama Musa, Farah Antoun, Jurji Zaydan, and Shibli Shumayal; and political leaders such as Ahmad Lutfi al-Sayyid, publicly known as ustadh al-jil, the master thinker of his generation.

(2006, p. 67)

Bibliography

Abu Rabi', Ibrahim M., *Intellectual Origins of Islamic Resurgence in the Modern Arab World*. State University of New York Press: Albany, 1996.

Al-Effendi, A. W., The killing of an activist masks the real conflict in Egypt, *Middle East Monitor*, 2 February 2015.

Dabashi, H., *Theology of Discontent: The Ideological Foundation of the Islamic Revolution in Iran*. Transaction Publishers: New York, 1993.

Dabashi, H., *Brown Skin, White Masks*. London: Pluto Press, 2011.

Egyptian President Abdel Fattah el-Sisi's speech on New Year's Day, 2015, available on YouTube, www.youtube.com/watch?v=QmA9-RDTpWs (4 January 2015), accessed on 22 June 2017.

Foucault, M., 'What is Enlightenment?' in *The Foucault Reader*, by P. Rabinow (Ed.), 32–50. New York: Pantheon Books, 1984.

Gilby, T., *Summa Theologiae*. Cambridge University Press: Cambridge, 2006.

Hourani, A., *Arabic Thought in the Liberal Age, 1798–1939*. Cambridge University Press: Cambridge, 1983.

Lilla, M., *The Stillborn God: Religion, Politics, and the Modern West*. Vintage Books: New York, 2007.

Maged, R. M., (An Egyptian Web based News Portal), www.masrawy.com, 2 July 2012.

Maghraoui, A., *Liberalism without Democracy: Nationhood and Citizenship in Egypt, 1922–1936*. Duke University Press: Durham, NC, 2006.

Makdisi, U., *Faith Misplaced: The Broken Promise of U.S.-Arab Relations: 1820–2001*. Public Affairs: New York, 2010.

Mitchell, R. P., *The Society of the Muslim Brotherhood*. Oxford University Press: Oxford, 1969.

Rabinow, P. (Ed.), *The Foucault Reader*. Pantheon Books: New York, 1984.

Said, E. W., *Orientalism*. London: Routledge & Kegan Paul, 1978.

The Economist, Islam in Egypt: Manipulating the minarets, 2 August 2014.

9 Internalized Islamophobia

The making of Islam in the Egyptian media

Sahar El Zahed

Introduction

On August 2016, images of veiled Muslim women forced to remove some of their modest clothes on French beaches and resorts, or leave, erupted a worldwide storm of criticism. The ban on the burkini (a two-piece swimsuit worn by Muslim women that covers the entire body) was challenged by human rights and women rights organizations, which considered the ban part of discriminatory restrictions against Muslim minorities (Rubin, 2016). The ban was suspended afterwards by a French court rule affirming that it is a violation of fundamental liberties to implement a law that forbids women from wearing burkinis (Dearden, 2016). No one suspected at that point that these same discriminatory restrictions are practiced against veiled Muslim women, in Egypt; a country with a Muslim majority where wearing a veil has been a common practice for more than 1,400 years. Not only was the burkini banned in some hotels and resorts, but also veiled women themselves have been forbidden from entering specific resorts, public beaches, hotels, restaurants and concerts since 2015. According to *al-Yawm el Sabi'* Egyptian newspaper, some women were also banned from working at some of these venues (Khalil, 2015). These uncommon restrictions on veiled women were protested by many Muslims, most of whom used social media to express their frustration not only over these limitations but also over the Ministry of Tourism's disregard of these restrictions. However, the ban on the burkini or veil in some Egyptian resorts, hotels, restaurants, concerts and beaches is not the only exclusive restraint against Muslim conservatives in Egypt.

Furthermore, Muslim veiled women were the target of a Facebook and media campaign that invited them to protest paternal guardianship by removing their veils in al-Tahrir Square. In 2015, Sherif el Shobashy, a controversial famous Egyptian journalist, publicly asked veiled Egyptian women, on his Facebook page, to organize a million-woman demonstration to take their veils off in al-Tahrir Square. Shobashy poses that the majority of the veiled women do not deliberately chose to wear the Islamic scarves but are rather forced to wear it by their fathers, husbands or guardians who threaten to beat them and lock them in if they don't wear it (AlHayah TV Network, 2016; 'Sherif el Shoubashi: The call to remove veil', 2015). Moreover, he stresses that the idea of wearing a veil is against freedom, and should, therefore, be countered by the state just like terrorism. Other journalists and policy-makers, including Egyptian journalist, Farida el Shubashi, former Minister of Culture, Jaber Asfoor, and many others, joined Al-Shubashy in his anti-hijab campaign that used the Western 'saver' discourse of Muslim women by depicting the veil as a sign of oppression (Al Jazeera Arabic, 2015).

On another occasion, on 19 June 2017, following the vehicular attack outside a London mosque, the Egyptian TV host Youssef Al-Husseini depicted the entire 1.6 billion Muslims worldwide of representing a menace to the world. He said:

> In all the previous vehicular attacks, at least in 2016 and 2017, the 'heroes' were, unfortunately, Muslims. And then people wonder why they hate us. Why do they hate us?! If they didn't, there would be something mentally wrong with them. [We] use weapons all the time, slaughter people all the time, flay people all the time, burn people alive all the time, run people over all the time, and plant explosive devices and car bombs all the time. Why do you still expect them to love you?
>
> (Memri, 2017)

Not is it only ironic, it rather brings to light a state of absolute confusion that, though Al-Husseini is commenting on an attack on Muslims as the victims and not the perpetrators, he continues to attribute terrorism to Islam and Muslims. Islam is blamed no matter what even when Muslims are the victims. These ongoing TV clips and anti-Islam incidents are only a few examples of the current debates on 'Islam' and 'Muslims' that are prevalent in Egyptian mainstream media today, which are shaping the national and public discourse. There has been an influx of accounts and debates over Islam's legacy and meanings focusing primarily on the relationship between Islam and terrorism. These accounts, which arguably intensified after President Mohammad Morsi of the Muslim Brotherhood came into power, are characterized by an unprecedented exaggerated hostility towards Islam. Although President Morsi's term was not very lengthy, the mass media has since then continued to be the primary platform for these Islamophobic debates that perpetuate and promulgate hatred and fear of Islam. Aiming to delegitimize President Morsi, the Egyptian mass media discourse on Islam has fuelled the so-called 'war on terrorism', while at the same time shaping and paving the way for public acceptance of the unprecedented government's violations of human rights. This disparaging discourse is arguably an offshoot of the derogatory Islamophobic and Orientalist narratives on Islam, constructing an image of it as an inherently violent religion that advocates terrorism, with global ramifications.

Through the analysis of segments of some of the most popular and widely viewed late-night TV shows, and segments of a presidential speech for President Abdel Fattah el-Sisi, this chapter elaborates on the ways in which various meanings of colonialism, Islamophobia and Orientalism influence the discursive construction of 'Islam' and 'Muslims' among policy-makers and secularized intelligentsia. It seeks to explore some of the vital features of internalized Islamophobia in the dominant debate on 'Islam' and 'Muslims', as well as the ways in which it differs from Western Islamophobia and Orientalism in 'Western' societies. This chapter argues that these television shows have deliberately constructed a hegemonic discourse that represents 'Islam' as a static, anti-modern and backward religion that propagates terrorism and irrationality; and paints 'Muslims' as inherently violent, fundamentalists and fanatics. The Egyptian intelligentsia, as seen in the role of TV hosts, producers, directors and owners of TV satellite channels, dominate and determine how this production of cultural troupes takes form. Although their rhetoric on Islam originates its vocabulary and ideas from Orientalism and Islamophobia, this chapter argues that Egyptian self-Orientalism still has its unique features.

Given that Islamophobia from within Muslim societies is indebted to Orientalism and a result and extension of Western Islamophobia, this chapter opens with a review of the relevant scholarly literature on the ways in which Islamophobia and Orientalist discourse on Islam emerged and developed over the centuries.

Islamophobia, Orientalism and internalized Islamophobia

Islamophobia here is not only understood as an exclusive attitude that portrays Islam as an un-Western and unmodern religion, as well as labelling Muslims as enemies or untrue citizens of the West (Shyrock, 2010), but also as a powerful tool of political mobilization that ruling elites use to advance their political and economic interests (Kumar, 2012; Shyrock, 2010). It has provided a discourse that represents Muslim as 'pure religious subjects separated from their race thus disarticulating Islamophobia from the field of racial bio-politics that had created it' (Tyrer, 2013, p. 146). This attempt of the West to rule the East has a long history and is built also on scholarly efforts to define 'Islam'. 'The term 'Islam' as it is used today seems to mean one simple thing but in fact is part fiction, part ideological label, part minimal designation of a religion called Islam' (Said, 1997, p. l). The difference between 'Islam' as the religion of more than 1.2 billion diverse people from all around the world and the term 'Islam' as used in conventional Western representations is enormous (Said, 1994). European and American anti-Islam discourses have played a significant role in widening this gap by constituting Islam as an alien 'Other' (Salama, 2011).

The core of these anti-Islam discourses and irrational set of associations about an imaginary unity of almost 1.5 billion diverse persons was originally constructed during the eleventh century, when the Catholic Church called on Europeans to unite together to fight a common enemy 'Islam' and has since then continued to instruct Western knowledge and shape its perceptions of Islam and Muslims (Kumar 2012; Lyons 2012). It was an excellent opportunity for the Catholic Church to use religion to lead Europe and create a European Christian identity that unites all Europeans. The same ideology was used again in 1492 to justify the massacres and expulsion of Muslims (Moriscos) – whose rule over the Iberian Peninsula lasted for eight centuries – from Spain. In the fourteenth and fifteenth centuries, the idea of a united Christian Europe was replaced by nationalism, and the Europeans began to define themselves not as Europeans but as English, French and so on (Kumar, 2012). When the Ottomans began to lose their military superiority over Europe in the seventeenth century, the idea of democracy for White West and despotism to non-White East began to take place (Kumar, 2012). By distinguishing between reason and emotions as well as debasing the emotional Eastern 'Other', the European Enlightenment, in the eighteenth century, has simultaneously elevated the intellectual European (Alquwaizani, 2012). The West has sought both to subordinate and devalue other societies, and at the same time to find in them clues to its own humanity (Asad, 1973). This task was given to enlightened scholars who began to classify humans according to race and colour producing an image in which whiteness was associated with cultural and racial superiority, and non-Whites were associated with savagery and unreason (Kumar, 2012).

Western interference

These stereotypical images were relegated to academics who turned them into a full-fledged science that (mis)-represents the Orient. Talking in its name as if it was a fixed entity, a label that could be conveniently applied to all of the Orientals as if they had no voices of their own and lacked the ability to represent themselves (Alquwaizani, 2012; Kumar, 2012). These joint efforts of academics and intellectuals succeeded in constructing Orientalism as a complete language, a discourse and an ideology, with the aim of maintaining Europe's domination of the Orient and making it look natural and inevitable (Dabashi, 2011). The way this discourse has been conceptualized produces an idea that validates the presence and the political engagement of the Western colonizer in the East by establishing a cluster of ideas or a body of thoughts that together construct a discursive formation that persuades people to accept and believe that colonization is better for them (Lal, 2014). It is a mode of thought that haunts those colonized, as an idea that an individual perpetually needs the colonizer to intervene and proceed with the individual's civilizational and representational scheme. It is in fact a reductionist, flattening and totalizing discourse that wipes away the identity and civilization of the colonized, dislocating their identity and creating a sense of inferiority encapsulated within the 'Eastern' self (Lal, 1014). As such, Orientalism is not simply a style of thought that describes the Orient to the West, but is also a self-reflection of the Orient in redefining and appropriating itself.

The uppermost share of this racist discourse was given to Islam as Western scholars translated the collection of *One Thousand and One Night* into a number of European languages, and it was used afterwards by novelists and poets to construct an image of the Muslim Orient that is associated with terror, sensuality and pleasure (Kumar, 2012). They played a vital role in representing Islam and Muslims as the enemy, and as Europe's 'Other' that should be chased out, whose lands should be invaded and colonized by the West to introduce him to modernity, enlightenment and democracy (Qureshi and Sells, 2003). Since then, Islam in European discourses continued to be perceived as a backward religion and as being at odds with modernity, globalism, democracy, freedom, etc.

A global discourse

In his discussion of the reasons that led the West to continuously represent Islam as a religion that does not belong to the West, Said (1997) attributes this long-standing hostility and constant fear of Islam to the historical relationship between Islam and Christianity. He points out that the West has always seen Islam as a persistent concern and challenge to Christianity because it is the only religion that has never entirely submitted to the West and has refused to submit to the concept of the separation between the State and Church. Accordingly, it could be said that just as the secularization of Christianity turned the West into a modern and Western place and turned the Western culture into a great culture, it was Islam's 'religio-cultural challenge' to secularism on the other hand, that has reduced Islam in the Western eyes to a 'monolithic entity' (Said, 1997).

> In one way or another that combination of fear and hostility has persisted to present day, both in scholarly and non-scholarly attention to an Islam which is viewed as belonging to a part of the world – the Orient – counter posed imaginatively, geographically, and historically *against* Europe and the West.
>
> (Said, 1994, p. 343)

It is paradoxical but profoundly true that the modern post-colonial world that condemns racism and discrimination remains loyal and tolerant to a 600 or 1,000-year-old racist language that 'otherizes' about one-quarter of the world populations (Lyons, 2014). This line of continuity was seen in the last few decades particularly at the end of the Cold War and especially post 9/11, which has shown a global and dramatic shift regarding the escalation and hostility towards Islam and Muslims, not only in the United States but also around the world. The events of 9/11 have reopened old debates on Islam as well as the 'West' bringing to the surface 'inconvenient questions' not only about the position of Islam in relationship to modernity and the European understanding of world history, but also the implications of this understanding in the world today (Salama, 2011, p. 9). Since then, Islam has been at the forefront of media discussions, and the intense focus on the role of Islam in terrorizing and threatening the West, its civilization and its ways of life has become greater than ever before. The same 'crafted' views of Islam were recycled and restored to be used again in contemporary critics of Islam (Salama, 2013). It was one of the moments that witnessed an ideological and intellectual construction of Islam as a problematic object (Lyons, 2014).

Although these anti-Islam discourses are constructed in the West by a few powerful political and intellectual elites and prominent Islamophobes, it has a universal quality that allows it to depict the 1.6 billion Muslims around the world as real potential enemies (Shryock, 2010). Such ideologies of constructing others as different and threatening led to a shared sense of legitimacy, of collective oppression and violent exclusion (Werbner, 2013). Anti-Islam post-colonial discourses furnished the ground for biased narratives to be acceptable to public opinion, creating a worldwide atmosphere of hatred, prejudice and racism that justifies violations and crimes against Muslims – in the name of the 'War on Terror'.

Indeed, it is this same anti-Islam discourse that set the foundation for the Egyptian President, Sisi, to be accepted by domestic, regional and international communities, despite his unprecedented violations of human rights, under the name of 'the war on terror'. The next section will elaborate and discuss a brief overview of Egypt with a focus on the recent political situation since the 2013 military coup d'état. This overview is believed to be necessary for an understanding of the circumstances that contributed to the recent formation of a Self-Orientalist discourse on Islam in Egypt.

Overview

Egypt is located in the Northeast of the African continent and is facing the Mediterranean Sea on the North and the Red Sea on the East. The Nile River, the longest river on the earth, runs through its land creating a fertile green valley across it. Along both sides of the Nile River and the Nile Delta, small cities and villages scattered where many generations of Egyptians have lived and farmed. By the Nile banks, Egypt's ancient Pharaoh civilization developed, which traced back to 3100 BC.

Close to the Nile Delta, Cairo, the city that never sleeps, as many like to call it, is located. It is the capital and the country's largest city and is home for about 19 million people. Egypt is one of the most populous countries in the Middle East with an estimated population of more than 90 million. Islam is the religion of about 90 per cent of Egyptians, but there is also a large minority of Christians (Copts) in Egypt whose numbers are estimated to be about 10 per cent of the population. Islam stretched back to the seventh century when Arab Muslims, under the leadership of Amr Ibin el 'As, defeated the Byzantines and introduced Islam to the country. Egypt or 'Misr' as the country is called in Arabic, was under the Byzantine Empire rule until the seventh century. Afterwards, the country became a part of the Islamic Caliphate and remained under its control until Napoleon Bonaparte invaded Egypt in 1798. The short-term French occupation of Egypt (1798–1801) allowed Mohammad Ali Pasha to take control of Egypt by separating it from the Ottoman Caliphate – the last Islamic Caliphate – and establishing his dynasty, which lasted from early nineteenth century to mid-twentieth century when the Egyptian revolution of 1952 took place ending both the British colonization and the Egyptian Khedivate.

Since then – with the exception of President Mohammad Morsi's short term (June 2012– July 2013) – Egypt has been controlled by the Egyptian military given that all of the presidents who served the country were former military offi-cers starting with President Mohammad Naguib, who was sworn in as the coun-try's first president in the aftermath of the revolution until President Mubarak. President Naguib's rule did not last long as Gamal Abdel Nasser, the second Egyptian President, seized control of the country in 1954 after removing Presi-dent Naguib. After President Nasser's death, his Prime Minister, Anwar Sadat, took office in 1971 and his rule lasted until his assassination in 1981. He was then followed by the fourth President Hosni Mubarak, whose rule of the country lasted for 30 years when he was swept from power as a result of the 2011 Egyp-tian uprising. This illustrates that all of the four Egyptian presidents who ruled the country between 1952 and 2011 were sworn in as presidents without elec-tions; under their rule, Egypt has never had free elections as the people had no saying on who controls the country. It is true that in 2005, under Mubarak's rule, Egypt had its first multi-candidate presidential election in the country's history, but this election was marked by fraud and boycotts. President Mohammad Morsi was the first Egyptian President ever to take office as a result of free elections. However, he only served from June 2012 to July 2013 as he was removed from power due to a coup d'état led by his then Defence Minister, General Abdel Fattah el-Sisi.

The case of ousting the first democratically elected President

On 13 July 2013, almost a year after the inauguration of Mohammed Morsi, the first civilian and democratically elected Egyptian President, a military coup led by his Defence Minister, and now President, Abd el-Fattah el Sissi, removed President Morsi and 'ultimately gave rise to precisely the kind of authoritarianism Egyptian revolutionaries had been railing against in January 2011' (Fahmy and Faruqi, 2017, p. 1). As a reaction to the removal of President Morsi, the oppon-ents of the military coup organized two massive sit-in protests in Rabaa' and El Nahda squares demanding the reinstatement of the elected president. One month later, on 14 August 2013, the Egyptian security forces raided the two camps opening fire on peaceful civilians killing hundreds of them in what was later described by Human Rights Watch as one of the world's most massive killings of demonstrators in a single day in recent history (Human Rights Watch, 2013).

Since this horrifying massacre, repression and unprecedented levels of human rights' violations against the regime's political opponents and Muslim Brother-hood members have continued to take place and have been largely tolerated in the name of 'war on terror'. According to Human Rights Watch, during the first year after the 2013 coup, at least 2,500 civilians were killed and 17,000 were injured (Dunne and Williamson, 2014). By March 2015, nearly 2 years after the coup, approximately 40,000 people, including leftists, journalists and students were arrested because they allegedly supported the Muslim Brotherhood (Human Rights Watch, 2015). 'It is not an exaggeration to say that every offense which President Morsi was accused of has been blatantly, and often shamelessly, com-mitted a hundred times over by President Sisi' (Abou el Fadl, 2017, p. 240).

However, most secular liberal groups that advocate democracy and freedom turned a blind eye to this unparalleled abuse of human rights and rather than condemning, let alone protesting it, they launched a vigorous campaign not only on political Islam but 'Islam' as a whole in order to justify not only the military coup that removed the first democratically elected president but also the human rights' violations that followed it. A few protested and suffered the ire of the repressive state, a few more fell silent, but most, accompanied by atonal narratives about the many shades of legitimacy, continued to support the Sissi regime' (Abou el Fadl, 2017, p. 241). Moreover, before the Rabaa' massacre took place, secular and liberal Egyptians were relatedly heard criticizing Sisi for not being brutal enough with protestors and rushing him to kill them (Hamid, 2015). Calls for the killing of the Muslim Brotherhood in particular and protestors in general were also heard on TV shows, as popular TV hosts were repeatedly urging President Sissi to retaliate from protestors; on one occasion a popular Egyptian TV host publicly urged for more blood and more protestors' corpses (Sada El Balad, 2015). This situation brings into question the position of the Egyptian secularized intelligentsia in regards to the concept of democracy, as well as shedding light onto how they often imagine themselves as

the one and only true possessors of legitimacy, not because they represent the sovereign will, but because they, and they alone, possess the civilizational and intellectual values necessary for a progressive order in which true democracy, unhampered by reactionary forces, can be achieved.

(Abou el Fadl, 2017, p. 241)

On the other hand, state and private Egyptian media represented the military coup as a legitimate move against President Morsi and the Muslim Brotherhood by amplifying the number of his opponents. The *tamarod* movement, which led the 2013 insurgence 'exaggerated its claims to have collected 22 million signatures in opposition to Morsi's presidency' (Fahmy and Faruqi, 2017, p. 2) They also emphasized the coup supporters' public reactions including renowned anti-Islam politicians claiming the legalization of the coup, and the cheering crowds on the *Tahrir* (Liberation) Square. They depicted the massacres as a necessary action in accordance with the 'war on terror' as well as a vital step towards the establishment of democracy describing the opponents of the coup, be they Islamists or not, as a national security threat. Despite the fact that removing a democratically elected head of state is not usually tolerated and accepted by local and international communities, and despite the insubstantiality of the official charges levelled by the military against President Morsi and his cabinet, the international community – with few exceptions – refrained from condemning the military coup, and the massacre that accompanied it. Ironically, rather than calling for the return of the first democratically elected Egyptian President, they advocated for a faster return to democracy.

In order to justify these human rights' violations, the political and secularized intelligentsia in Egypt resorted to a well-crafted Islamophobic discourse originating from Western Orientalism, with a deliberate representation of Islam as inherently problematic, violent and non-democratic. This image was reinforced by the characterization of Islamic culture as static, hence lacking dynamism and growth, and consequently an uninspiring model for any civilization. Subsequently, this narrative created a widespread consensus that it is through downgrading the role of Islam – let alone political Islam – in shaping the Egyptian society that Egypt be restored and safeguarded.

Modernization and Islamic identity

The previous section highlights the political conditions under which narratives on Islam in general and political Islam, in particular, were constructed. It reveals the ways in which Egyptian secular liberals went against their liberal values by supporting the removal of the first democratically elected president, the return of the military to power and the persecution of political Islamists under the claim of the 'war on terror'. Islam in Egypt has been an object of change and the source of heated debates since the nineteenth century and attempts to modernize Egypt have taken place on many occasions over the past two centuries since the country came into direct contact with the European civilization. This issue raised enormous debates creating two opposing trends; one argued that Islam and modernization do not conflict, and the other rejected the idea, stressing that Egyptians should adhere to their Islamic identity.

However, modernization attempts were not only limited to Egypt nor were they advocated just by Egyptian modernists. In the post-colonial era, a move towards modernization and secularization started to take place in the entire Muslim world, which paved the way for a gradual displacement of Islam as the basis of Muslim society and for an acceptance of secularism in its place (Kumar, 2012). These modernizing reforms resulted in the creation of a new secular and Western-oriented middle class that were given positions of importance in government, education and law. They eventually led the early national liberation struggles in various Islamic countries (Kumar, 2012). This Arab class was a Western by-product that was formed through a discourse that made them feel inferior to the West (Moore-Gilbert, 1997). They viewed themselves through the lenses of the 'Oriental' and thus exercised their hegemony in the region through the borrowed language of Orientalism, and through the vocabulary of modernization (Dabashi, 2011). Their desire to be modern led them to see religion as dispensable to society and see modernization and secularism as the only option (Bayoumi, 2010). With Western support and media propaganda, this class gradually succeeded to construct a sense of devaluation of Islam in countries with Muslim majorities. They used the same Orientalist discourse to serve the Western interests in the Middle East on the one hand and to advance their own ideological and political gains on the other hand.

Interestingly, the emergence of this Western-oriented class was not a coincidence; the colonizer has always been aware that controlling the masses would not be possible without the help of native intellectuals. The colonial officer, Thomas Macaulay, revealed this concept when he stated,

> We must at present do our best to form a class who may be interpreters between us and the millions whom we govern – a class of persons Indian in blood and colour, but English in tastes, in opinions, in morals and in intellect.
>
> (Cutts, 1953, p. 825)

This is precisely what has been happening in the Muslim world, including Egypt, from the time when the Western colonizer decided to control people with 'sociology' rather than troops (Asad, 1973).

Since then, debates over the relationship between Islam and modernization are ongoing. Both for the advocates and opponents of modernization, stripping Egypt from its Islamic identity was not an option as the central question was how to modernize while remaining Muslim (Najjar, 2014). Their aim was to marginalize the role Islam plays in society but not to distort it, or to form a link to terrorism and violence. However, the last few years have presented a dramatic shift in the discourse of Egyptian secularized intelligentsia on Islam, who unlike their predecessors, do not only call for a separation of Islam from politics, or a marginalization of its role, but rather for a separation of Islam from the Egyptian society. Attempts to secularize the society and shift Egyptians' perceptions of the place and nature of religion in their everyday life have occurred before under Presidents Nasser and Mubarak, but arguably, at no other time in Egyptian history has Islam been reduced to a handful of negative generalizations and stereotypes, as has been the case in recent years. A brief look at the contemporary situation in Egypt – where Gamal al-Din al-Afghani and Muhammad Abduh planted the first seeds for an Islamic reform that sought to advance and modernize the system without stripping its Islamic identity – reveals how far Muslim modernists are today from these early attempts. In the following pages, this chapter attempts to investigate the ways in which various meanings of Orientalism inform the making of Islam among the secularized intelligentsia in Egypt. It is particularly interested in sketching some of the salient features of 'Self-Orientalism' in the dominant discourse on Islam in the Egyptian media.

Focusing now on the primary objective, which is to briefly elaborate on the discursive construction of Islam in the media and policy circles, I draw upon Fairclough's Critical Discourse framework. The following three sections focus on both micro and macro sociological analysis by deconstructing the linguistic and discursive characteristics of the texts, through word-choice and style of argument, and exploring whether the texts under analysis challenge or reproduce the order of discourse (Fairclough, 1992). Given that the main focus of discourse analysis is on how certain discourses are constructed, it 'is most often linked to small studies based on theoretical/intentional selection of cases' (Lindekilde, 2014, p. 210) Hence the chapter limits itself to a few selected cases.

The data gathered for the textual analysis is collected from the most popular and widespread TV shows in Egypt, including two different segments from Amr Adeeb's TV shows *Al Qahera Wannas* and *Kul Yawm*; Youssef Al-Husseini, on *ONTV*, the Egyptian intellectual and journalist, Khaled Muntasser on *Sky News Arabia*, and the Egyptian secular writer and thinker, Sayed el Qemy on *Al-Hurra TV*. The chapter also analyses a segment of a political speech for the Egyptian President Sisi. Both Adeeb and El Husseini are very popular in Egypt and their shows are widely viewed. Adeeb's shows in particular are among the leading programmes in Egypt due to his simple and sarcastic style; he is an iconic TV host and one of the highest paid. Like most of the Egyptian TV show hosts, Adeeb is also known to be a mouthpiece of the regime. All of my selected data are accessible online as I retrieved the TV shows' episodes online from YouTube. The reason behind my selection of these particular TV shows is based on their diverse ownership as well as their ratings given that they are considered among the highest ranked and most viewed TV shows in Egypt. While *ONTV* and *Al Qahera Wannas* private satellite TV channels are owned by Egyptian businessmen, *Sky News Arabia* is a joint venture between Abu Dhabi Media Investment Corporation and UK-based Sky plc, and Al-Hurra Channel is a US-based public Arabic-language channel. Another reason behind my selection is based on the political stand of these TV channels as most – if not all – of the Egyptian state and privately owned TV channels are regarded as propaganda tools to the Egyptian regime.

Using the various mediums of the media as tools of propaganda is not new to the government; since the country gained its independence from the British colonization in 1952, Egyptian rulers have recognized the significant influence of the media in mobilizing the people and shaping their views (Abdullah, 2014). And since the television has been deemed more powerful and influential than both the press and radio (Amin and Napoli, 1999), the government highly relied on it to shape public opinion and establish consent. In the name of national development, a top-down media policy was adopted in Egypt and the government was allowed full control over both radio and television (Chiba, 2009). As a result of the high rates of illiteracy in Egypt, both the radio and television were used as means to reach Egyptians and 'evoke enthusiasm for the social, political, and economic changes' (Abdullah, 2014; Rugh, 2004, p. 188). It is true that the introduction of the private satellite TV channels and cable TV to Egypt have played a role in providing diversified voices and providing some outlet within the state control, yet these channels did not affect the democratization process (Elouardaoui, 2013). Due to the state's censorship laws, as well as the impact of the close ties between the TV private channels and the ruling regimes in Egypt, the level of neutrality of these channels in relation to news coverage is very questionable (Elouardaoui, 2013). 'Instead of being an agent for democratization, the nascent bourgeoisie [particularly the business owners] in Egypt has become, in fact, a major foundation of support for an authoritarian regime' (Abdel-Khalek and Al Sayyid, as cited in Elouardaoui, 2013, p. 107).

I identified three dominant discourses propagated in the media. One is suggesting that Islam creates problems, and the other two argue that Islam reinforces terrorism and backwardness. Along with a number of other sub-discourses, they depicted Islam as a religion that causes problems on a global scale by radicalizing its adherents and reinforcing, ignorance, irrationality and superstitious among them. Together these three frames constructed Islam as a religion that is incompatible with modernity, sciences, reform and co-existence with others. The following pages examine these three discourses, suggesting that the construction of Islam among politicians and secularized intelligentsia in Egypt is informed by meanings of Orientalism and Islamophobia.

Islam as reinforcing terrorism

This discursive pattern, which noticeably attributes terrorism to Islam, is an example of a series of narratives that began long before the 2013 military coup. In the aftermath of the brief rise of the Muslim Brotherhood-linked Freedom and Justice Party (FJP) in 2012, the discourse of 'terrorism' was aggressively stressed and was attributed not only to the political stance of certain Islamists groups but rather Islam as a whole was taken within its fold. At this time, Egyptian political elites and secularized intelligentsia – who were disturbed by the arrival of President Morsi from the FJP to office – used the mass media expansively to circulate their hostile debates on Islam with the aim of justifying the military coup and its human rights' violations. In order to further strengthen this narrative of terrorism, two additional sub-discourses were used; the first being 'terrorism as exclusively Islamic' and the second 'Islamic history as bloody'.

For instance, on 8 April 2018, speaking of the Syrian regime's chemical attacks on Douma, the Egyptian news network ONTv, the privately owned and widely watched news network, Adeeb projected the attack as a religious or specifically Islamic attack, rather than a political attack by the Syrian authoritarian regime against its people. He said:

> At the end of the day, there is a tragedy, a disaster. At the end of the day, there is a human massacre, by all levels. Such a thing does not occur elsewhere except in the Arab and Muslim world. In this world where the earth planet exists and billions of people live, such dirty tragedies, which are humiliating to humanity, do not happen anywhere else in the 21st century except for the Arab Muslim countries. Therefore, we Arabs whether Muslims or Christians need to take a look at ourselves. Honestly, we have become a source of shame for ourselves. Honestly, it does not matter who is behind the attack. You say: It's the regime, the opposition, the Al-Nusra Front, ISIS. Say whatever you want, but ultimately, we have become a source of shame! We are a source of shame! We are a source of shame for the world and humanity, by what we are doing to ourselves. Nowhere else in the world do people do to themselves what we are doing to ourselves. Such thing has become beyond belief and beyond tolerance. It seems that

we have within us things that are not merely wrong but also horrifying. We have to confront ourselves, and realize that besides all the talk about international interests, imperialistic conspiracies and so on, we have become a source of shame for ourselves by what we do to ourselves. I'm serious. Honestly, we have reached the lowest level in terms of humanity. We have reached a level that is beyond any expectation because what we are doing to ourselves is beyond all standards.

(ON Ent, 2018)

Adeeb's use of the 'we' versus 'they' or 'us' versus 'them', a very transparent Orientalist discourse – with 'we' referring to Arab Muslims and 'they' referring to the remaining of the world – suggests that Adeeb sees the world as divided into two camps; Muslims, and the remainder of the world, which implies that Muslims are different in essence from everyone else on the entire planet. Moreover, he portrayed them as a 'source of shame', and as 'bringing shame to themselves, the world, and humanity'. He did not clarify as to why all Muslims should be blamed for this tragedy, or why they should be held accountable for a crime they were not responsible for. He severs the story from its larger context and conveniently reduces it to look more like a religious problem rather than a political conflict. It is true that both the attacker and the attacked are Muslims; nonetheless the victims have been killed for political reasons. Moreover, Adeeb's inability to connect what he calls 'filthy tragedies, which are humiliating to humanity' to the Syrian authoritarian regime – which is backed by Russia, Iran and a number of other Arab regimes, including Egypt – is a not a blatant logical fallacy but a complete distortion of facts. Not only did he avoid discussing who the attacker is, he also defended the Syrian regime by claiming that it has no reasons to attack Douma.

Moreover, Adeeb argues that the problem is caused by things that 'we' (Muslims) seem to have within 'us', things that are not merely wrong, but also horrifying'. He did not declare what these horrifying things that exist only within the 'Arab and Muslim world' are. He left it ambiguous and up to the viewers to draw a conclusion. He also made it very clear that it is something that exists solely among Muslims. To prevent this problem, Adeeb suggests that Muslims need to confront themselves and, rather than blaming this on 'international interest' or 'imperialistic conspiracies', they should realize that 'they have become a source of shame'. Furthermore, in his enthusiastic attempt to prove that violence and terrorism are exclusively a Muslim phenomenon, Adeeb overlooked such horrific atrocities, for example: the thousands of Bosnian Muslims killed, injured raped and tortured in the twentieth century by their Croatians Christian neighbours; the persecution, killing and imprisonment of Palestinian civilians in the twentieth and twenty-first centuries at the hands of the Israeli Jewish government; the continued ethnic cleansing of Burmese Muslimsand brutalities of the Rohingyas at the hands of Buddhists. However, this is not the first time Adeeb uses the discourse of terrorism as exclusively Islamic in discussing terrorist attacks.

On 22 March 2016, on his live show *Al Qahira al Yawm*, on *Al-Yawm* TV channel, commenting on the terrorist attacks in Brussels, Adeeb blamed Islam, though this time directly, for terrorism. He argued that neither ISIS, nor Al-Qaeda or Islamists, but solely Islam, should be held accountable for these acts of terror, stressing that terrorists around the world adopt their ideologies from Islam. When his co-host, Rania Badawi, told him that these terrorist assaults are committed by a group of Muslim individuals and not religion, Adeeb invited her to look at history stating that it was Muslims who killed Hussein and three of the righteous (*rashideen*) caliphs while performing their prayers. He asked sarcastically, 'Who killed them? Was it Belgium or Britain or maybe the CIA?' Adeeb then asked her why we do not hear about Jews or Christians shooting innocent people anywhere in the world, and why Muslims are the only perpetrators of these crimes (Coptic Eagle, 2016)? Adeeb here is not merely pointing to Islam as the source of terrorism, but is also claiming that the Islamic history is full of blood. By using words like 'solely', 'neither' and 'the only', and connecting them to Islam and Muslims, again, this suggests that terrorism is exclusively Islamic. Also, by connecting these terrorists attacks to the Islamic history and inviting his co-host to 'look at the history', Adeeb implies that Islam has been a source of violence since its early days and that Muslims have been the sole perpetrators of terrorist acts since the birth of Islam. As usual, the solution he suggests is that 'we must confront ourselves' and 'look at ourselves' with 'we' referring to Muslims.

Another example was on 19 June 2017, following the vehicular attack outside a London mosque. It is for the Egyptian TV host Youssef Al-Husseini on ONTV on the day of the attack. He said:

> In all the previous vehicular attacks, at least in 2016 and 2017, the 'heroes' were, unfortunately, Muslims. And then people wonder why they hate us. Why do they hate us?! If they didn't, there would be something mentally wrong with them. [We] use weapons all the time, slaughter people all the time, flay people all the time, burn people alive all the time, run people over all the time, and plant explosive devices and car bombs all the time. Why do you still expect them to love you?
>
> (Volokh, 2015)

By changing the question from 'why did they kill us (Muslims)?' to 'why do they hate us', Al Husseini victimizes the oppressor and criminalizes the victim. Meanwhile, his statement suggests that attacks against Muslims are justifiable because 'they' (the world) have the right to hate 'us' (the Muslims) or otherwise 'there would be something wrong'. So their hate is rational and justifiable mentally because 'we slaughter them'. By using words and phrases such as, 'slaughter', 'use weapons', 'flay', 'burn alive', 'run over' and 'plant', Al Husseini suggests that Muslims are not only extremely violent but are also skilful in using their violence. His use of the present continuous tense with words such as 'all the time' in verbs such as 'slaughter', 'flay' or 'burn', indicates that Muslims are perpetually killing their 'others'. Furthermore, by using the indefinite word 'people', Al Husseini suggests that Muslims' terrorism has no limits; they kill anyone and everyone at all times. He portrays it as a war between 'them' (the Muslims) and 'people'. To give terrorism in Islam an exclusive and historical nature, and to add to the Islamic history a bloody trait, Al Husseini later questions whether Muslims have ever contributed anything to the West other than slaughter and massacres. Then he adds, 'It's true. That's what the Turks did in Europe in the 16th and 17th centuries' (Memri, 2017).

As the previous discursive units show, to feed this discursive construction of 'terrorism as Islamic', words and phrases like 'nowhere', 'does not happen anywhere in the world', 'except in the Arab and Islamic world', 'do not occur elsewhere', were excessively used, which suggests that terrorism is an exclusively Islamic phenomenon. It is also established through recurring words and phrases such as 'only', 'sole', 'nobody else', 'nowhere else' and so on. By polarizing the world into 'Muslims' versus 'others', and exclusively attributing terrorism to Muslims, this discourse propelled a causal relationship between Islamism and terrorism, and subsequently portrays Islam as the only generator of terrorism.

Islam as a source of problems

Another frequent discourse in regard to Islam that propagated in many media outlets is 'Islam as a source of problems'. According to this rhetoric, Islam is conceptualized as a burden and a source of trouble not only to Egypt and Egyptians, but also to the 'entire world'. For example, on 1 January 2015, Sisi addressed a speech at Al-Azhar University in the anniversary of the Prophet. He said:

> I am referring here to the religious clerics. We have to think hard about what we are facing – and I have, in fact, addressed this topic a couple of times before. It's inconceivable that the thinking that we hold most sacred should cause the entire umma [Islamic world] to be a source of anxiety, danger, killing and destruction for the rest of the world. Impossible! That thinking – I am not saying 'religion' but 'thinking' – that corpus of texts and ideas that we have sanctified over the centuries, to the point that departing from them has become almost impossible, is antagonizing the entire world. It's antagonizing the entire world! Is it possible that 1.6 billion people [Muslims] should want to kill the rest of the world's inhabitants – that is 7 billion – so that they themselves may live? Impossible!
>
> (Volokh, 2015)

In this speech, Sisi's recurrent use of words such as 'inconceivable', 'impossible', 'antagonizing' and 'we are in need' suggests that there is an enormous problem that needs to be taken into consideration. Like Adeeb, Sisi is relying here on the 'we' versus 'they' binary discourse with the first representing the Muslims and the latter representing the remainder of the world. This exclusionary discourse suggests that Muslims are not a part of, nor do they belong to, the remaining world. It polarizes the world into 'dangerous Muslims' versus 'endangered others'. The causes of the problem according to Sisi's speech is the Islamic 'thinking' or 'the corpus of texts and ideas' that Muslims have been carrying throughout the centuries, which implies that the entire Islamic 'thinking' or 'ideas' without any filtration or exception reinforces violence and terrorism. Sisi is not directly blaming Islam; however, he is blaming the legacy of Islam – which he refers to as the 'entire Islamic thinking' – and is blaming the 'entire Muslim *ummah*' with no exceptions. By saying this, Sisi is assuming that every single person among the 1.6 billion Muslims including moderates, non-practicing or even seculars wants to kill 'the others'. Furthermore, he regards every one of them to be 'a source of destruction' to the entire world. The question here is what is the common thing that connects all these people other than their Islamic identity? Apparently, it is enough for one to be a Muslim to be regarded as a menace or threat to 'the others'. Additionally, the recurrent use of absolute in words and phrases like the 'entire *ummah*', the '1.6 billion Muslims' or 'the world's inhabitants' highly emphasizes the impression that Muslims 'otherize' non-Muslims, and thus are at war with these 'others'. This makes it look as if there is a conflict of values and a clash of civilization between the two camps. On the other hand, Sisi did not specify which 'corpus of texts and ideas' he is referring to. By putting everything in the same basket, Sisi's statement implies that Islamic texts altogether, since the seventh century onwards, reinforces othering, violence, and terrorism.

To prevent this problem, and save the 'entire world', Sisi is calling for a 'religious revolution'. He demonstrates:

> I say and repeat again that we are in need of a religious revolution. You, imams, are responsible before Allah. The entire world, I say it again, the entire world is waiting for your next move … because this umma is being torn, it is being destroyed, it is being lost – and it is being lost by our own hands.
>
> (Volokh, 2015)

However, these are only a few examples among many others. Political figures and Egyptian secularized intelligentsia took turns implying that Islam and Muslims have become a source of troubles and problems to the entire world. This particular understanding flows from connecting Islam or Muslims with words and phrases like 'a source of anxiety', 'a source of shame', 'a source of killing and destruction to the rest of the world', 'a shame upon ourselves and humanity', 'filthy tragedies', 'humiliating' and so on. The linguistic constitution of Islam or Muslims as a source of problems was further constituted through recurrent use of phrases and sentences that suggest that the Islamic thought has created a worldwide dilemma, and that the world is waiting for Muslims to repair this form of damage. Some of these phrases were 'antagonizing the entire world', 'the rest of the world', and other phrases such as, 'we have to think hard about what we are facing', or 'the entire world is waiting for your next move'.

Islam as a backward religion

Despite the long and sophisticated history of Islamic science, the role of Muslims in science has been downplayed not only by Western Orientalists but Egyptian Self-Orientalists as well. This trend emphasized in the last decades enabled the construction of an image of Islam as a backward religion that has contributed and still contributes to the decline of Muslims and the Muslim world. Speaking of the Quran's scientific *i'jaz* (miraculous nature) to Sky News Arabia on 20 April 2018, Khaled Montaser, an Egyptian intellectual and journalist projected Muslims as 'lazy', 'feel inferior', 'paralyzed' and in need of someone to reassure them. He states:

> This (Qur'an's scientific miraculous nature) is a man-product for those who feel inferior and feel the huge gap that exists between them and the West. What is the solution? Can we become like the West. They ask themselves. But requires a very long time and effort, and they are lazy – lazy in mind, lazy in body, and lazy in all aspects. Therefore, the solution is to say that every existing or newly invented thing in the West has already existed in the Quran and the Hadith.
>
> (Sky News Arabia, 2018)

The previous statement reveals that not only did Montaser use the colonial binary division of 'they' and 'the West', he also attributed all the negative traits and characters to 'they', which refer to Muslims and did not use any adjectives to depict the 'West'. This is simply because the 'West', according to him, is the opposite of the Muslim world. His use of phrases and questions such as a 'huge gap', 'what can we do?' or 'can we become like the West', suggests that the Western model is superior to the Muslim model and thus should be followed by everyone. Moreover, he added, 'scientific-miraculous' nature (*i'jaz*) served as an anaesthetic or a nice sedative for the Arabs and the Muslims to make them feel superior: 'we are superior', 'we are the best', 'we are the greatest'. By using words and phrases such as 'sedative', 'aesthetic' and 'making them feel superior', Montaser echoes the Western theory of the clash of civilization by suggesting that Muslims' backwardness and ignorance created an inferiority complex among Muslims that led them to envy the West for their civilization and rationality. Their only reason to study the *ijaz* of the Qur'an is to overcome this inferiority complex and prove that they 'are superior' and 'the best'. Montaser's use of words such as, 'delusion', and phrases such as 'We are at the tail end of the nations' and 'lowest level of humanity', suggests that Islam reinforces particular types of actions and attitudes such as 'ignorance', 'laziness of body', 'laziness of mind', 'undemocratic means', 'superstitions' and so on. To feed this discursive construction, he attributes Muslims' laziness in both body and mind to their *fatwa*-style and their reliance on the Qur'an and Hadith in everything they do. Montaser here suggests that whereas the Western model encourages science, rationality and modernity, the Islamic model reinforces laziness of mind and body, irrationality and deficiency and is thus incompatible with modernity. He said that, unlike *fatwas*, 'the scientist cannot provide' Muslims with the 'reassurance' they need. Asked by his host what makes him attribute the 'backward' phenomena to the Arabs and Muslims alone, Montaser replied that this is because 'in the Islamic world, superstitions constitute a sweeping current'.

Another profoundly hostile example on the relationship between Islam and science is the Egyptian TV host Youssef Al-Husseini, on ONTV, on 19 June 2017, where he was asking what Muslims have contributed to the world other than violence. He said:

> What have the Islamic countries contributed to the world? Nothing. What have they contributed in the field of scientific research? Two, three, four, or ten scientists in the course of 1,435 years? C'mon, man! Let's forget about 435 years and keep just one millennium. Ten important scientists in 1,000 years?
>
> (Memri, 2017)

Here, Husseini is boldly downplaying the role of Islamic sciences, philosophers and scientists over the past 1,435 years. His use of words like 'nothing', 'two, three, four, or ten' and 'C'mon, man' is a glaring example of undermining Muslims' contributions to science and a flagrant denial of the enormous intellectual contributions of Muslim scholars over several centuries in many different fields, including Algebra, astronomy, geography, physics, chemistry, mathematics, medicine, pharmacology, architecture, linguistics and so on. By using a question and answer format, Husseini gives the impression that he is discussing historical facts, not personal views and misconceptions. In a very direct way, he stressed that the Islamic model has contributed nothing to science and subsequently has not provided any good to the world. It has only provided 'terrorism', as he emphasized in the previous pages. So, why follow it? Why follow a model that is at odds with science and modernity?

This aligns with the Egyptian secular writer and thinker, Dr Sayed el Qemny who, in a statement on Islam in an interview aired on *Al-Hurra TV* on 24 January 2018, stated that Islam stopped adding anything 1000 years ago. He said:

> This [Islamic] heritage froze a thousand years ago; it froze in the fourth century of Islam as it has not moved forward, has not evolved, and has not been renewed since then. Therefore, and because it [religion] still constitutes the main source for the thinking of regular citizens, regular citizens do not turn to the natural sciences, mathematics and the like in order to resolve their problems. Instead, they turn to religion. Just imagine relying on a religion that stopped a thousand years ago adding anything, stopped changing anything, and stopped renewing itself.
>
> (Al-Hurra TV, 2018)

In this statement, el Qemny is echoing the Orientalist's claim of a static Islam that has been frozen since the fourth century, versus a dynamic West that relies on natural sciences. By attributing to Islam words and phrases like 'froze', 'stopped adding anything', 'stopped changing', 'stopped renewing itself', 'at odds with our times' and 'think according to the logic of a thousand years ago', el Qemny asserts that Islam is incompatible with modernity, democracy and natural sciences and subsequently is at complete odds with our times. Rahter, it is a backward religion that froze 1,000 years ago. He added:

> Because the door of ijtihad has been closed since Al Ma'moun's death, the way Muslims think is at complete odds with their time and era, because they think according to the logic of a thousand years ago. An entire millennium is no trivial matter because mankind and sciences have tremendously progressed and the in a way that no one could have anticipated. This great progress has made it impossible for Muslims to grasp and understand.
>
> (Al Hurra TV, 2018)

By using phrases like 'Muslims think', and 'they find it impossible to grasp', el Qemny is representing the 1.6 billion Muslims as a single homogenous unprogressive and underdeveloped entity that lacks the ability to make the right choices. They need someone, like el Qemny, to observe them, study them, think for them and represent them. Furthermore, el Qemny here is creating a causal relationship between Islam and the problems of the Muslims by claiming that it is Islam itself alone that should be blamed for the backwardness, defeat and regression of the Muslim world. He asks, 'We are among the most backward countries in the world. Why should anybody conspire against us? They can just leave us to our own devices. Our heritage is the best way to bring defeat, backwardness, and regression upon us.' Again, el Qemny's statement is a call for a total displacement of Islam from the Egyptian society.

Discursive analysis

The narrative on Islam is mostly constituted and reproduced by the mixing of three pre-existing discourses, which were formerly separated, namely the discourse of 'security versus chaos', the 'discourse of secularization' and the discourse of 'terrorism'. Whereas, the 'security' discourse is pre-occupied with the national stability of the state in the aftermath of the military coup, and the chaos that Muslim extremists have created in the Arab region, the 'secularization' discourse is interested in modernizing Egypt and getting it out of its darkness and backwardness. On the other hand, the discourse on 'terrorism' was mainly interested in terrorism as an explicitly Islamic phenomenon, political Islam and the bloody history of Muslims. For instance, in his discussion of the chemical attacks on the Syrian city of Douma, Adeeb fed the rhetoric of 'security' by using sentences such as, 'let's make our priority to protect the state', 'if you can't play a role in the Arab region, at least protect the state', 'Let's not allow what happened in Syria to be repeated in Egypt', 'We need to realize that we should not be lenient with and easy on violent groups' and 'the nation is the only side that has the right to use violence to resist violence' (ON Ent, 2018). To sum up, in all of the examined discursive units, Islam was constructed via particular words and phrases as violent, backward and problematic. These problems were presented as caused by the nature of Islam, which is inherently violent, reinforces terrorism and is incompatible with modernity.

Mixing these three discourses together in the texts portrays Islam in a particular light, a light in which violations of the human rights of the so-called 'terrorists' become national security and allowing Islam in the public sphere becomes a potential security problem. Furthermore, it portrays those who pose a challenge to Egypt's secularization and modernization as a potential security challenge because Islam is theorized as inherently problematic and violent according to this debate. By using these Islamophobic forms of discourses, Egyptian policy-makers and secularized intelligentsia furnished the ground for biased narratives on the Muslim Brotherhood to be acceptable by public opinion, creating a national atmosphere of fear of Islam that justifies human rights' violations – in the name of the 'War on Terror'. In sum, it was these discourses that paved the way for the military coup and the regime's massacres against its political opponents to be accepted by the Egyptian society and seen as legitimate moves and necessary steps towards the establishment of democracy and national security.

Conclusion

This chapter makes the argument that since President Morsi of the Muslim Brotherhood-linked Freedom and Justice Party took office in June 2012, the discursive construction of Islam in Egypt has been strongly informed by various discursive elements of Orientalism and Islamophobia. This is evident in the examined TV shows and political speeches with their continuous attempts to link 'Islam' to popularized notions of terrorism and backwardness, portraying the religion as a source of agony and despair for the Egyptian society and the entire world. It is also seen in their depiction of the vast and varied adherents of Islam as inherently violent fundamentalists and fanatics. Arguably, the discourse used to circulate this message is intended to serve the benefits of the Egyptian policy-makers and secularized intelligentsia by legitimizing the military coup against the first democratically elected president and normalizing the unprecedented human rights violations against any form of opposition to the current regime. As a consequence it goes even further in eradicating Islam from the public sphere by spreading fear of the religion in the Egyptian society.

Although the rhetoric on Islam in Egypt originates its vocabulary and ideas from Orientalism and Islamophobia, this chapter argues that Egyptian self-Orientalism still has its unique features: (1) with Egyptian self-Orientalism, the pronoun 'we' refers to the conservative or practicing Muslim 'other' and the pronoun 'they' refers to the remaining of the world; (2) unlike Western Orientalism, by including themselves with the 'other', self-Orientalists are more likely to be approved by the Muslim audience and their Orientalists' thoughts are more likely to be accepted by the society since it comes from within; (3) self-Orientalist discourse constructs an image of 'good' Muslims and 'bad' Muslims with the first referring to the one who separates his religion from the public sphere; (4) Egyptian self-Orientalists are bolder and offensive without attempting to be politically or historically correct; (5) their information is often inaccurate, and they have many historical and logical fallacies, which is a general feature of the discourse on Islam even in the West; (6) the journalists and presenters involved are not professionals, nor are they trained in journalism. They do not practice investigative journalism and rather present their personal views as facts. In conclusion, there is no doubt that Western Islamophobia has hugely harmed Islam, Muslims and the Muslim world by distorting the image of Islam and its legacies over the centuries. Regrettably, Muslim Egyptian self-Orientalists could even provide a more significant threat than their fellow Western Orientalists because they are people within the Egyptian community who speak the same language and have the same skin colour. Furthermore, they know how to communicate the message because they understand the culture and the behaviour, and have a grasp on the sociology of the country. In order to grab people's attention, they praise Islam and even repeat verses from the Qur'an, attempting to show respect. Through their fear-mongering tactics and narratives on Islam, this chapter argues, Muslim self-Orientalists are successfully pushing their agenda of normalizing Islamophobia within the Egyptian society.

Bibliography

Abdulla, R. (2014). Egypt's media in the middle of a revolution. *Carnegie Endowment for International Peace*. Retrieved from http://carnegieendowment.org/files/egypt_media_revolution.pdf, date of access: 24 May 2018.

Abou el Fadl, K. (2017). Egypt's secularized intelligentsia and the guardians of truth. In D. F. Fahmy and D. Faruqi (Eds), *Egypt and the contradictions of liberalism: Illiberal intelligentsia and the future of Egyptian democracy* (pp. 235–252). London: Oneworld Publications.

AlHayah TV Network (2016, 11 January). بوضـــوح - شـــريف الشوباشـــي : الحجـاب" اهانة" (Buwduh-Sherif el Shubashi: Hijab is an insult to the Islamic religion! Most veiled women wear hijab without conviction). الاسـلامي للــدين !! واغلـب المحجبـات يرتـدون الحجـاب بـدون اقتنـــاع Retrieved from www.youtube.com/watch?v=DwrgzFpG1pk, date of access: 24 May 2018.

Alhurra Channel (2018, 24 January). سـيد القمـني فـي حلقـة ناريـة: لـدي الجـرأة لكسـر كلّ الخطـوط الحْمـراء (Syed El Qemni: I have the audacity to break all the red lines). [Video file]. Retrieved from www.youtube.com/watch?time_continue=263&v=_p5BjcQ7cE4, date of access: 24 May 2018.

Al Jazeera Arabic (2005, April 17). دعوات فـي مصـر لخلــع الحجـاب (Calls in Egypt to remove the veil). [Video file]. Retrieved from www.youtube.com/watch?v=VlX4KNzjTSI, date of access: 24 May 2018.

Alquwaizani, M. (2012). *Orientalism and postcolonialism in modern Arab thought.* Beverly Hills, CA: Toppington Publishing.

Amin, H. and Napoli, J. (1999). Media and power in Egypt. In J. Curran and M. J. Park (Eds), *De-Westernizing media studies* (pp. 178–188). London: Routledge.

Asad, T. (Ed.) (1973). *Anthropology and the colonial encounter.* London: Ithaca Press.

Bayoumi, M. (2010). The god that failed: The neo-Orientalism of today's Muslim com-
mentators. In A. Shylock (Ed.), *Islamophobia Islamophilia beyond the politics of
enemy and friend* (pp. 79–93). Bloomington: Indiana University Press.

Chiba, Y. (2009). Media history of modern Egypt: A critical review. University Research
Information Repository. Retrieved from https://repository.kulib.kyoto-u.ac.jp/dspace/
bitstream/2433/155745/1/ssh_084.pdf, date of access: 24 May 2018.

Coptic Eagle. (2016, 1 December). العـــالم فـــي الارهاب مصـــدر الاســـلام/اديـــب عمرو (Amr
Adeeb: Islam is the source of terrorism in the world). [Video file]. Retrieved from
www.youtube.com/watch?v=a3GyCxBMztE, date of access: 24 May 2018.

Cutts, E. H. (1953). The background of Macaulay's minute. *The American Historical
Review*, 58(4), 824–853. Retrieved from www.jstor.org/stable/1842459?seq=1#page_
scan_tab_contents, date of access: 24 May 2018.

Dabashi, H. (2011). *Brown skin, white masks*. London: Pluto Press.

Dearden, L. (2016, 26 August). Burkini ban suspended: French court declares law forbidding swimwear worn by Muslim women 'clearly illegal'. *Independent.* Retrieved from
www.independent.co.uk/news/world/europe/burkini-ban-french-france-court-
suspends-rule-law-forbidding-swimwear-worn-muslim-women-seriously-a7211396.
html, date of access: 24 May 2018.

Dunne, M. and Williamson, S. (2013). *Egypt's unprecedented instability by the numbers.*
Report prepared for Carnegie Endowment for International Peace. Retrieved from
www.carnegieendowment.org/2014/03/24/egypt-s-unprecedentedinstability-by-numbers/
h5j3, date of access: 24 May 2018.

Elouardaoui, O. (2013). The crisis of contemporary Arab television: Has the move
towards transnationalism and privatization in Arab television affected democratization
and social development in the Arab World? *Global Societies Journal*, 1, 100–114.
Retrieved from www.global.ucsb.edu/gsj/sites/secure.lsit.ucsb.edu.gisp.d7_gs, date of
access: 24 May 2018.

Fahmy, D. and Faruqi, D. (2017). Egyptian liberals, from revolution to counterrevolution.
In D. F. Fahmy and D. Faruqi (Eds), *Egypt and the contradictions of liberalism: Illib-
eral Intelligentsia and the future of Egyptian democracy* (pp. 1–27). London: Oneworld
Publications.

Fairclough, N. (1992). *Discourse and social change*. Cambridge: Polity Press.

Hamid, S. (2015). Islamism, the Arab Spring, and the failure of America's do-nothing
policy in the Middle East. *The Atlantic.* Retrieved from www.brookings.edu/blog/
markaz/2015/10/14/islamism-the-arab-spring-and-the-failure-of-americas-do-nothing-
policy-in-the-middle-east/, date of access: 24 May 2018.

Human Rights Watch (2013). Egypt: Security forces used excessive lethal force.
Retrieved from www.hrw.org/news/2013/08/19/egypt-security-forces-used-excessive-
lethal-force, date of access: 24 May 2018.

Human Rights Watch (2015). UN human rights council: Adoption of the UPR report on
Egypt. Retrieved from www.hrw.org/news/2015/03/20/un-human-rights-council-
adoption-upr-report-egypt, date of access: 24 May 2018.

Khalil, F. (2015, 31 July). اقلـــع إتصيّفى؟ يعـــاوزة (Do you want to go to the beach? Then take
off your clothes). *El Yawm el Sabi'.* Retrieved from www.youm7.com/story/2015/7/31/
فـــى-ذروتهـــا-تصـــل-المحجبـــات-علـــى-الشـــواطئ-حرب-اقلعـــى-تصيّفى-عاوزة/2285578, date of
access: 24 May 2018.

Khiabany, G. (2008). The Iranian press, state, and civil. In Semati, M. (Ed.), *Media,
culture and society in Iran: Living with globalization and the Islamic state* (pp. 17–36).
New York: Routledge.

Kumar, D. (2012). *Islamophobia and the politics of empire*. Chicago: Haymarket Books.

Lal, V. (2014, 25 January). History of British India [Video file]. Retrieved from www.youtube.com/watch?v=Y0uh9uUGvlM, date of access: 24 May 2018.

Lindekilde, L. (2014). Discourse and frame analysis: In depth analysis of qualitative data in social movement research. In D. D. Porta (Ed.), *Practices in social movement research* (pp. 195–226). Oxford: Oxford University Press.

Lyons, J. (2014). *Islam through Western eyes: From the Crusades to the war on terrorism* (Reprint edition). New York: Columbia University Press.

Memri TV (2017, 19 June). Egyptian TV host Youssef Al-Husseini following London mosque attack: The Muslims have contributed nothing but terror, so why do you expect them to love you? [Video file]. Retrieved from www.memri.org/tv/egyptian-tv-host-following-london-attack-muslims%20contributed-terror/transcript, date of access: 24 May 2018.

Moore-Gilbert, B. (1997). *Postcolonial theory: Contexts, practices, politics* (1st edition). London: Verso.

Najjar, M. (2014). Whither the Islamic religious discourse? *Middle East Policy*, 21(1), 87–97. Retrieved from https://doi.org/10.1111/mepo.12059, date of access: 24 May 2018.

ON Ent (2018, 8 April). كاملة الحلقة 2018. أبريـل 8 الأحد – يـوم كل (Kul Yawm-Sunday, April 8, 2018 – Full episode). [Video file]. Retrieved from www.youtube.com/watch?v=9ZWl2wpA348, date of access: 24 May 2018.

Qureshi, E. and Sells, M. (Eds) (2003). *The new crusades: Constructing the Muslim enemy*. Karachi, Pakistan: Columbia University Press.

Rubin, A. J. (2016, 24 August). French 'burkini' bans Provoke backlash as armed police confront beachgoers. *New York Times*. Retrieved from www.nytimes.com/2016/08/25/world/europe/franceburkini.html?mcubz=0, date of access: 24 May 2018.

Rugh, W. A. (2004). *Arab mass media: Newspapers, radio, and television in Arab politics*. Westport, CT: Greenwood Publishing Group.

Sada el Balad (2015, 26 January). ارهاب دكوا " الهواء علـى ينفعـل موسـى احمد الاعلامـى المطريـة" (Ahmad Moussa: Destroy of El-Matarriyyah's terrorism). [Video file]. Retrieved from www.youtube.com/watch?v=fFSuRdf9mZM, date of access: 24 May 2018.

Said, E. W. (1994). *Orientalism* (25th edition). New York: Vintage.

Said, E. W. (1997). *Covering Islam: How the media and the experts determine how we see the rest of the world* (Revised edition). New York: Vintage.

Salama, M. R. (2011). *Islam, Orientalism and intellectual history: Modernity and the politics of exclusion since Ibn Khaldun*. London and New York: I.B.Tauris.

Sherif el Shoubashi: Calls to remove veil is directed against political Islam (2015, 18 April). *CNN*. Retrieved from https://arabic.cnn.com/middleeast/2015/04/18/calls-hijab-remove, date of access: 24 May 2018.

Shryock, A. (Ed.) (2010). *Islamophobia/Islamophilia: Beyond the politics of enemy and friend*. Bloomington: Indiana University Press.

Sky News Arabia (2018, 20 April). العـرب حـديث فـي منتصـر خالـد المصـري المفكـر (The Egyptian intellectual Khaled Muntasir at Hadeeth Al Arab). [Video file]. Retrieved from www.youtube.com/watch?v=6nT50KIfijM, date of access: 24 May 2018.

Tyrer, D. (2013). *The politics of Islamophobia: Race, power and fantasy*. London: Pluto Press.

Volokh, E. (2015, 4 January). We are in need of a religious revolution. *Washington Post.* Retrieved from www.washingtonpost.com/news/volokhconspiracy/wp/2015/01/04/we-are-in-need-of-a-religiousrevolution/?noredirect=on&utm_term=.452371b9f135, date of access: 24 May 2018.

Werbner, P. (2013). Folk devils and racist imaginaries in a global prism: Islamophobia and anti-Semitism in the twenty-first century. *Ethnic and Racial Studies*, 36(3), 450–467. Retrieved from https://doi.org/10.1080/01419870.2013.734384, date of access: 24 May 2018.

10 The confluence of race and religion in understanding Islamophobia in Malaysia

Mohamed Nawab Osman[1]

Introduction

You are taught what they (ulama) want you to know. They did not tell you that your Prophet has sexual relations with a nine year old child. They did not tell you that your Prophet encourages his followers to perform anal intercourse with their wives. They did not tell you that your Prophet wanted you to view women as land that can be used and sold as you wish and not as human beings who should be respected. Your religious scholars did not tell you the truth about how your Prophet died as a result of poisoning by one of this wives.

(David Orok, Politician from the Malaysian state of Sabah)

The above remarks by the Sabahan politician posted on his Facebook page are reflective of growing Islamophobia within Malaysia. David Orok was subsequently arrested and sentenced to 16 months imprisonment by the Malaysian courts. Subsequent reactions from many Malaysians were equally problematic. Many Malaysian Muslims not only criticized Orok but hurled insults against Christianity. On the other hand, some of Orok's supporters felt that the sentencing was too harsh and represents politicization of Islam in the Malaysian state that has curtailed the rights of non-Muslims in the country. This chapter seeks to understand Islamophobia in the context of Malaysia by examining the historical and contemporary structures of power that has enabled the rise of Islamophobia, the factors that have rendered Islamophobia increasingly normalized, as well as the manifestations of Islamophobia in Malaysia. This shall range from an examination of discriminatory policies, hate speech in cyberspace and the construction of dehumanizing political narratives. This chapter argues that Islamophobia in the Malaysian context needs to be understood from the lens of racism. Previously held cultural and racial biases against the Malay–Muslim majority populace in Malaysia is now viewed from the lens of religion. At the same time, Islamophobia in Malaysia has also been triggered by a strong sense that political Islam has encroached on the lives of many non-Muslims in the country. This chapter consists of three parts. First, the chapter will critically analyse the literature on race and Islamophobia. Second, the chapter will highlight some key factors that have led to the rise of Islamophobia in the country. Last, it will explain how Islamophobia in the Malaysian context should be viewed from the lens of cultural racism.

Islamophobia underpinned by cultural racism

Outside of academia, race is often treated as a teleological category. It is assumed that race is a 'tell-all' social identifier. A person is deemed to behave in a particular way because of his race. While race emerged as a pseudoscientific concept during European colonialism, claiming biology as a deterministic factor of a person's behaviour (Stoler, 1997), the notion of what race entails has since evolved – though the assumption of determinism still prevails. Here, the notion of cultural racism is relevant. Cultural racism involves the discrimination of people on the basis that their culture makes them inferior (Meer and Modood, 2012). Significantly, culture is assumed to be an inherited and thus *permanent* facet of one's life, rendering it impossible for a person to free himself from the prejudice that comes with being deemed to belong to a particular cultural group (Meer and Modood, 2012). Discrimination on the basis of religious membership functions similarly. Whereas one can technically leave Islam, and theoretically sidestep the Islamophobia accompanying it, 'no one chooses to be born into a society where to look like a Muslim or to be a Muslim creates suspicion, hostility, or failure to get the job you applied for' (Meer and Modood, 2012, p. 42). In other words, whether or not one leaves Islam is immaterial. One need only be perceived as a Muslim to suffer Islamophobia. In this vein, Islamophobia is thus a form of cultural racism that treats the norms, values and beliefs of Muslims as immovable characteristics of their existence (e.g. sexist, violent, dogmatic), with Islam as the totalizing source of all their convictions and behaviours (Grosfoguel, 2012).

This does not mean that Islamophobia manifests itself homogeneously across different contexts. There are particularities unique to the ethno-religious composition of a given society. Nonetheless, it can be understood through the lens of cultural racism. Within many societies in Southeast Asia, Islamophobia is expressed through the lens of racism. In Singapore, Malay–Muslims were treated as potentially treasonous for decades by the state – it believed that Malay–Muslims oriented their loyalties towards the Ummah, not other Singaporeans (Rahim, 2012). As a result, they were excluded from the system of mandatory conscription into the armed forces for nearly two decades (Rahim, 1999), and were generally excluded from units and appointments deemed sensitive to national security (e.g. pilots) (Hill, 2004). Additionally, the state characterizes the prevalence of diabetes among Malay–Muslims as a function of the diet specific to Malay–Muslims (Tan, 2017) without taking into account socio-economic status. The oversimplification of this discourse makes it appear that health issues are individual problems, not structural ones. Muslims in India are portrayed as unquestionably oppressive towards Muslim women because it is deemed that Islam permits them to divorce their wives instantly without offering recourse for women (Agnes, 2016). They are also characterized as violating the religious sensitivities of the Hindu-majority because they eat beef and thus endorse the slaughter of cows – an animal deemed holy in Hinduism (Sharma, 2009). In Myanmar, Rohingya Muslims have for decades been denied citizenship – thus forcibly rendered stateless and at the mercy of state and non-state persecution – because they are treated as descendants of Bengali migrants who were brought into Burma by the British (Ibrahim, 2016).

The Muslims in the Southern Philippines were first pejoratively termed Moros by the Spanish colonizers because their religious practices resembled the Muslims Moors, with whom they had warred repeatedly against in the crusades (Gowing, 1979). In each of these examples, the Islamophobia is patterned along culturalist lines peculiar to each of the contexts. The apparent affront felt by Hindus towards Muslims' consumption of beef is particular to the context of Hindu–Muslim relations in India. One would be hard pressed to find a similar dynamic between Hindus and Muslims on the issue of beef outside of India. Being treated as the symbolic Other to the national imaginary is a common form of Islamophobia Muslims face in many countries.[2] Some examples of this include India (Thapar, 2014), Thailand (Dorairajoo, 2009), the US (Ali *et al.*, 2011; Alsultany, 2012; Bazian, 2014; Dubosh, Poulakis and Abdelghani, 2015; Joseph and D'Harlingue, 2012), France (Louati, 2015), Germany (Hafez, 2014) and Norway (Døving, 2015). However, the Rohingyas are perhaps the only straightforward example of Muslims being victims of systemic exclusion from citizenship because of an Islamophobic regime. This particularity is a function of the historical and cultural context within which Rohingyas are located in – one that Muslims elsewhere do not necessarily share.

In another example, American Muslim student Ahmed Mohamed, whose home-made clock was confused as a bomb, was treated exceptionally well after the media uproar that came from the fact he was a victim of racial profiling. He went on to be granted a visit to the White House and President Obama, invited to visit Facebook and invited to a science fair by Google (Vincent, 2015). This has been described as Islamophilia, or an attempt to treat specific Muslims exceptionally well in order to overcompensate for – but do nothing substantive about – the systemic discrimination of Muslims at large (e.g. narrativizing Muslims as terrorists) (Kazi, 2015). It is arguable that this occurred in the US because the permutation of contextual factors enabled it to manifest. That an explicit form of racism occurred so unabashedly meant that it needed to be responded to with measures that maintained the veneer of equality. Thus, treating Islamophobia as an underpin by a form of cultural racism enables an analysis of contextual factors that account for the emergence of particularized forms of anti-Muslim racism as will be demonstrated later in the chapter.

Factors for the rise of Islamophobia in Malaysia

Islamophobia in Malaysia differs compared to its other expressions elsewhere. While it might seem strange that there would be Islamophobia in Malaysia given the fact that the phenomenon is often understood and studied in the context where Muslims are a minority, Malaysia offers a unique case study of Islamophobia especially because of the unique state of race relations in the country. The state of race relations can be traced to the historical legacy of British colonial rule.

The legacy of history

The context of Islamophobia must be understood from the prism of history. Malaysia's multicultural mix came about largely due to immigration encouraged by the British colonialists to further their economic interests. The policies were responsible for enacting changes that has had lasting consequences in Malaysian society, namely to segregate relations between the different ethnic groups. The British had allocated the different ethnic groups in Malaysia to specialized occupations and segregated Malaysian cities according to race. In doing so, the colonial master created divisions between the *bumiputera* group (natives of Malaysia, which includes the Malays and indigenous peoples) and immigrant races (Chinese and Indians) (Hefner, 2001). Much of the British policy was also driven by strong cultural biases held against the Malays. As Alatas noted, the British considered the Malays to be lazy and stupid (Alatas, 2013). Likewise, with the exception of the English educated Malay intelligentsia, the British distrusted the Malay community. The non-English educated were distrusted, especially those with strong religious feelings, because their thinking quite obviously did not harmonize with the British pattern of thought and action (Khoo Kay Kim, 1974, p. 197). For British officials, Islam represented a backwardness that needed to be addressed. Stamford Raffles, an important British colonial official in the Malay World, chastized the practice of polygamy among Malay which he deemed to be injurious to population growth and happiness in family life (Aljunied, 2008).

In the later years of colonial rule and the post-colonial period, a competitive attitude developed between the Malay rulers (and their political elites) and the non-Muslim minorities, as each group sought political power and rights. Following the end of the Second World War that saw the end of Japanese Occupation of Southeast Asian countries, the British enacted a plan known as the Malayan Union to transfer the sovereignty of the sultans to the British Crown and confer equal citizenship rights to non-Malays, effectively overturning any past privileges and protection given to the Malay race and religion (Ahmad Fauzi, 2007, p. 386). This plan faced massive political challenge from the Malay leadership, forcing the British to adopt a more tempered version of the original plan that makes it more difficult for the other ethnic groups to attain citizenship. The Malayan Union episode heightened ethnic tensions between the Malays and non-Malays that would subsequently culminate into open conflicts between the Malays and Chinese. Colonial rule shaped the thinking of and reinforced the latent feelings of many Chinese about the Malay population. Given the close links between the colonial system and the recognition of the traditional Malay aristocracy as the nominal rulers of the country, British colonialism was often seen as a prop for a 'backward' and feudal Malay society (Hirschman, 1986).

Privileged position of the Malays and the ethnic discrimination of non-Malays

The primacy of the Malays was enshrined in the Constitution of the new Malaysian state in exchange for the recognition of ethnic minority rights. These privileges recognize the Malay rulers as heads of the religion of Islam, accords the Malay language and religion (Islam) official status, and provides special rights to protect the Malays. A tacit understanding that Malays will be dominant in the political sphere and non-Malays in the economic sphere also developed.

The governments 'failure to address adequately the problems of Malay poverty in the rural areas and the lack of a Malay capitalist class in the early post-independence years sparked off post-election ethnic violence between the Malays and Chinese in 1969' (Zawawi, 2004). A policy known as the New Economic Poliicy (NEP) was introduced with the aim of minimizing the inter-ethnic tensions caused by income inequality (Sundaram, 2004). The NEP further granted rights such as the establishment of quotas in the public service, university enrolment and granting of scholarships and bursaries to Malay students. Far from eradicating inter-ethnic tensions, the NEP was responsible for further heightening the ethnic distinctions between Malay and non-Malay citizens (Peletz, 2005). Many within the minority ethnic groups were unhappy over the codification of unequal treatment based on 'race'. One of the key unintended outcomes of the NEP is the perception that Malays are overly reliant on assistance from the government, without which they would be unable to sustain themselves. Many among the minority communities also feel that it is unfair that a significant portion of their taxes are used to assist Malays.

Intolerance towards minorities

Since the 2008 Malaysian general elections, which saw the ruling Barisan Nasional (BN) coalition hold on power weakened, there has been a number of instances of violence against minorities. The 2008 election also saw for the first time in more than five decades that minority communities voting en masse against the ruling coalition triggering politicians within the government to start attacking minorities, especially the Chinese community, for being disloyal to the government (Mohamed Osman, 2016). This has led to politicians within the United Malays National Organisation (UMNO) overtly threatening violence against minority communities. One such example is the Red Shirt rally held in September 2015. The rally was held by Malay nationalist groups close to the government in defence of the Malay political position in the country. The group claimed that the country is under threat from the Chinese community. The rally saw participants displaying anti-Chinese banners and evoking violence against the Chinese community if they threatened the position of Malays in Malaysia. One racially charged posters circulated prior to the rally read, 'Cina Turun Bersih, Sedialah Bermandi Darah' (China Down, Just Like Blood), depicted a person in a Bersih T-shirt, made to look like a Chinese individual, about to be decapitated by a man holding a machete, who is depicted as a Malay warrior.[3]

The rally received tacit support from the ruling UMNO party with several senior UMNO leaders attending the rally. The former Prime Minister Najib Razak defended the rally and claimed that it was neither racial nor malicious in nature. Despite the obvious racial overtones, racist remarks hurled at Chinese reporters, and provocative banners and slogans, an investigation concluded there was no ill will or malice and no further police action was taken (Provocation, racial slurs mar 'red shirts' rally', 2015). One UMNO leader, Annuar Musa even remarked that Islam obliged him to be racist against anyone attacking the religion (in reference to the Chinese community). He was quoted as saying:

> Being racial is endorsed in Islam as long as you are not cruel towards other people. This rally if you say is racist, yes. What are you scared of? Islam has put in place guidelines, what is not allowed is racism that is cruel towards other races.

(Mayuri, 2015)

Following the Red Shirt rally, China's ambassador to Malaysia had called for the Malaysian government to end overt discrimination against the country's Chinese minority. In response to this statement, Malaysia's Deputy Agriculture and Agro-Based Industry Minister, Tajuddin Abdul Rahman, remarked that Malaysian Chinese should stop dreaming that China could defend their interests and threatened to slap any Chinese person complaining about the state of the country's ethnic politics outside Malaysia ('Deputy Minister "threatens to slap" Chinese who complain outside Malaysia', 2015).

The politicization of Islam in Malaysia and rising religious intolerance

The process of politicization of Islam in Malaysia can be understood as the adoption of stricter Islamic practices and principles working in tandem with a more exclusionary attitude towards non-Muslims. The process of Islamization in Malaysia can be traced to the Islamic resurgence that first occurred in the 1970s. The 1970s saw a rise in political Islam within the Malay community in Malaysia. Primarily driven by international political developments within the Muslim world, such as the Saudi Arabian financial support to Malaysian Islamic movements as well as the Islamic activism of Muslim student movements, the focus of these groups is to bring about a greater awareness of Islamist politics. In the 1980s, the focus of this movement became more political when demands for Malaysia to implement Islamic criminal laws and establish an Islamic state became more prominent. The politicization of Islam led to the government adopting a more Islamic outlook through the expansion of the religious bureaucracy and the implementation of stricter Islamic laws and policies that began to curtail the rights of non-Muslims. Another impact of Islamic resurgence is the political competition that developed between the ruling UMNO party and the Pan-Malaysian Islamic Party (PAS) where both parties sought to out-Islamize the other group. In an attempt to out-Islamize PAS, religious bureaucrats and politicians within the government have adopted policies that curtail the rights of non-Muslims in Malaysia. An example of this is the controversy surrounding the use of the word 'Allah'.

Through judicial verdicts and administrative decisions, Malaysians were denied the use of the Arabic word for God 'Allah' in a religious sense. In a highly contested judicial process, the Malaysian Court of Appeal finally decided to overturn a High Court decision in 2009 permitting the use of word 'Allah' as a reference to God in the Malay language section of *The Herald*, a Catholic publication. In spite of widespread protestations against usurpation of an age-old native religious custom, the Malaysian government's official spokesman for Islam has been uncompromising in insisting on the exclusive use of 'Allah' for Muslims (Hoffstaedter, 2013, pp. 475–489). In more recent times, restrictions have included not allowing the cross to be too prominently displayed to 'respect the sensitivities of Malaysian Muslims'. In 2015, a group of Muslim demonstrators led by local members of the then ruling UMNO party staged a protest against a new church for putting up a cross on its façade forcing the church owners to remove the cross. The group argued that Taman Medan where the church is located is a Muslim area and that putting up a cross in a Malay majority area is a challenge to Islam and could influence young Muslims (Palansamy, 2015).

The media portrayal of Islam

In an interesting article examining the portrayal of Islam and Muslims in Malaysia by the *Wall Street Journal* and *Guardian*, it was concluded that the articles overwhelmingly portrayed Islam and Muslims in Malaysia negatively (Hassan and Omar, 2017). Another study suggested that the English language media in the country tends to portray Islam and Muslims in a negative fashion. One such example of this is an opinion article that was featured in 'Yoursay' column in the news portal Malaysiakini. This column features opinions by readers that are deemed newsworthy. One such article, mischievously titled 'Having sex on camel needs gymnastic skills, no?', mocked and ridiculed a religious bureaucrat in Malaysia for allegedly saying that a Muslim woman provides sex for their husband even on a camel (Malaysiakini, 2015). The remark, which was taken out of context, resulted in a flurry of negative comments about Islamic law governing marriage and sexual relations. Another example is an article featured in a Malaysian English daily. In an article published in May 2017, the top half of the page featured the headline 'Malaysian terrorist leader', referring to the emergence of a Malaysian, Mahmud Ahmad, as a top regional Islamic state leader. Beneath it, separated by a thin line, was a picture of Muslims praying at the beginning of Ramadan, the Islamic holy month (Razak, 2017). This was deemed to be an attempt to ridicule Islam. While there have not been any studies conducted on the impact of local media portrayal on non-Muslims in Malaysia, one study did find that the international media has a significant effect on the mindset of Malaysians (Abdul, 2010). It can thus be averred that such reporting is likely to shape the perception of some non-Muslims towards Islam.

Islamophobia in Malaysia can thus be traced to the overt racial policies of the Malaysian government, the racist stances of politicians within the government, and the negative portrayal of Islam in local and foreign media. The politicization of Islam has seen the curtailment of the religious rights of many non-Muslims (Mohamed Osman, 2017). As such, unlike in its permutations in other parts of the Muslim world, Islamophobia in Malaysia arose from non-Muslims equating an exclusivist understanding of Islam to Islam as a religion.

Understanding Islamophobia in Malaysia

This chapter contends that Islamophobia among non-Muslim Malaysians are a direct reaction of increasing politicization of Islam that has translated to the religious and racial discrimination of these communities. This can be clearly seen from the manifestation of Islamophobia within the Malaysian context. Most expressions of Islamophobia occur in the cyber space normally in response to articles related to racist actions against non-Malays in the country or actions by the Muslim majority populace that seeks to curb the rights of non-Muslims. Anti-government and anti-Islamic sentiment is found in the margins of society and media, as traditional broadcast and print media is heavily regulated in Malaysia. Comment sections of online news articles and social media posts generally contain these views, especially if the article is related to something Islamic or to do with an imposition of Malay norms. This may be due to fear of backlash, considering that Malaysia is a Malay–Muslim majority country and the examples made of Islamophobes such as Alvin Tan who previously likened Islam to Nazism (*Malay Mail*, 2015). Islamophobia is not, however, limited to the cyber space, it has been expressed within intellectual circles and the legal fraternity.

Islamophobia in the cyber space

Online religious and racial vitriol in Malaysian mainstream discourse persists, though negative comments directed towards minority faiths and ethnicities in Malaysia can be viewed as an expression of Islamophobic sentiments. Islamophobic sentiments in response to the alleged creeping Islamization gaining ground in Malaysia can be seen in the local media via websites such as Free Malaysia Today and Sinar Harian. These platforms receive more active commentary than others via their Facebook-linked comments sections. Overall, barring a miniscule vocal minority, Malaysians commenting on Islamization are generally able to dissociate between Islam and Malaysian Muslims on one hand, and key figures who utilize exaggerated Islamic issues for political mileage. Several themes in the expression of Islamophobia can be noted in this regard. First, the notion that Islam and Muslims are inherently violent and that terrorism cannot be separated from Islam. In an article titled 'The rise of Islamophobia', which discusses the impact of the phenomenon on Islam, one Tony Soprano wrote:

Why is it that Islam is entirely at fault when a person with an Arabic name terrorises the masses?' Because westerners don't hijack commercial jets and fly them into Middle Eastern buildings. Because there are hardly any non-Muslim terrorists. Because from China to Thailand to all over Europe to the United States and all the countries in between where terrorism occurs, the last word on the murderers' lips is Allahu Akbar. That's why.

(Ahmad, 2016)

Another Islamophobic narrative that is often expressed is the intolerance within the Islamic faith. In an article discussing the introduction of shopping trolleys that are exclusively for Muslim use in a supermarket, comments were made ridiculing the initiative. In one comment, a reader Steven Ong said:

Soon a religious apartheid in Malaysia. For Muslims Only or Untuk Muslimin Saja signs will be seen around Bole land. Wait a minute, is this not Bolehland? But it seem that all is boleh (permissible) for Muslims and tak boleh (prohibited) for non- Muslims. That is why it is called a religion of submission. Where ever it goes, all must submit to it. Actually it had already been in force in some areas. Yea, god is great, great at persecution.

(Mokhtar, 2016)[4]

Another expression of Islamophobia that is often seen in the Malaysian context is the support for violence against Muslims elsewhere. For some Malaysian non-Muslims, the intolerance shown to them in Malaysia justifies violence against Muslims elsewhere. In response to an article titled 'Critical thinking needed on issue of Allah Ban', which discussed Malaysia's decision to ban non-Muslims from using the word Allah to describe God, a reader Bai Yun Sheng remarked:

And the Muslims wonder why there are no prompt actions and outpouring of sympathy and help for the Rohingyas …. Because Muslims like to tell other people of faiths on what to eat, wear, see and hear and how this should be done or cannot do, finding every donkey ways to oppress others way of life etc….. I don't see Muslims come out in droves across the world to help the Rohingyas … let along Melayu (Malay) Muslims. Muslims are just bad people with a warped sense of justice and rights … sorry my two cents.

(Malaysiakini, 2017)

One can also discern covert racism in the expression of Islamophobia in the Malaysian context. In all the remarks made by Malaysian Islamophobes, Muslims are linked to Malays and the linkage between the cultural and religious identities cannot be separated. The belief that Malays are stupid and as such Islam is a religion of the irrational and stupid is clearly manifested in these remarks. New traits associated with being Muslim such as intolerance and violent can be seen in these remarks.

Islamophobia as defending a secular constitution

Beyond social media, Islamophobia has also seeped into mainstream society with some members of the non-Muslim community in Malaysia being quick to react against any view or issue that centres around general morality and responded to as an emphasis of Islamic values 'forced' onto general members of society. In an incident that sparked a controversy within Malaysia, a Malaysian Muslim man was videoed giving a lecture to a group of foreigners in a housing area explaining to them the religious sensitivities of Malaysian Muslims, urging them to refrain from drug abuse, gambling and public consumption of alcohol. In response, a member of the Malaysia bar, Sankaran Nair, accused the man of committing an alleged criminal offence by imposing his values on others and having breached Section 298(A) of the Malaysian Penal Code that stated that no Malaysian should be 'causing disharmony, disunity, or feelings of enmity, hatred or ill will, or prejudicing, the maintenance of harmony or unity, on grounds of religion'.

Nair noted that such acts are indicative of attempts by some Muslims to impose their values on others and stressed that Malaysia was a secular nation with a sizeable multi-racial and multi-religious population (Anbalagan, 2017). In criticizing Nair, a Haniff Khatri (a prominent Muslim lawyer) noted that calls to curb social ills should not be viewed as an imposition of the Islamic faith on adherents of other religions (Khatri, 2017). The case cited above is indicative of a trend that has grown significantly in Malaysia where some non-Muslims have become quick to view Muslims as intolerant and seeking to impose their values on others, in particular to change the Malaysian Constitution which is inherently secular.

Islamophobia among intellectuals

Islamophobia in Malaysia has also grown as a result of the inability to differentiate between the politicization of Islam and Islam as a religion. Dr Ng Kam Weng, a Malaysian Protestant theologian and founder of the Kairos Research Centre, was critical of the term 'Islamophobia' as he felt that it is a tactic to suggest that Christians are fearful of Muslims and as such becomes an excuse to put down Christians.[5] He felt that the fear of Islam and Muslim is not an irrational fear (i.e. Islamophobia) as there have been attempts by Muslims to impose Islamic practices and teachings on Malaysian Christians. Ng noted that Islam in Malaysia has shifted from being a largely folk religion in Malaysia to an Islamist variant (Mohamed Osman, 2017). He opined that there are elements within Islamic teachings that suggest the religion has total desire to dominate over the rest of society but that the anti-Chinese attitude that used to plague the mindset of many Malays is today transformed to an anti-Christian one (Personal Communication, 2016). Another public intellectual informed the author that Islam as a religion is intrinsically political and as such there is little reason to differentiate between political Islam and Islam as a religion. Politics, he argued, is part of the

Islamic faith. As such, attempts by exclusivist Muslim groups to promote the implementation of Islamic criminal law should be viewed as an attempt to simply impose a tenet that is clearly stipulated in the Koran at the national level in Malaysia (Personal Communication 2017). It was further added that the Malay supremacist attitude is now replaced by an Islamo-facist world-view of many Malaysian Muslims.

As highlighted earlier, Islamophobia within some segments of the non-Muslim Malaysians constitutes an ideological reaction against and a negative perception of an increasingly exclusivist bend in Islamization of Malaysian politics and society. A key issue related to this is the equating of Islam as a normative religion with this exclusivist brand of Islam. This variant of Islamophobia is mediated through a combination of ignorance on Islamic teachings, real concerns of rights of non-Muslims by a shrinking secular space due to encroaching Islamization and an existent mindset of being part of a minority in a Malay–Muslim majority country (Ali, 2016). It can be added that there is an increasing perception among some non-Muslims in Malaysia that a pious practicing Muslim will pose a problem to Malaysia's social fabric.

Conclusion

The issue of Islamophobia in Malaysia is indeed interesting and unique. The confluence of race and religion within the Malaysian socio-political domain has resulted in the increasing constriction of both racial and religious rights for many non-Muslims in the country. In turn, this has resulted in an increasing Islamophobic attitude expressed against Malaysian Muslims, especially on social media, within academic circles and in the legal realm. For many Malaysian Islamophobes, Islam is often seen as a religion of intolerance and violence that is inward-looking and has sought to impose its values and ideals on members of other faith communities; that a politicized expression of Islam is just an expression of the Islamic faith; and that a pious practicing Muslim poses a challenge for contemporary society. Such views are a continuation of cultural racism against Malays that have long been perpetuated by the British colonial masters, historical baggage of policies of the Malaysian government and the role of the media. While such views are limited to a minority within the non-Muslim community in the country, the intolerance towards Islam and Muslims is likely to increase with the increasing exclusivist turn within Malaysian Islam. This could potentially impact the social fabric of Malaysia, which has long seen peaceful co-existence between different religious communities.

Notes

1 The author would like to thank Amalina Anuar and Prashant Waikar for research assistance rendered for this chapter.
2 For an excellent analysis of the links between Islamophobia and anti-Muslim attitudes and violence see Arosoaie, 2018.

3 Bersih refers to the Alliance for Free and Fair Elections, a civil society group formed with the aim of ensuring that the conduct of elections are done in a free and fair manner in the country.

4 One of the key taglines of the Malaysian state is, 'Malaysia Boleh' or 'Malaysia can do it', indicating that Malaysia is a land of possibility. Hence the author is making a reference to Malaysia as a land of negative possibility.

5 The Kairos Research Centre is an evangelical organization that seeks to promote Christian and interdisciplinary scholarship to advance the development of Christianity in contemporary Malaysian society. See Kairos Research Centre, www.kairos-malaysia.org/.

Bibliography

Abdul, H. K. (2010). Globalisation, 'in-between' identities and shifting values: Young multi-ethnic Malaysians and media consumption. *Journal of Communication, 32*(2).

Abdul Hamid, A. F. (2007). Malay anti-colonialism in British Malaya: A re-appraisal of independence fighters of peninsular Malaysia. *Journal of Asian and African Studies, 42*(5).

Agnes, F. (2016). Muslim women's rights and media coverage. *Economic & Political Weekly, 51*(20), 14 May.

Ahmad, R. (2016). 'The rise of Islamophobia', *Malaysiakini*, www.malaysiakini.com/letters/348884, date of access: 18 July 2018.

Alatas, S. H. (2013). *The Myth of the Lazy Native: A Study of the Image of the Malays, Filipinos and Javanese from the 16th to the 20th Century and Its Function in the Ideology of Colonial Capitalism*. Oxford: Routledge.

Ali, R. (2016). 'The threat to UMNO posed by M'sia's rising Islamophobia', *Today*, 19 April.

Ali, W., Clifton, E., Duss, M., Lee, F., Keyes, S. and Shakir, F. (2011). Fear, Inc.: The roots of the Islamophobia network in America. *Center for American Progress*.

Aljunied, S. K. (2008). *Rethinking Raffles: A Study of Stamford Raffles' Discourse on Religions amongst Malays*. Singapore: Marshall Cavendish.

Alsultany, E. (2012). *Arabs and Muslims in the Media: Race and Representation after 9/11*. New York and London: New York University Press.

Anbalagan, V. (2017). 'Flora Damansara man must be investigated, says lawyer', *Free Malaysia Today*, 23 September. Accessed from www.freemalaysiatoday.com/category/nation/2017/09/23/flora-damansara-man-must-be-investigated-says-lawyer/, date of access: 29 July 2018.

Arosoaie, A. (2018). Understanding the creation and radicalisation of the Students Islamic Movement of India (SIMI) and the Indian Mujahideen (IM), South Asia. *Journal of South Asian Studies*. Published online 22 May 2018, https://doi.org/10.1080/00856401.2018.1469205.

Bazian, H. (2014). National entry–exit registration system: Arabs, Muslims, and Southeast Asians and post-9/11 'security measures'. *Islamophobia Studies Journal, 2*(1).

'Deputy Minister "threatens to slap" Chinese who complain outside Malaysia'. (2015). *The Rakyat Post*, 1 October.

Dorairajoo, S. (2009). Peaceful Thai, violent Malay(-Muslim): A case study of the 'problematic' Muslim citizens of Southern Thailand. *The Copenhagen Journal of Asian Studies, 27*(2).

Døving, C. A. (2015). The way they treat their daughters and wives: Racialisation of Muslims in Norway. *Islamophobia Studies Journal, 3*(1).

Dubosh, E., Poulakis, M. and Abdelghani, N. (2015). Islamophobia and law enforcement in a post 9/11 world. *Islamophobia Studies Journal, 3*(1).

Gowing, P. (1979). *Muslim Filipinos: Heritage and Horizon.* New Day: Quezon City.

Grosfoguel, R. (2012). The multiple faces of Islamophobia. *Islamophobia Studies Journal, 1*(1).

Hafez, F. (2014). Disciplining the 'Muslim subject': The role of security agencies in establishing Islamic theology within the state's academia. *Islamophobia Studies Journal, 2*(2).

Hassan, F. and Omar, S. Z. (2017). Illustrating news bias towards Islam and Muslims in Malaysia and Indonesia by Wall Street Journal and The Telegraph. *Asia-Pacific Media Educator, 27*(1).

Hefner, R. (Ed.) (2001). *The Politics of Multiculturalism: Pluralism and Citizenship in Malaysia, Singapore, and Indonesia.* Honolulu: University of Hawai'i Press.

Hill, M. (2004). The rehabilitation and regulation of religion in Singapore. In J. T. Richardson (Ed.), *Regulating Religion* (pp. 343–358). New York: Springer.

Hirschman, C. (1986). The making of race in colonial Malaya: Political economy and racial ideology. *Sociological Forum, 1*(2).

Hoffstaedter, G. (2013). Religious pluralism in Malaysia: Can there be dialogue? In J. Camilleri and S. Schottmann (Eds), *Culture, Religion and Conflict in Muslim Southeast Asia: Negotiating Tense Pluralisms* (pp. 41–51). Abingdon: Routledge.

Ibrahim, A. (2016). *The Rohingyas: Inside Myanmar's Hidden Genocide.* London: C. Hurst & Co.

Joseph, S. and D'Harlingue, B. (2012). The Wall Street Journal's Muslims: Representing Islam in American print news media. *Islamophobia Studies Journal, 1*(1).

Kazi, N. (2015). Ahmed Mohamed and the imperial necessity of Islamophilia. *Islamophobia Studies Journal, 3*(1).

Khatri, H. (2017). 'Is Islamophobia slowly creeping into Malaysian society?', *Free Malaysia Today*, 24 September. Accessed from www.malaysia-today.net/2017/09/24/is-islamophobia-slowly-creeping-into-malaysian-society/, date of access: 29 July 2018.

Khoo Kay Kim (1974). *Malay Society: Transformation & Democratisation: A Stimulating and Discerning Study on the Evolution of Malay Society through the Passage of Time.* Petaling Jaya: Pelanduk Books.

Louati, Y. (2015). *L'Exception Française*: From irrational fear of Muslims to their social death sentence. *Islamophobia Studies Journal, 3*(1).

Malay Mail (2015). 'Bigot, troublemaker, agent provocateur? Alvin Tan prefers "free speech activist"', 19 April. Accessed from www.malaymail.com/s/889519/bigot-troublemaker-agent-provocateur-alvin-tan-prefers-free-speech-activist, date of access: 30 March 2018.

Malaysiakini (2015). 'Having sex on camel needs gymnastic skills, no?', *Malaysiakini*, 16 June. Accessed from www.malaysiakini.com/news/301962, date of access: 3 August 2018.

Malaysiakini (2017). 'Critical thinking needed on issue of "Allah" ban', *Malaysiakini*, 24 October. Accessed from www.malaysiakini.com/news/399275, date of access: 30 March 2018.

Mayuri, M. L. (2015). 'Annuar Musa: "I am racist, Islamically"', *Malay Mail*, 16 September.

Meer, N. and Modood, T. (2012). For 'Jewish' read 'Muslim'? Islamophobia as a form of racialisation of ethno-religious groups in Britain today. *Islamophobia Studies Journal, 1*(1).

Mohamed Osman, M. N. (2016). The Islamic conservative turn in Malaysia: Impact and future trajectories. *Contemporary Islam, 11*(1).

Mohamed Osman, M. N. (2017). Understanding Islamophobia in Asia: The cases of Myanmar and Malaysia. *Islamophobia Studies Journal, 4*(1).

Mokhtar, M. (2016). 'Halal trolleys? What next?', *Free Malaysia Today*, 27 January. Accessed from www.freemalaysiatoday.com/category/opinion/2016/01/27/halal-trolleys-what-next/, date of access: 28 April 2018.

Palansamy, Y. (2015). 'For non-Muslims in Taman Medan, discretion is the better part of valour', *Malay Mail*, 22 April. Accessed from www.malaymail.com/s/882735/for-non-muslims-in-taman-medan-discretion-is-the-better-part-of-valour, date of access: 28 April 2018.

Peletz, M. G. (2005). Islam and the cultural politics of legitimacy: Malaysia in the aftermath of September 11. In R. W. Hefner (Ed.), *Remaking Muslim Politics Pluralism, Contestation, Democratization* (pp. 240–272). Princeton: Princeton University Press.

'Provocation, racial slurs mar "red shirts" rally'. (2015). *Malaysiakini*, 16 September.

Rahim, L. Z. (1999). Singapore-Malaysia relations: Deep-seated tensions and self-fulfilling prophecies. *Journal of Contemporary Asia, 29*(1).

Rahim, L. Z. (2012). Governing Muslims in Singapore's secular authoritarian state. *Australian Journal of International Affairs, 66*(2).

Razak, R. (2017). 'Mixing Islam and terrorism: A blunder too far for Malaysia's Star?', *South China Morning Post*, 3 June.

Sharma, J. (2009). Digesting the 'other': Hindu nationalism and the Muslims in India. In V. Lal (Ed.), *Political Hinduism: The Religious Imagination in Public Spheres*. New Delhi: Oxford University Press.

Stoler, A. (1997). Carnal knowledge and imperial power. Gender, race, and morality in colonial Asia. In R. Lancaster, M. Di Leonardo and M. D. Leonardo (Eds), *The Gender/Sexuality Reader. Culture, History and Political Economy* (pp. 13–36). New York: Routledge.

Sundaram, J. (2004). 'The New Economic Policy and Interethnic Relations in Malaysia' for *Identities, Conflict and Cohesion (2000–2009)*, United Nations research Institute for Social Development, Programme Paper No 7, September.

Tan, G. Z. (2017). 'Today article on diabetes targets Malay & Indian eating habits, S'poreans call it out as racist', *Mothership*, , 28 August. Retrieved from https://mothership.sg/2017/08/today-article-on-diabetes-targets-malay-indian-eating-habits-sporeans-call-it-out-as-racist/, date of access: 20 March 2018.

Thapar, R. (2014). *The Past as Present: Forging Contemporary Identities through History*. New Delhi: Aleph Book Company.

Vincent, J. (2015). 'Ahmed Mohamed hangs out with Sergey Brin at Google Science Fair', *The Verge*, 22 September. Retrieved from www.theverge.com/2015/9/22/9369921/ahmed-mohamed-sergey-brin-google-science-fair, date of access: 20 March 2018.

Zawawi, I. (2004). Globalization and national identity: Managing ethnicity and cultural pluralism in Malaysia. In Y. Sato (Ed.), *Growth and governance in Asia*. Honolulu: Asia-Pacific Centre for Security Studies.

11 Securitization of Islam in contemporary Ethiopia

Jemal Muhamed

Introduction

The end of the Cold War has witnessed the rise of the discourse about a potential 'clash of civilizations' along with the consequent paradigm of security anchored in the perceived threat of Islam to the West. Apart from claiming to be facilitating multiculturalism, political discourse in the West has created public sermons that have tied Islam with terrorism (Krume, 2010). Interestingly, this Western trend of threat framing in relation to Islam has appeared in other parts of the world as well (Cesari, 2009).

With about 100 million people, Ethiopia is home to multiple religions and Orthodox Christians, Muslims and Protestants respectively represent 43 per cent, 33 per cent, and 18 per cent of Ethiopians (Central Statics Agency, 2007). For the most part, the historical accounts of the country demonstrate the harmonious existence of different religious communities within the state. However, the history of the relations between different religious groups and between religious groups and the state have been highly troubling (Muhamed, 2016). Orthodox Christianity was the official state religion and the main provider of political ideology to the Ethiopian state from the fourth century CE to 1974 (Abbink, 2014). Other religions, including Islam, were subject to assimilation into the state religion (ibid.) Islam in Ethiopia is as old as Islam itself, ushered in with the first contact of the two in 615 when the *Sahaba* (the first followers and companions of the Prophet Muhammad) received asylum in the Abyssinian state and were welcomed by its Christian king when they were persecuted by their *Quraish* countrymen in Mecca (Dereje, 2011; Erlich, 1994; Trimingham, 1952).

The 1974 socialist revolution had brought a paradigm shift in the long-established Ethiopian state: State and Church were divorced and Ethiopia has been a secular state ever since (Dereje, 2011). Moreover, the 1991 regime change and the coming of the ruling Ethiopian People's Revolutionary Democratic Front (EPRDF) to power with its liberalized socio-cultural policies brought ample opportunities to Ethiopian Muslims (Abbink, 2014). As a result, the latter enjoy enhanced access to education, economic and political participation, and religious freedom (ibid.). Despite this welcoming initial phase, the nature of the relations between Muslims and the Ethiopian government has gradually changed from accommodation to confrontation and the attitude of each to the other has transformed over time (Dereje, 2011). Since 2011, the declining nature of the relations between the two has scaled up to open confrontations and accusations, with the Muslim community protesting against the government's interference in its internal affairs and the latter labelling Muslims and their activities as an attempt to establish an Islamic state in Ethiopia (Muhamed, 2015).

The government officially identified the threat as 'Islamic fundamentalism' a challenge for Ethiopia's secular order (Muhamed, 2015). The government's securitized views and narrations of Muslims drew new patterns of relationships in the Ethiopian society and within the Muslim community itself. This work attempts to analyse the securitization of Islam that has come to affect the life of Muslims as both individuals and a community, as well as shape their relationships with their representatives, the government and the society at large in Ethiopia. The work refers to and adopts 'securitization' as the logic of security based on the constructivist knowledge claim of securitization theory as framed by The Copenhagen School (CPS).

The condition of securitization of Islam and Muslims through the security discourse of 'Islamic fundamentalism' in Ethiopia deserves scholarly attention. This work is based on the assumption that securitization of Islam and Muslims through the security semantic of fundamentalism in Ethiopia has turbulent effects on religious and societal stability, the national peace and the state-building process at large. Cesari (2009) argued in her study of Muslims in the West that the politicization and securitization of Islam essentially impoverishes and threatens the survival of the religion, while leading the religious community to feel resentful of the interference of non-religious actors.

This chapter aims to analyse the securitization of Islam and its multidimensional implications and its contributions can be partly justified by the following considerations. First, although the post-1991 political order in Ethiopia widens the social space for religious revivalism, there have not been serious academic discussions on the nature of the relationships between the religious community and the multicultural Ethiopian state. Second, this chapter is a systematic analysis of practical developments and their theoretical implications for the securitization theory in an effort to address the following research questions:

- How has Islam been securitized in Ethiopia?
- What are the contextual factors for the securitization of Islam in Ethiopia?
- To what extent has Islam been securitized in Ethiopia? How can this securitization be evaluated?
- How significant is the audience in the securitization of Islam in Ethiopia?
- What are the implications of the securitization of Islam for the life, relations, and interactions of Muslims both as individuals and as a community?

Research methods and theoretical context

This study is based on qualitative research methods. Moreover, the theoretical base of this study, securitization theory, which views security as a multidisciplinary and socially constructed phenomenon, seeks the consideration of the individual's psychological behaviours and the group's social behaviours like attitudes, perceptions, point of views and motivations that best deserve qualitative approaches. A variety of qualitative methods: content and document analysis, discourse analysis, policy frameworks and security practices will be utilized to address the research questions. While discourse analysis is used to study the actor's securitizing speech acts, a qualitative content analysis is employed to serve the documentation of securitizing moves. Moreover, the study also makes use of policy frameworks and institutional practices as indexes for the securitization of Islam in Ethiopia. Policy frameworks and institutional practices serve as important indicators in measuring and understanding the securitization process and the extent to which the issue is securitized (Bourbeau, 2011).

Theoretically, this chapter adopts securitization theory as framed by CPS to address the research questions based on information from both primary and secondary sources. This theory is primarily applied for its instrumental values for practical security analysis. Securitization theory as a tool of analysis enables the researcher to draw on occurrences of securitization and to facilitate practical analysis of political statements (Taureck, 2006). However, the chapter does not relate securitization theory in its original form. Rather, it adopts and modifies the theory in order to ensure it serves the purpose of this study according to contextual variations.

Securitization theory is tested to work for security studies in Europe, whose political and cultural settings are completely different from those of Ethiopia. As securitization is composed of securitizing claims by the government and legitimate acceptances of the claim by the public, securitization theory as a method of analysis relies on democratic political culture. This means that securitization is a political culture-bounded activity that relies on the nature of the relationship, meaning the trustworthiness of the securitizing agent in the eyes of its audience. Moreover, securitization has been successfully applied to various issues including environment, migration, political dissidence, ethnic identity claims and religious revivalism in Western countries where the political culture is highly participatory (Kaya, 2009). However, this study partly examines how securitization occurred in authoritarian political cultures where audiences are cynical about the securitizing claims of political agents whose legitimacy is in doubt. Thus, this chapter applies securitization theory partly to discover the nature of securitization in the contexts of political cultures other than democracy, such as in Ethiopia. In terms of social set ups, securitization has been successfully employed to securitize Islam in the West, where fewer people have religious affiliations and interactions with Muslims. Since the attacks of 9/11, it is obvious that Muslims and their religion have been considered as the enemy of the state, with epithets such as 'violent', 'threatening', 'fanatic' and 'terrorist' applied to them, and have been under sharp scrutiny in Europe and USA alike (Krume, 2016; Kaya, 2009). On the other hand, the social realities in Ethiopia are highly diverse and accommodative, allowing various religious communities to co-exist along with a shared history, kinship and experiences of mutual assistance. With due consideration of these discrepancies, this study strives to evaluate how securitization can be carried out under such cultural and socio-political conditions.

Discussion and analysis

The term contemporary Ethiopia is used here to refer to the period of three decades of EPRDF rule. The initial period of EPRDF's rule was marked by the liberalization of the country's political, economic and cultural spheres. These political reforms have created enabling fields for all religious communities in Ethiopia. Particularly, the trend has paved way for the historically marginalized Ethiopian Muslims to enjoy greater degrees of religious freedom, as well as better political and economic engagements (Østebø and Wallelign, 2015). The new political climate had allowed the institutionalization of Islam at the national level with the de-jure establishment of the Ethiopian Islamic Affairs Supreme Council (hereafter EIASC) in 1991 (Haustein and Østebø, 2011). Moreover, the new policy has ended the previous restrictions on the pilgrimage to Mecca and the import of religious texts, also allowing the construction of more mosques and the establishment of Islamic organizations, magazines and newspapers, facilitating the modification of Friday office hours in accordance with the weekly Muslim congregational prayer, as well as enhancing endorsement for the legal status of Sharia courts in the country (Hussein, 2002). The government institutionalized religious freedom with the new Constitution under secular political order (Abbink, 2011). Articles 11, 27 and 33 of the Constitution respectively declare the separation of state and religion, the right of religious freedom and the right for religious communities to enjoy associational life. All these developments lead to the revival of religious activities among Ethiopian Muslims (SIDA, 2002). However, the government's hospitability towards Muslims did not last for long and most of these developments were lost after 1995 (Østebø and Wallelign, 2015).

Towards securitization since 1995

Securitization is the process of transforming normal political developments into matters of security and survival by speech acts that label the latter as a threat to value's survival (Poutanen, 2015). While most of securitization studies focus on the phenomenon primarily through speech, this chapter analyses securitization both in terms of speech acts, policy and practical security developments, along with contextual factors that contributed to the securitization of Islam in Ethiopia. In adopting the social constructivist approach of securitization theory, this study does not claim that the actor's speeches are mere inventions. Rather, it argues that there might be real occurrences that are subjected to different interpretations by various agents.

As highlighted above, the mid-1990s were an important turning point in the study of the hostile relationship between Ethiopian Muslims and the government, which has actually soured since 2011. The US ambassador to Ethiopia from 1996 to 1999, David Shinn, (2002, p. 1) stated that the late Prime Minister Melese Zenawi told him 'The most significant long term threat to Ethiopia's security is "Islamic fundamentalism" '. According to Dereje (2011), the view of the premier represents the introduction of 'Islamic fundamentalism' into Ethiopia's security discourse. The above claim of the premier consisted of the core components of securitization theory; the actor and speech act, the existential threat and the referent object, meaning the late Prime Minister and his expression, Islamic fundamentalism, and Ethiopia's security respectively. The premier's argument established a framework for the securitization of Islam and Muslims. In this regard, people like Zekarias (2014) argue that the speech of the premier is not about Islam but Islamic fundamentalism, which employs the magical power of language in constructing security discourse. Larzillière (2012, p. 19) argued that 'the use of a security semantic tends to produce frames of reference and categories that concentrate on the "threatening" aspect of the societies in question and thus format the analysis of these societies'. Securitization takes place through security discourse that integrally ties to the securitization of the society and its institutions (Poutanen, 2015). According to securitization theory, the aim of the elite's speech act is to convince the domestic audience. However, in this instance, the audience of the Prime Minister's words is an ambassador, and not the Ethiopian general public. Regardless of the audience, the late Prime Minister had employed the security semantic of 'Islamic fundamentalism' that creates the threatening aspects of the Muslim identity. In this sense, securitization of Islam through speech act in Ethiopia had appeared even long before the 9/11 global discourse of Islamic fundamentalism and international terrorism (Dereje, 2011). As the speech had not been made to the general public, it deviates from securitization theory's claim that securitization is primarily speech acts to convince the broader audience.

Contextual factors for securitization of Islam in Ethiopia

Contextual factors are facilitating conditions in reference to which the securitizing actor presents a danger to the referent object's survival (McDonald, 2008). Likewise, the securitization of Islam in Ethiopia has been facilitated by various factors that in one way or the other justified the change in the government's policy towards Muslims. CHS's initial thought of securitization as a single phenomenon of speech act is not the focus of this chapter; rather how a combination of different contextual factors like historical, domestic, regional and global contribute to the process of securitization in different times.

Domestic social dynamic as a factor of securitization of Islam in Ethiopia

The political liberalization of 1991 and its accommodative socio-cultural policies had brought transformative effects within Ethiopian Muslims (Abbink, 2011; Østebø, 2007). This led to the rise of religious activities and the renaissance of religious affiliations among Muslims, which had been suppressed for a long time in imperial and socialist Ethiopia (Sida, 2003). The regime's open policy towards religion, its relaxation of press freedom, and rapid improvement in literacy and communication technologies, and most recently social media, contributed to the reawakening of Islam in the post-1991 Ethiopia (Jawar, 2012). Islamic revivalism in Ethiopia has manifested itself through the growth of spiritual interest and increasing religious teachings, the construction of religious institutions, intellectual movements, and the production and circulation of religious literatures (Hussein, 1994). These developments, in turn, increased the visibility of Muslims in the public sphere (Haustein and Østebø, 2011). However, people in government circles and even some members of other religious communities did not welcome this revivalism and visibility (Østebø and Wallelign, 2015).

Islamic reawakening and public visibility as manifestations of political Islam

The sharp visibility of Muslims and its symbolic representation of Islam in the Ethiopian public space following the political reforms of 1991 to accommodate Ethiopia's religious diversity have produced a dual sense of reactions in what Haustein and Østebø (2011, p. 10) referred to as 'feelings of hope and expectations as well as discomfort and fear'. The development of hope is relegated to Muslims, while fear and discomfort are attributed to Muslims by governments and some members of other religious communities. The tension among the latter has come from the misinterpretation of social dynamisms within the Muslim community, socio-economic empowerment and religious revivalism as a result of the politicization of Islam (Dereje, 2010. The discomfort about Muslims' new position has manifested itself at both the governmental and societal levels. Government officials and prominent Christians alike have viewed and narrated the expansion of mosques and religious activism and the claims of Muslims for more rights as trends of radicalization (Haustein and Østebø, 2011). In this regard, Østebø (2007) argued that, while higher representation of Muslims in public life and an increased number of mosques could hardly qualify as proof of politicization of Islam in Ethiopia, it has been common to equate the activities of the Muslim community with politicization of Islam. The government's unhappiness is revealed through a serious of measures taken against Muslims presented in subsequent sections.

The historical harmonious relations of Muslims and Christians were mostly at the 'micro-level', while macro-level relations have been more antagonistic

(Haustein and Østebø, 2011, p. 10). Christians were becoming gradually anxious about the increasingly visible role of Islam in public places 'with reference to the growth in the number of mosques all over the country and the increasing number of Muslims holding governmental and public positions' (Østebø, 2007, p. 11) One of the Christians' discursive resistances towards Muslims can be attributed to their labelling of all aspects of Islamic revival in Ethiopia as 'growth of Islamic fundamentalism under the influence of Saudi Arabia' (Dereje, 2011, p. 16). Another form of resistance was physical violence against Muslims, particularly in the areas of mosque construction. According to Hussein (2006, p. 12)

> the construction of almost all the major mosques in Addis Ababa (and those elsewhere in the country) was invariably preceded by opposition from the Christian residents and Churches of the areas in which the mosques were intended to be built.

Likewise, the construction of mosques faced protracted legal battles from the side of government departments responsible for the permissions. In this regard, the most notable controversy was observed in 2003 when Muslims attempted to build a mosque in Axum in the Tigray region, when a large group of Christians tore down the unfinished building. (ICG, 2016) Likewise, the federal government denied Muslims' requests for land to build a mosque in Axum, which still remains a source of grievance until today (ibid.). As these negative actions produced dissident voices from Muslims, the government moved to frame these dissident claims as evidence of further radicalization. A speech by the then Ministry of Federal Affairs Shiferaw Teklemariam on 12 October 2014, delivered to the Ethiopian diaspora community in the United States in a conference coordinated by American Muslims, reveals how history is used to securitize Islam in Ethiopia:

> while our constitution has corrected historical religious discriminations and clearly outlined about the separation of state and religion under Article 11, these groups want to have a government based on Sharia law as a way to balance historical injustice and claiming 'it is our turn'.

The point to be made here is that in the speeches of the minister, historical injustices against Muslims serve as a contextual factor to securitize Muslims' advocacy movement since 2011 as a political move to establish a Sharia-based government. Haustein and Østebø (2011, p. 15) contend:

> As the new political developments since 1991 have contributed to Islamic revivalism in Ethiopia, it needs to be noted, though, that Muslim views on politics has taken a different form than the often portrayed notion of seeking power based on Islamic political preferences.

Although the revival of Islam post-1991 and the increasing movements by Muslims to assert their Ethiopian citizenship have never taken a political form, the government and religious leaders of the Ethiopian Orthodox Church have viewed the former as a phenomenon resulting from radicalization (Abbink, 1998; Dereje, 2011) According to Abbink (2014, p. 356), 'in government circles there is a myth that such an overall radicalization of all Ethiopian Muslims is ongoing, even inevitable, and that it is a danger'. Erlich (2013) attributed it to the 'Ahmed Gragn Syndrome' in the Christian elites, meaning the mentality of fear of Islam in memory of Ahmed Gragn, who unified and led the forces of Muslim Sultan-ates and waged devastating war against Christian kingdoms during the sixteenth century. This shows that the historical antagonism between Muslim communities and the Ethiopian state is used by the government to shape its policies towards Muslims. In regards to this, Buzan (1983, p. 226) argued that logical problems in security policy-making imply that 'the perceptual problem is fundamental because affects the entire information base on which the decision-making process rests'. Although changes are normal and inevitable with the opening of more political space and they have facilitated the way for revival among the reli-gious community, the government has utilized these developments for the pro-duction of security norms.

Violent incidents as a factor of securitization

The government's threat articulation of radicalization of Muslims has made use of violent incidents to justify concern over Muslims communities. The first violent incident occurred on 21 February 1995, in the compound of Anwar Mosque in Addis Ababa, when clashes between Muslims in the mosque and the police who used excessive force left 9 people dead and 129 wounded (Abbink, 1998). While the conflict might have been the result of certain internal issues within the religious community, the hasty intervention of the government with strong use of force revealed the latter's intention to exploit the condition and interfere in the affairs of Muslims (ibid.). Following the incident, hundreds of Muslims were imprisoned and all Muslim organizations and NGOs were closed by the government. The measure was intended to curb Islamic revivalism, which the government actually perceived as a radicalization of Muslims (Abbink, 1998). The action of the government left EIASC (or Mejilis) as the only institu-tion representative of Ethiopian Muslims (Haustein and Østebø, 2011). The second violent incident occurred on 26 June 1995 when an unsuccessful assassination attempt was made against Egyptian President Hosni Mubarek who was to attend an Organisation of African Unity (OAU) leaders' summit in Addis Ababa (Medhane, 2004). The attempt had reportedly been carried out by Muslim Brotherhood-affiliated Egyptians who were supported by the government of Sudan (ibid.). The third incident occurred in the shape of various bomb attacks in 1995–1996 by *Al-Itihad Al Islamiya* in the Ethiopian territory (Jep, 2014). While the mosque incident was not presented for judicial inquiry and no investi-gation had been carried out to determine whether Ethiopian Muslims were involved in the other violent incidents, the government utilized the incidents to take over the EIASC (Mejilis) leadership and assign its loyalists (Abbink, 1998).

Moreover, the government has utilized both inter and intra-religious tensions for its securitization of Islam. As religious revivalism often involves rivalry between traditionalists and reformists, the state has exacerbated this rivalry in order to weaken Muslim communities (Jawar, 2012). The inter-religious tension that facilitates the government's securitization of Islam and Muslims occurred in 2011, when Muslims and Christians of Jimma were said to have entered into physical conflict. In relation to these conflicts, the late Ethiopian Prime Minister Meles Zenawi said 'Muslim radicalization and activism might grow out of hand and needed a state response'. Accordingly, 'specific reasons cited were the violent incidents in the Jimma area in 2011, as well as the mounting public and cyberspace polemics between Muslim Orthodox and Protestant preachers and "intellectuals", denigrating and attacking each other's faith' (Abbink, 2014, p. 353).

Despite different explanations that have been provided by different entities about the above conflictual incidents other than purely religious motives, the premier exclusively accused Muslims in relation to the conflict. In this regard, ICG (2016) has reported that conflicts in Jimma have been associated with long-established ethnic-based political and economic domination in the course of historical ethnic interactions, as there are ethnic fault lines between Muslims and Christians in the area. On the other hand, Østebø (2007) has argued that faith-based violence in Jimma was caused by competition over ownership claims and allocation of land to build religious institutions rather than motives of religious extremism. Unlike the above explanations, Jep (2014) has attributed inter-religious contentions in Ethiopia, including those in the Jimma area, to the post 9/11 global condition of 'war on terror' as the latter was considered to be the worldwide confrontation between Muslims and Christianity, in which the Ethiopian government stands by the side of Western powers. While the inter-religious contentions were subject to different interpretations, the Prime Minister associated the former with the radicalization of Muslims in the way that is quoted above.

Securitization of Islam in the regional context of the Horn of Africa

The nature of the relations between and among regimes in different countries of particular regional settings influences the patterns of peace and hostility and the formation and structure of security policies (Buzan and Wæver, 2004). Likewise, the relations and interactions of the Ethiopian government with regimes and political forces in neighbouring states of the Horn of Africa have facilitated the securitization of Islam in Ethiopia. The Ethiopian government was in military confrontations with the Somalia-based *Al-Itihad Al Islamiya* who had laid claim to the Ogden region of Ethiopia in 1995–1996 (Østebø, 2007).

As *Al-Itihad Al Islamiya* is supposed to have an Islamist agenda in the region, the government used it as a pretext to control the organized life of Ethiopian Muslims. As stated by Vaughan and Tronvoll (Sida, 2003, p. 62), 'the Muslim community in Ethiopia has been put under a strong political focus in recent years due to armed political resistance from various Islamic organizations, most notably *Al-Itihad Al Islamiya'*. Moreover, the rise of an Islamist party in Sudan (National Islamic Front) in 1995 and its regional policy orientation of supporting Islamic movements in neighbouring states, such as for revival of Islamist insurgents in Eritrea, was used by the Ethiopian government to develop suspicious views to control Ethiopian Muslims' organizational life (Dereje, 2011). Grebrewold (2014, p. 4) further argued that the rise of 'Islamic fundamentalism' in Somalia and Eritrea, both of whom Ethiopia had developed hostile relations with, shaped security understandings in Ethiopia and the government's security policy. Although these regional developments contributed to the regime's securitized approach towards Muslims, none of these events were reported to be linked with Ethiopian Muslims. Overall, these developments resulted in 'effective control of EIASC (Majilis) by the government' to provide institutional support for the regime's security discourse of 'Islamic fundamentalism' (ICG, 2016). The main point I would like to make here is that developments in the regional settings of the Horn of Africa were exploited by the Ethiopian government in order to securitize Islam and Muslims in Ethiopia, not to argue whether these developments posed objective threats to the Ethiopian state.

The role of the global war on terror for securitization of Islam in Ethiopia

The 9/11 incident and the subsequent global discourse of 'war on terror' have appeared to be a blessing in disguise to the already hostile position of the Ethiopian government towards Muslims. In this regard, Dereje (2011, p. 17) has argued that while the discourse on Islamic fundamentalism in Ethiopia started in the mid-1990s, it largely magnified after 9/11 when the Ethiopian government enthusiastically joined Bush's 'coalition of the willing' to assert itself with strategic importance in the 'US led post-cold war global order'. Ethiopia joined the Western camp mainly to secure strategic gains and economic developments from the United States (US) and European Union (EU) partnerships (Belachew, n.d.; Kłosowicz, 2015). As the Islamic Court Union became powerful in Somalia in 2006, the United States encouraged Ethiopia to strike against the Union by supporting the operation financially and militarily (Kłosowicz, 2015). Since then, the United States, the leading gospel of the 'war on terror', sees Ethiopia as an important partner for its operations in the Horn of Africa (Jep, 2014). In exchange, the US government offered Ethiopia economic, military and political assistance, amounting to 700 million US dollars every year (ibid.). All in all, the Ethiopian government manipulated both internal and external threats and developments in order to change its approach against Ethiopian Muslims (Haustein and Østebø, 2011). In this line, Jep (2014) argues that the government has been employing the global discourse of 'Terrorism' in order to justify its repressive actions against religious actors and their activities.

Policy frameworks and institutional practices as index of securitization

Securitization, by its very nature, needs institutions devoted to uphold security discourse and claims against the matter at hand (Poutanen, 2015). The work of these institutions serves a dual purpose both to understand the process and to evaluate the extent of securitization (Bourbeau, 2011). Policy frameworks and institutional practices are important to explain power relations and security sub-jectivities among different actors in the securitization process. Moreover, securi-tization policies and practices, again by their very nature, infringe basic human rights values under normal political circumstances, which are in turn countered by dissident voices from victims of security policies (Cesari, 2009). This goes with what Buzan (1983) describes as how modern bureaucratic states exercise large-scale institutional and legal powers against their people in the name of ensuring common good, referring to national security. Therefore, it would be valuable to shed light on institutional frameworks and policy orientations rel-evant to the topic.

Foreign affairs and national security policy and strategy (2002)

CHS conceptualizes securitization as the ultimate prioritization of national security from all political concerns. Likewise, the Ethiopian national security strategy document outlines national security as the supreme yardstick for security matters; 'In a fundamental sense, security policy is a matter of ensuring national survival'. Indeed, 'unless the overall policy direction pursued by the government takes this basic reality into account, our national existence and security will face grave danger' (FDRE, 2002, p. 5). This shows that security policy is inclined towards national security, whereas human security is a matter of secondary importance. The purpose of this study, however, is to show how Islam is treated as a source of insecurity in policy documents. The policy docu-ment emphasizes the negative aspects of Ethiopia's relations with neighbouring states based on Islamic religious sense when it points out that, while there are no benefits Ethiopia can expect from its neighbours for its national interests, the negative role of the latter should not be underestimated, reading as:

> By promoting religious extremism or providing the territory for religious extremists, they could sorely test our young democracy which is based on the separation of state and religion and religious tolerance.
>
> (FDRE, 2002, p. 60)

Apart from presenting empirical evidence to articulate the danger of religious extremism imported from the neighbouring states, the document relies on antici-pation of the phenomena in the future. Stating Ethiopian long-established histor-ical, linguistic and cultural ties with the Middle East, the document further stresses the negative aspect of the country's relationship with the latter in reference to Islam. In this regard, the document (2002, p. 113) states that 'while religion is not free of casting negative influences', 'Islamic extremism' and 'Ethiopia's susceptibility to danger' are the main sources of challenge in Ethiopia's relations with the Middle East.

Another aspect of securitized narratives about Islam in the policy document is the vague interpretation of Islamic history about the ancient Abyssinian King Nejashi. Ethiopia has played a crucial role in Islamic history for various reasons. Among others, the benevolence of the Christian Abyssinian King towards Islam and Muslims and his conversion to Islam have been widely circulated in Islamic history. Nejashi has a special place in religious accounts, not only as the first king abroad who recognized and converted to Islam, but also 'due to the prophet's issuing of Islam's first special funeral prayer in absentia (*salat al-ghaib*) to the King' when the latter passed away (Dereje, 2011, p. 27). In this way, Ethiopia has a special place both in the hearts of Muslims worldwide and the Ethiopian Muslims in particular (ibid.). Regardless of this piece of Islamic history cherished by Muslims across the world, the national security and strategy document has criminalized Islamic narrations of King Nejashi as an Ethiopian king who accepted Islam (2002, pp. 113–114):

> One of the differences between Muslim extremists and moderate Muslims concerns their differences on the subject of Ethiopia. The moderate Muslim believes that Ethiopia is a country that received the first followers of the Prophet, the first hijra (pilgrimage) destination, a respected country in which a believer should not touch if it does not touch him. As a result of this, he considers it to be a special place different among other countries. The extremist, on the other hand, preaches that it was the Ethiopian King who provided refuge to the followers of the Prophet and that the latter had been converted to Islam, although he did not make it public for fear of the people. So, the people are the enemy. Ethiopia should be categorized as the first 'Andalusia', the land which betrayed Islam.

According to the policy document, a Muslim who believes in and preaches King Nejashi's conversion to Islam is to be categorized as an extremist, thereby denying the Islamic history memorized by Muslims of the world. Furthermore, while Islam preaches about the positive instruction of the Prophet, who was reported to have said 'leave the Abyssinians in peace, so long as they do not take the offensive', the document reports him to have said 'the people are the enemy of Islam', an assertion which is not substantiated by even a single reference from Islamic sources. Dereje (2011, p. 27) refutes this claim, as Muslims' narration about King Nejashi's conversion to Islam is universally known among all the Muslims of the world. Moreover, he goes on to argue that Ethiopian Muslims' narratives on Nejashi could be positively utilized to cultivate national pride and belongingness, as well as considered to be Muslims' reassertion to the Ethiopian state.

The above views presented in the policy document can be interpreted in three dimensions. First, the way Ethiopian security strategy looks at neighbouring states and the Middle East reflects a centuries-old siege mentality in the security culture of the country, anchored in Christian Ethiopia as an 'Island of Christianity in the sea of Islam'. Second, the policy document reveals the influences of the works of intellectuals who have adopted the Western lens of the 'Clash of Civilizations' to explain the conditions and interactions of Ethiopian Muslims in their motherland. In this regard, one example worth mentioning is a self-proclaimed Zionist, Israeli professor named Haggai Erlich (1994) who serves as an architect of the interpretation in which the Nejashi tradition of Islam somehow transforms Islam into Ethiopia's historical enemy, as it can be seen in the policy document. Erlich (2007, p. 17), in another instance, also warns about the operation of what he called 'Wahhabi Muslims' for the 'political victory of Islam' in Ethiopia. Jep (2014) notifies the need to consider the position of Erlich and his intention as an Israeli historian who has specialized in Islam in Ethiopia. The works of Erlich emphasize the 'Salafi/Wahhabi' doctrine to link Islamic movements in Ethiopia with terrorist organizations such as Al-Qaida. Erlich had 'significant influences' on the government's policies towards Islam as 'he has given various lectures to various government officials' (Jep, 2014, pp. 104–105).

Most of Erlich's publication recounts and accentuates the conflictual aspects of the relationship between Ethiopian Muslims and Christians by adopting offensive coinages like the 'Ahmed Gragn Syndrome' to present Christians' views on Muslims, as well as 'the enemy of the Ethiopian state to Islam' as the Muslims' perspective towards Ethiopia. In this way, he misreads the harmonious historical interactions between Ethiopian Christians and Muslims at the societal level. This can be attributed to his mission and interest in Ethiopia read as:

> A major aspect of Ethiopian Christianity is a sense of closeness and full identification with 'Israel' as a religious and historical notion.
>
> (Erlich, 2013, p. 10)

> The Jewish state, working to find allies and friends in what was defined as the 'periphery' of the Middle East and the Arab world, invested in Ethiopia's development more than in any other country. The Ethiopians, for their part, trusted the Israelis and asked them to help and guide in nearly everything. These special relations ended due to Arab pressure on Ethiopia which proved more effective around the 1973 war in the Middle East.
>
> (Ibid., pp. 2–3)

The influence of Erlich on government policy clearly proved effective in 2011 when he suggested the introduction of a so-called moderate version of Islam called Ahbash to be practiced and followed by Ethiopian Muslims as a counter-radicalization strategy. Muslim activist and commentator Muhamed (2013, p. 2) denounced the government's collaboration with Erlich as:

> The government apparently is showing complete contempt for Ethiopian Muslims by inviting an Israeli Zionist to help in its nefarious project. As

Muslims over the world know, the Zionists of Israel have been involved in the systematic ethnic cleansing, indeed the uninhibited genocide, of the predominately Muslim people of Palestine for more than half a century.

Another scholarly contributor is Methane Tadesse, who has served to stimulate the government's cautiousness about the potential rise of Islamic extremism in Ethiopia. In a conference on federalism, conflict and peace-building organized by the then Ministry of Federal Affairs and the German Development Agency (GDA) at the Institute for Peace and Security Studies at Addis Ababa University, Medhane had reportedly said that 'the religious equilibrium [in Ethiopia was] collapsing very quickly' and that the religious status quo in the country was being 'dramatically eroded, incubating violent confrontations' (quoted in Ramos, 2013, p. 22). The claim of Medhane consists of dual targets of 'the enormously successful proselytizing efforts of the P'ent'ay Churches in Southern Ethiopia and the growth of Sunni fundamentalism in Somalia' (ibid.). He had blamed both the Ethiopian government and the Orthodox Church in the words of Ramos (2013, p. 23) as they 'were failing the country in offering at least mitigating solutions to the social and economic ills of the poorest quarters of society, thus giving way to other religions'. While he has referred to both Protestantism and Islam, the content of his speech gives much more focus to the so-called 'Wahhabism'; in his words, 'the hour of the miracle worker religion had finally come', and 'the contemporary religious militancy should be seen as a wholly new phenomenon and a threat to the peace, stability, and independence of the country' (quoted in ibid.). In accordance with the academic discourse of the 'Clash of Civilizations' in the West, the views and the contributions of Medhane and Erlich have played a crucial role for the securitization of Islam in Ethiopia. This can be revealed in the words of an officer in the Ministry of Federal and Pastoralist Development Affairs who replied to the question 'What indicators does the government use to identify "Islamic extremism" as a security threat in Ethiopia?' thus:

> A lot of scholars including Dr. Medhane Tadesse of Addis Ababa University have warned and alarmed the government to prepare and take important steps for the future inevitable problem of radicalism among Ethiopian Muslims.

Third, as the policy document has been issued after 9/11, the discourse of 'moderate and extremist Muslims' can also be seen in its text as the Ethiopian government's expression of its alliance with the West in its 'war on terror'. In this regard, Jep (2014, p. 78) argues that, based on its divisive narration of Muslims as 'Sufi' and 'Salafi', the Ethiopian government openly engaged in the post 9/11 global discourse of 'the good' and 'the bad' Muslim. Accordingly, the 'Sufi' represents 'the good or a moderate Muslim', while the 'Salafi' refers to 'the bad or a radical or an extremist Muslim' who is invariably associated with 'Salafism and Islamism'. The functionality of the policy framework and its divisive and exclusive effects on Muslims was witnessed in January 2004, when the

EIASC (Mejilis), in the presence of representatives from the Ministry of Foreign Affairs, held a meeting and removed all executive members of the council, replacing them with the so-called 'anti-Salafists' (Haustein and Østebø, 2011, p. 12). The presence of the United States' hand in these developments can be detected from the 'Thank You' letter, S/C/1883/60/2008, sent to the American Embassy in Addis Ababa in January 2008 by the former Vice President of Mejilis Elias Redman, reading as:

> It is to be recalled that, the sole representative organization of Muslims, the Ethiopian Islamic Affairs Supreme Council, and the Embassy are working together in order to eradicate Wahhabis from Ethiopia and strengthening the visit of Islamic shrines, which were neglected by Muslims due to the influence of Wahhabi teachings. So far, what we have done for Dire Sheikh Hussein [in Oromia] and [...] al-Nejashi mosque [in Tigray] are major witnesses for our close cooperation. Recently, we are in progress to do the same for Jamma Nigus, Qatibarie, and Albuko [mosques]. The promise of the Honorable Ambassador [Donald Yamamoto] to open Sufi Islamic colleges in Addis Ababa and Tigray are historic and always to be remembered. The historic support, both in advice and financial aid, which the Embassy is providing for me and my colleagues to enhance our acceptance [as a leader] and the legitimacy of Mejilis in the eyes of the Ethiopian Muslim community, is so immense. Assuring our commitment in the fight against religious extremism once again, we request the Embassy to keep up your support in the future.
>
> (As translated by and quoted in Muhamed, 2016)

The letter clearly discloses the Council's position as an agent and loyal instrument for the joint interest of the EPRDF government and its American partner.

The ban on the public manifestation of Islamic identity in 2008

Securitization is a process of transforming an issue from normal politics into a security agenda in order to adopt policies that can be justified in security terms (Poutanen, 2015). One of the debauched measures of the Ethiopian government against the Muslim community is the restriction of public spaces (Østebø and Haustein, 2001). The policy directive, adopted by the Ethiopian Ministry of Education in 2008, prohibits Muslim students from attending congregational prayers in the university compounds and prevents Muslim female students from wearing the niqab, affirming a securitization of Islam both in terms of policy frameworks and institutional practices that negatively affect Muslims. The policy is against normal legal, political and social norms in the contexts of the Ethiopian legal regime of multiculturalism. In terms of legal provisions, the public manifestation of religion is guaranteed under Article 27(1) of the Constitution as:

Everyone has the right to freedom of thought, conscience and religion that include the freedom to hold or to adopt a religion or belief of his choice, and the freedom, either individually or in community with others, and in public or private, to manifest his religion or belief in worship, observance, practice, and teaching.

In spite of the fact that freedom of religious public expression through worship, observance, practice and teaching are guaranteed constitutionally, the directive compromises the normal law of the land. In contrary to the constitutional regulation, the directive has prohibited female Muslim students from wearing niqab and prevented communal worship for both male and female students in public universities (Muhamed, 2016).

The Constitution, under Article 27/5, sets the grounds for the limitation of the public manifestation of religion as 'Protection of "public safety, peace, health, education, public morality or the fundamental rights and freedoms of others, and to ensure the independence of the state from religion"'. It follows that, in the eyes of the government, the wearing of niqab by female Muslim students and Muslims' communal prayer in the compounds of public universities are to be considered contrary to any of the above cherished values of the state, meaning public safety, peace, education, public morality, the fundamental rights and freedoms of others, and the country's secular order at large.

On 23 January 2013, Bahir Dar University prohibited female Muslim students from wearing the niqab or the hijab on campus, forcing many of them to put down their education (Abbink, 2014). In this way, the directive refutes the constitutional right of religious freedom, the right to education and the notion of multiculturalism that had previously existed in the Ethiopian context. Considering the legal framework of religious freedom and the Ethiopian context of multiculturalism, the directive has caused one of the visible institutional practices of securitization as it goes beyond the normal political circumstances.

Like other securitization policies, the ministry's directive has provoked resistance from Muslim communities who viewed the policy as a violation of the constitutional rights of religious freedom and called on the government to respect constitutional rights (Dereje, 2011). From his side, the government argued that the directive's measures and restrictions are applied equally to all religious communities, not solely targeting Muslims (ICG, 2016). However, if we look into actual occurrence, the policy has neither prohibited non-Muslim students of public schools from wearing ostentatious religious symbols, nor faced protests from students other than Muslims.

Anti-terrorism proclamation and the new Ethiopian civil societies law of 2009

In 2009, the Ethiopian government officially proclaimed its own anti-terrorism policy and thereby officially joined the international discourse on terrorism. Under Article 3, the proclamation states that Ethiopia's survival is at stake if it fails to fight terrorism, which by its nature is international. The law outlines multiple reasons for the need to adopt and implement the anti-terrorism laws that are entwined in the global, regional and local insecurity formation. Accordingly, the primary reason is the emerging danger of 'terrorism as the serious threat for the peace, security and development of the country' and 'the peace and security of the world at large'. The second reason is the insufficiency of the country's existing regular laws to effectively address the problem of terrorism.

The third and fourth reasons of adopting the proclamation mention the need to enhance investigations and information on suspected individuals and to cooperate with other governments' anti-terrorism efforts. The regime was accused by both domestic politicians and Western right advocacy groups of using the proclamation to suppress opponent groups; the latter has ultimately brought enormous challenges to Ethiopian Muslims. Jep (2014, p. 90) argues that the anti-terror law in Ethiopia serves to justify the government's scrutiny of Muslims' daily life.

Although the definitions of terrorism in the proclamation have invited criticisms for being vague, immediate developments and contexts to the issuance of the law proved to be in relation to Islam. In January 2009, an Ethiopian newspaper reported on the arrest of 18 armed Islamist militants who sought to enforce a theocratic state in Ethiopia and prepare for terrorist actions (USCIRF, 2013). On 23 February of the same year, the government issued a ban on 'all Muslim religious' activities that had not received a prior approval by the EIASC (Haustein and Østebø, 2011, p. 13). In the same year, with the aim of monitoring the activities of the Muslim community, the government 'issued through the EIASC (Mejilis) a registration-form to the country's mosques, ordering them to submit information on how they were run, on their sources of income, and whether the mosque was linked to any outside donor' (ibid., pp. 12–13). Securitization laws and policies always result in violations of rights and produce an internal resistance from the victims of extraordinary measures (Cesari, 2009). Likewise, the securitization of Islam in line with the global discourse of the 'war on terror' and the consequent change in the policies and actions of the government have generated dissident voices from Ethiopian Muslims but not from other religious communities. For example, the letter written by the Ethiopian Muslims Solution Finding Committee members who had been in jail for anti-terrorist charges since 2012, to the then President of the United States of America, Barack Hussein Obama, on 22 October 2014 states:

> We are 19 Ethiopian Muslims writing to you from within the Ethiopian gulags. Since we were arrested and detained on fabricated charges under the country's notorious anti-terrorism laws more than two years ago, we have been going through Stalinist political show trial designed to intimidate and silence us into submission in the face of the government's audacious and grotesque program of re-indoctrinating Ethiopian Muslims. We categorically reject the ridiculous allegations against us.

The message of the letter is that, while Ethiopian anti-terrorism law is a by-product of post-9/11 global security formation based on the securitization of Islam and the role of the United States in the securitization process, the dissident voices from victims of securitization have targeted both the domestic actor and its external partner. In this regard, Buzan and Wæver (2004) argue that the securitization process in a certain state might be influenced by the interests of another state, even if the latter is out of the regional security complex.

Another policy indicator of securitization of Islam in Ethiopia is the new civil society law issued in 2009. Accordingly, the EPRDF government has required Muslim religious organizations in the country to 'register and periodically renew their licenses' (ICG, 2016, p. 10). The discriminatory effects of the civil society law come from the fact that the Ethiopian Orthodox Church is exempt from the registration and renewal of its licenses as established by law during the Imperial Ethiopia (ibid.). Overall, the parallel issuance of anti-terrorist and Ethiopian civil society laws in 2009 created the 'rule by law' effects based on which the government cracked down on all Islamic NGOs. In this regard, Finensi (2011) argues that Islamic civil society organizations in Ethiopia have been dying out following 9/11 due to the government's suspicion of these organizations as if they were tied to global terrorist groups. Moreover, the government has closed down all Islamic periodicals in the country that have contributed to Islam's presence in the Ethiopian public sphere by spreading Islamic ideas to all of the Ethiopian population (Jep, 2014, p. 135). These actions contradict the country's proclamation to provide freedom of the mass media and access to information No. 590/2008 issued in 2008 which states that 'freedom of mass media is constitutionally guaranteed' and 'censorship in any form is prohibited'.

Securitization of Islam in the contexts of the Arab Spring and the Ahbashism mandatory training of 2011

According to securitization theory, securitization can be studied in terms of speech acts that present the issue as a security problem, as Wæver (1995, p. 54) states that 'security is not of interest as a sign that refers to something more real; the utterance itself is the act'. According to McDonald (2008), the contexts in which securitizing speech acts are made are also crucial in the study of securitization. Although the securitization of Islam in Ethiopia already started in 1995, it was largely publicized with the incidents following the Arab Spring in 2011. In addressing the question about Muslim protests against the government during the parliamentary session of 17 April 2012, the late Prime Minister Melese Zenawi stated:

> Unless the government takes timely and appropriate measure over these extremist groups, the danger is clear and imminent from what they are doing in Yemen, Libya, Syria, and Tunisia. [...] Some of these extremist groups are creating trouble in such countries and are trying to bring the Arab Spring to Ethiopia.
>
> (Quoted in Muhamed, 2016, p. 259)

For the events of the Arab Spring, Ethiopia resembled Egypt since 'both had long serving authoritarian systems' and 'important ties to the US security interests' (Lyons, 2015, p. 2). The Arab revolution resulted in the loss of the United States' power in Egypt, with the toppling of America's key ally regime and the political rise of the Muslim Brotherhood (Kłosowicz, 2015). This increased the value of Ethiopia for the United States and, and as compensation for the its loss in North Africa, the United States started looking for partners in the Horn of Africa (ibid.). Three important developments in 2011 were identified by Kłosowicz (2015, p. 92) to indicate the formation of new alliances between Ethiopia and the United States in the context of the Arab Spring as:

> The US embassy in Addis Ababa was opened in a new, impressive building, which is currently the biggest US diplomatic mission in Sub-Saharan Africa, military assistance was radically stepped up by 256% compared to the previous years, and a base for American drones was opened in Arba Minch in Southern Ethiopia.

In exchange for all these developments, the Ethiopian government planned to introduce the new sect called Ahbash, seeing it as a moderate Islam to be practiced by Ethiopian Muslims at the national level. Abbink (2014, p. 353) summarized this move in the following way:

> The 'Ahbashism' campaign, was started in the summer of 2011 when teachers from the Lebanese Al Ahbash organization (officially the 'Association of Islamic Charitable Projects', founded in 1930 in Lebanon and led by Ethiopian-born Sheikh Abdullah al Harari, 1910–2008), were invited to head an outreach training program to counter perceived radicalization tendencies among Muslims. The campaign was prepared with the EIASC, formally the instigator and implementer. Whatever its intrinsic nature, Al Ahbash was perceived as a moderate, non-radical Muslim group without a formula of political Islam, and thus superficially seen as suitable to 'teach' the government's preferred form of Islam. Affiliated religious instructors were mobilized for this campaign, to be rolled out in the country via religious schools and mosques. Some 16,000–18,000 Muslim community leaders underwent training.

The trainings were mandatory for Muslims recruited by the government to accept the *Al Abash* teaching throughout the country (Østebø and Wallelign, 2015). At this juncture, the government's approach to Muslims completely changed from tight institutional control to forceful indoctrination for new sects, what Haustein and Østebø (2011, p. 12) referred to as 'From repressive policies to interferences in the internal affairs of the religious community' and what Østebø (2013, p. 23) called 'from containment to the production of a governmental Islam'.

The act of the government at this moment clearly demonstrates the extraordinary measures taken towards Islam and Muslims beyond dehumanizing speech acts and repressive policies. This act of the government was in violation of the country's normal legal regime i.e. the Federal Democratic Republic of Ethiopia (FDRE) Constitution that is stated under article 11(3) as 'the state shall not interfere in religious matters and religion shall not interfere in state affairs'.

Securitization, by its very nature, involves security framing that constitutes the 'domains of political interaction by distributing and administering fear and trust among human interactions' (Huysman, 2006, p. 51). Likewise, the Ethiopian government created Sufi–Salafi dividing narratives among Muslims. While the government alarmed the Muslim community about the rise of 'Salafism/ Wahhabism' in the course of the training, it forced them to adopt the moderate doctrine of the 'Ahbash' sect of Islam. By dividing Muslims into 'Wahhabi/ Salafi' and 'Sufi', the government created a dichotomy and distinguished those that can be trusted from those that should be feared.

As a reaction to accusations of the government's interference, the late Prime Minister argued that the presence of the government in the training session was to teach constitutional values so that Muslims would not join Salafi groups. He tried to justify the position of the government as a disciplinary power to teach Muslims about constitutional norms and values. However, a disciplinary power is one that promotes unity and integration through inclusive trainings rather than select and divide the subjects of the disciplinary training (Foucault, 1995, p.132) in contradiction to the government's Sufi–Salafi dividing narratives of Muslims.

Conclusion

Securitization of Islam in contemporary Ethiopia is ascertained through speech acts, policy frameworks and institutional practices that have negatively affected the lives and interactions of Ethiopian Muslims both as individuals and as a community. The phenomenon is a by-product of various factors at the domestic, regional and global levels and a result of the roles of multiple actors ranging from leading academicians to foreign powers that have strong geopolitical interests in the Horn of Africa. Accordingly, increasing religious revivalism due to post-1991 political liberalization, intra and inter-religious tensions, the political rise of Islamists in the Horn of Africa (Sudan in 1995, Somalia in 2006), the post-9/11 global 'war on terror' and the events of the Arab Spring of 2011 have all contributed to the securitization of Islam in Ethiopia. The government interpreted these developments, both domestic and external, as if they had implications for the security matters of the Ethiopian state in relation to Ethiopian Muslims. The securitization process was followed by many changes in the government's actions and policy towards Ethiopian Muslims. Among others, the introduction of the 'Islamic fundamentalism' discourse resulted in the government's close scrutiny of the Muslim community's institutional life and its leadership, the banning of Islamic civil societies and periodicals, and the restrictions on religious public manifestations. Furthermore, the government violated the fundamental democratic and human rights of Muslims granted by the Ethiopian Constitution, the worst of these violations being the forced indoctrination of

Ethiopian Muslims to the so-called 'Ahbashism' Islamic sect, which the former imported from abroad in 2011. It has been discussed that securitization, by its very nature, gives rise to resistance and dissident voices as it violates basic human rights under normal political circumstances.

This characteristic of securitization has also manifested in the Ethiopian context of securitization of Islam, as both the government's narratives of 'Islamic fundamentalism' and its counter measures have faced counter claims and swift resistance from Ethiopian Muslims.

As per securitization theory, although the ultimate aim of securitization is to produce extraordinary approaches to labelled existential threats, the success of securitization depends on the people's approval of the issue as a threat. As the government's discourse about the rise of extremism among Ethiopian Muslims faced swift resistance from both Muslim and other religious communities and advocacy organizations at the national and global levels, this chapter argues that the role of audiences for securitization processes in non-democratic political systems is irrelevant.

However, the case of the securitization of Islam in Ethiopia has sought deviations from the original principles of securitization as presented by CHS securitization theory. First, the primary step of securitization in accordance with securitization theory is the speech acts in which the issue is presented as an existential threat to particular referent objects in order to convince the significant portion of audiences so that the actor can use extraordinary measures against the issue at hand. On the contrary, the Ethiopian case of securitization of Islam demonstrates that securitization in terms of speech act is largely a post-securitization phenomenon, that speech acts have been made after the policy formulations and several extraordinary measures have taken place. The aim of speech acts in this case is to suppress counter-securitizing claims. According to securitization theory, public approval or acceptance of the security component of the issue serves as a standard to evaluate whether the issue is securitized and whether it deserves extraordinary means. This study demonstrates that the role of the public is not relevant in taking extraordinary measures against the securitized issue. Therefore, it is arguable that in the case of political cultures that are not democratic, the measure of the changes in public policies and extraordinary actions better serve as indexes of securitization instead of the audience's approval of the issue as an existential threat. If we consider the audience's role in the contexts of CHS securitization theory, it would follow that securitization of Islam in Ethiopia is not successful. However, if securitization is to be evaluated based on its ends (extraordinary measures) rather than its means (an audience's agreement), securitization in that context has been successful as the government has been undertaking several extraordinary measures against Muslims and Islam under the justification of fighting terrorism. However, the security discourse of 'Islamic fundamentalism' in Ethiopia lacks general agreement from a significant portion of the Ethiopian society. This can be attributed mainly to two ways in which Ethiopia varies from Western countries where securitization of Islam has received popular support. First, the Ethiopian society is highly heterogeneous; almost equally distributed religious compositions do not facilitate in creating tensions of fundamentalism as the Ethiopian society has already built societal trust in multicultural social settings. The second reason is the absence of the political culture of transparency. As the elites are not accessible to people, the audiences are always cynical about the actor's securitizing claims. This implies that, while securitization in the contexts of securitization theory is supported by security discourse among the significant level of general public, in pseudo-democratic systems, the security discourse is only represented at the elitist understanding of the phenomenon.

Bibliography

Abbink, J. (1998). An Historical-Anthropological Approach to Islam in Ethiopia: Issues of Identity and Politics, in *Journal of African Cultural Studies*, Vol. 11.

Abbink, J. (2011). *Religion in Public Spaces: Emerging Muslim-Christian Polemics in Ethiopia*. Oxford University Press, African Affairs, 110/439 No. 2.

Abbink, J. (2014). Religious Freedom and the Political Order: The Ethiopian Secular State and the Containment of Muslim Identity, in *Journal of Eastern African Studies*, Vol. 8.

Bourbeau, P. (2011). *The Securitization of Migration. A Study of Movement and Order*. London, Routledge.

Buzan, B. (1983). *People, States, and Fear: The National Security Problem in International Relations*. Brighton, Sussex, Wheatsheaf Books.

Buzan, B. and Wæver, O. (2004). *Regions and Power: The Structure of International Security*. Cambridge, MA, Cambridge University Press.

Cesari, J. (2009). *Securitization of Islam in Europe*. Challenge Research Paper No. 15.

Dereje, F. D. (2010). *Setting a Social Reform Agenda in the Homeland: The Identity Politics of the Ethiopian Muslims in the Diaspora*. Diaspeace WP3 Working Paper.

Dereje F. D. (2011). *The Transnational Politics of the Ethiopian Muslim Diaspora. Ethnic and Racial Studies*. Oxford: Routledge.

Erlich, H. (1994). *Ethiopia and the Middle East*. London, Lynne Rienner Publishers.

Erlich, H. (2007). *Saudi Arabia and Ethiopia: Islam, Christianity and Politics Entwined*. Boulder and London, Lynne Rienner Publishers.

Erlich, H. (2013). Islam, Christianity, Judaism, and Ethiopia: The Messages of Religions. The Fifth Annual Levtzion Lecture was delivered at the Hebrew University, 30 April 2009.

Finessi, M, (2011). Muslims' Participation in Ethiopian Civil Society: Findings from Field Research in Addis Ababa. MA Thesis, Hogskolan Dalarna.

Foucault, M. (1995). *Discipline and Punish: The Birth of the Prison*. New York: Vintage Books.

Gebrewold, B. (2014). The Ethiopian Dilemma between State Security and Human Security, in *Human Security Perspectives Journal*, Vol. 1.

al Hashimi, M. A. A. (2013). *Ethiopian Muslims and the Ahbash Controversy in the Civil Rights Movement of Ethiopian Muslims: Context, Defining Features and Implications (Selected Articles)*. Belgium, LEBMA vzw.

Haustein, J. and Østebø, T. (2011). EPRDF'S Revolutionary Democracy and Religious Plurality: Islam and Christianity in Post-Derg Ethiopia, in *Journal of Eastern African Studies*, Vol. 5.

Hussein, A. (2002). 19th Century Islamic Revival in Wallo, Ethiopia. Historical Approaches. ISIM Newsletter 9/02. East Africa.

Hussein, A. (2006). Coexistence and/or Confrontation?: Towards a Reappraisal of the Christian-Muslim Encounter in Contemporary Ethiopia, in *Journal of Religion in Africa*, Vol. 36.

Huysman, J. (2006). *The Politics of Insecurity Fear, Migration and Asylum in the EU. The New International Relations Series.* The Taylor & Francis e-Library.

International Crisis Group (ICG) (2016). Ethiopia: Governing the Faithful Crisis Group Africa Briefing No. 117 Nairobi/Brussels, 22 February.

Jawar, M. (2012). Growing Muslim Activism and the Ethiopian State: Accommodation or Repression?, 4 April 2012.

Jep, S. (2014). Ethiopian Muslims in the Public Space of Addis Ababa since 1991. Universiteit Gent.

Jorg, H. and Østebø, T. (2011). EPRDF'S Revolutionary Democracy and Religious Plurality: Islam and Christianity in Post-Derg Ethiopia, in *Journal of Eastern African Studies*, Vol. 5.

Kaya, A. (2009). *Islam, Migration and Integration: The Age of Securitization.* London: Palgrave Macmillan.

Kłosowicz, R. (2015). The Role of Ethiopia in the Regional Security Complex of the Horn of Africa, in *Ethiopian Journal of Social Sciences and Language Studies*, Vol. 2.

Krume, T. (2010). *Islam – Religion Or Security Threat? An Analysis of the Securitization of Islam in the West.* Paper conducted for a course in International Security at the University College Dublin.

Larzillière, P. (2012). Production of Norms and Securitization in Development Policies: From Human Security to Security Sector Reform. The Issam Fares Institute for Public Policy and International Affairs, American University of Beirut.

Lyons, T. (2015). The Arab Uprisings and Ethiopia: Diffusion and Local Models. AUCP Workshop, ISA.

McDonald. (2008). Securitization and the Construction of Security, in *European Journal of International Relations*, Vol. 14.

Medhane, T. (2004). *Turning Conflicts to Cooperation: Towards an Energy-Led Integration in the Horn of Africa.* Addis Ababa, Ethiopia: Friedrich-Ebert-Stiftung.

Muhamed, D. (2015). Secularism and Politicized Faith in Ethiopia, 2015, Tana Forum University Essay Competition Essay No. 2.

Muhamed, D. (2016). Contested Secularism in Ethiopia: The Contention between Muslims and the Government. PhD dissertation, Adiss Ababa University. School of Graduate Studies, unpublished material.

Østebø, T. and Wallelign, S. (2015). The Intellectualist Movement in Ethiopia, the Muslim Brotherhood and the Issue of Moderation, Norwegian Peace Building Resource Center, NOREF Report.

Østebø, T. (2007). *The Question of Becoming: Islamic Reform Movements in Contemporary Ethiopia.* CMI Working Papers, Chr, Michelsen Institute, Bergen.

Østebø, T. (2013). Islam and State Relations in Ethiopia: From Containment to the Production of a Governmental Islam, in *Journal of American Academy of Religion*, Vol. 81.

Poutanen, M. (2015). Critical Discourse Analysis; Policy and Power. 'Surrounded by Threats; How Securitization Research Can Be Complemented by Critical Discourse Analysis to Uncover Relations and Conceptualizations of Power', 10th International Conference in Interpretive Policy Analysis (Lille, France).

Ramos, M. J. (2013). From Beleaguered Fortresses to Belligerent Cities. In A. Magnólia Dias (Ed.), *State and Societal Challenges in the Horn of Africa: Conflict and Processes of State Formation, Reconfiguration and Disintegration* (pp. 14–31). Lisbon: Center of African Studies (CEA)/ISCTE-IUL, University Institute of Lisbon.

Shinn, D. (2002). Ethiopia: Coping with Islamic Fundamentalism before and after September 11, in *Africa Notes, Africa Program, Center for Strategic and International Studies*, No. 7.

Sida (2003). Structures and Relations of Power in Ethiopia. Background Documents Country Strategy 2003–2007, by Sara Vaughan and Kjetil Tronvoll.

Taureck, R. (2006). Securitization Theory and Securitization Studies, in *Journal of International Relations and Development*, Vol. 9.

Trimingham, J. S. (1952). *Islam in Ethiopia*. Oxford University Press, London.

USCIRF (2013). *Other Countries and Regions Monitored: Ethiopia*.

Wæver, O. (1995). Securitization and De-Securitization. In R. D. Lipschutz, *On Security* (pp. 46–86). New York, Columbia University Press.

Zekarias, S. (2014). Religious Extremism as a National Security Threat: The Case of Ethiopia. MA Thesis, Adiss Ababa University.

List of materials used for discourse and content analysis

Speeches of leaders and motions

Speech by Prime Minister Meles Zenawi, During FDRE Parliamentary Session (2012), broadcasted through Ethiopian Television (ETV), 17 April 2012, downloaded from YouTube on 1 March 2017, accessed on 25 June 2017.

Speech by Dr Shiferwa Teklemariam, in a conference held in USA (on 12 October 2014) organized by Ethiopian Diaspora in USA in coordination with American Muslim show, downloaded from YouTube on 16 March 2017. 116 www.youtube.com/watch?v=h3 OphgAsPPo, accessed on 20 June 2017.

Ethiopian Muslim arbitration committee letter to President Obama, President of the United States of America, 22 October 2014. Posted by: ecadforum 30 October 2014.

National official documents

Anti-Terrorism Proclamation No. 652/2009, of the Federal Democratic Republic of Ethiopia. (2009). Federal Negarit Gazeta No. 57.

Central Statistics Agency (2007). 'Summary and Statistical Reports of 2007 Population and Housing Census: Population Size by Age and Sex'. FDRE Population Census Commission, December 2008, Addis Ababa.

Federal Democratic Republic of Ethiopia (2002). Foreign Affairs and National Security Policy and Strategy. Ministry of Information, Press and Audio-visual Department.

Ministry of Education (2008). 'Directive that Govern Worship Codes of Conduct in Educational Institutions'.

12 Islamophobia from within

A case study on Australian Muslim women

Derya Iner and Katy Nebhan

Problematizing the use of the term Islamophobia

The study of Islamophobia in the past decade has been a study of dichotomies informed by long-held prejudices, fears and stereotypes located within a largely Western context. Following the landmark publication of *Islamophobia: A Challenge For Us All*, the report of the Runnymede Trust Commission on British Muslims and Islamophobia (1997), numerous studies have sought to add to the growing body of research and commentary on Islamophobia that has centred on the nature and nurture of anti-Muslim racism. 'Location' has been relevant principally as an indicator that situates the Islamophobic experience within a Western context. As such the 'West', with its transnational media, has not only been the focal point for the experience and dissemination of anti-Muslim racism and marginalization, it has become the space where public, political as well as academic discourses relating to Islamophobia operate on the premise that this experience is between 'Muslim' and 'non-Muslim'. The contribution to Muslim civilian risk mitigation made by this binary presumption is manifold. As well as overlooking the experiences of Islamophobia *among* Muslims living in the West and their root causes, it fails to differentiate between the differing levels of religious identification among Muslims and the levels of assimilation resulting from the influence of Western Islamophobia.

This problematizes the use of the term Islamophobia when describing similar racist and discriminatory behaviours of some Muslims towards other Muslims. It raises the question of why the term Islamophobic is acceptable to use for non-Muslims but not so for Muslims who display the same prejudicial behaviour. In this study the term Islamophobia is used within a context that perceives this behaviour as stemming from a form of 'internalized oppression' (David, 2013). The instances referred to in this chapter reflect, to varying degrees, the contemporary reality of oppression which occurs at a sophisticated, often subconscious level. David's reflections on the 'taxonomy of microtransgressions – subtle, everyday communications of discrimination and prejudice' are particularly critical to this approach (David, 2013). This framework allows for the understanding of Islamophobia from 'within' to be seen a by-product of the 'hidden injury of oppression that is often ignored or minimised' (Pyke, 2010), in this case, by traditional Islamophobic discourses.

This chapter will analyse the experiences of a group of Australian Muslim women in order to explore the ways in which the intricate nuances of internalized oppression are expressed through intercommunal racism, sexism and criticism of particular 'Muslim practices', which are negatively portrayed within the Western Islamophobic discourse. It will look at the ways non-Muslim Islamophobic discourses have infiltrated and influenced Australian Muslim attitudes and their experiences with/towards the hijab, religious practice and religious identification. The impact of colonialism, secularism, nationalism and generational differences will also be explored. The chapter will conclude with an analysis of the multiple levels of religious identification and the differences between Islamophobic 'judgement' within the Muslim community and legitimate criticism of it.

Much has been written about the source and development of Islamophobia as well as its implications for the Muslim experience in the West. While Islamophobia is becoming increasingly prevalent in the political, economic and sociocultural discourses within these 'non-Muslim' societies especially in the wake of the events of 9/11, the theoretical studies focus on certain aspects of Islamophobia. For instance, Erik Bleich defines it as 'indiscriminate' negative attitudes and emotions directed at Islam and/or Muslims (Bleich, 2011). Jorg Stolz provides a more comprehensive definition through his recognition of the 'emotional, cognitive, evaluative as well as action-oriented elements' of Islamophobia (Stolz, 2005) while Salman Sayyid defines it as a form of racism 'in response to problematisation of Muslim identity' (Salman, 2014). Within the Western context the tendency to associate Islamophobia with 'anti-Muslim racism' remains widespread particularly in public discourses (Runnymede Trust, 2017). This compressive and reductive definition of Islamophobia overshadows the increasing prevalence of Islamophobic behaviour that exists and functions within the Australian Muslim population.

The danger here is the tendency to 'define' and 'understand' Islamophobia through reductionist binarisms. In his analysis of the 'war on terror' Robert Beshara refers to its 'State-centric' legitimacy which relies on the reduction: terrorists = Muslims and acts like an 'unconscious mantra' that is both foundational to the binarism of this discourse and which in turn 'positions 'postcolonial' subjects as either 'counterterrorists' (us) or 'terrorists' (them)' (Beshara, 2017). The use of dichotomous categories, with their origins in the Saussurean belief that the basic structuring principle in all human language is through binary oppositions, is most notable in media discourses that utilize binary signs to reduce 'reality' to distinct, dichotomous facts.

In doing so, the politics of internalized oppression evident through anti-Muslim social exclusion *within* the Muslim community is overlooked. This view, which has been central to studies of Islamophobia in general, requires further study if we are to understand the full impact of anti-Muslim discrimination on Muslims, between Muslims, across West/East borders and their root causes.

This chapter uses empirical data collected from a series of interviews with Muslims mothers to investigate the impact of Western Islamophobia on these women and their children in Australia. Although 'internal' Islamophobia was beyond the scope of the initial research, repetitive references to anti-Muslim sentiments and experiences within the community highlighted the need for reflective analysis of this neglected face of Islamophobia. What was evident from the outset was that these experiences were not defined by factors traditionally associated with religious discrimination like sectarianism (Sunni/Shia) and ethnicity. All the participants were Sunni Muslim who came from diverse backgrounds and identified with different levels of religious commitment. What was common to all the participants was the experience of forms of anti-Muslim discrimination within the Muslim community and their reflections on this experience in relation to exposure to Islamophobia outside of it in contemporary Australia.

The Muslim presence in Australia predates the dispossession of Aboriginal people by the British. While Macassan–Aboriginal relations have been, until recently, absent from Australia's historical narrative, their stories are preserved in rock art from the Kimberley to the Top End of the Northern Territory to parts of Northern Queensland with evidence suggesting first contact may date as far back as 1664 (May, 2013). The 'Afghan' cameleers, Australia's first Muslim settlers, followed from the mid- and late-nineteenth century. They were originally employed by the British colonialists to assist in the expeditions attempting to cross Australia's harsh interior. While colonial Australia was politically and socially progressive, racism and xenophobia was rife with blatant opposition to the 'sneaking, crawling, insidious Mohammedan invasion now going on' (Markus, 1979). The opposition to Asian/coloured immigration which increased in the mid-nineteenth century had, by the time Australia became a nation in 1901, led to the implementation of the White Australia Policy. This policy, along with the development of a national identity based on White exclusiveness and the superiority of one race and culture, was paramount in casting these early immigrants as 'coloured races' and a 'coloured problem' with no regard to the diversity within their community which was made up of Syrians, Indians, Malays, Turks, Afghans and Arabs (Lyng, 1927).

While Australia's 'agitation' and 'commitment' to a white Australia has been well documented, intercommunal conflict within minority communities is less so (Jupp, 1998). The lack of sufficient evidence stands in the way of making an informed reflection on intercommunal relations among Australia's Muslim communities in the early decades of the twentieth century. The Turkish Cypriots who came from a highly secularized society and the Syrian Muslims who migrated after the Second World War were discouraged from establishing any faith-based organizations due to the White Australia Policy as well as the linguistic/cultural barriers that existed within the small and geographically fragmented Australian Muslim population. Muslims did not become more visible as a community until after the arrival of large numbers of Turks in the late 1960s and the Lebanese in the late 1970s. The 2016

Census reveals that 2.6 per cent of the Australian population identify as Muslim, a significant increase from 1.7 per cent in 2006, 0.88 per cent in 1991 and 0.17 per cent in 1971 (Australian Bureau of Statistics, n.d.).

The Whitlam Labour government made a series of amendments in 1973 that saw the legal end of the White Australia Policy. While this may have theoretically put an end to the enforcement of racial aspects relating to immigration law, the lived experience of Australia's Muslims and the portrayals of them in media would suggest that anti-Muslim discrimination was far from absent. (For instance, in political discourse see Akbarzadeh, 2016; Cheng, 2017; in media discourse see Akbarzadeh and Smith, 2005; Poynting and Noble, 2003; Rane and Ewart, 2012; as part of everyday experiences see Dunn, Atie, Mapedzahama, Ozalp and Aydogan, 2015; Dunn, Klocker and Salabay, 2007; Johns, Mansouri and Lobo, 2015; for interpersonal type of Islamophobia see Hassan and Martin, 2015; Iner, 2017; for institutional Islamophobia see Iner, 2017; and for cyber Islamophobia in Australia see Iner, 2017; Jakubowicz *et al.*, 2017; Oboler, 2016.) What has been missing from the discourse, and what this chapter will now analyse, are the dynamics of Islamophobia within the Australian Muslim community.

The impact of non-Muslim Islamophobia on the Australian Muslim community

One of the key issues that arose from the data collected during the interviews centred on the experience of Islamophobia at the hands of other Muslims, referred to as intercommunal Islamophobia throughout this chapter. The types of Islamophobia recounted mirrored the forms of anti-Muslim racism prevalent in Western and other non-Muslim discourses. Some of the anti-Muslim sentiments described by the interviewees were explicitly identified as 'Islamophobic'. Other incidents and some of the statements made by the interviewees themselves mirrored the growing normalization of Islamophobia. The prevalence and influence of Islamophobia through the media, political and mainstream social discourses is evident in the variety of examples of anti-Muslim discrimination given that include forcing women and girls to wear the hijab and niqab; Islam is an oppressive religion and the desire of some Muslims to be publicly disassociated with Islam.

The true extent of the damage caused by non-Muslim Islamophobia on Australian Muslim women is evident in the explicit references to 'Islamophobia' as experienced *between* Muslims. One of the interviewees expressed it quite bluntly when she stated:

> I actually found that more common. Internal Islamophobia from Muslim to Muslim. From in my personal experience, is more common. I have to fend off and explain myself more to Muslims that I have to non-Muslims. And my children as well.

(Alia, 2017)

The hijab is often at the centre of Islamophobic discourses. The 'Australian' entry included under 'Freedom of Expression' in the *Encyclopaedia of Women and Islamic Cultures*, points to the wearing of the hijab as a source of daily religious racism. This is partly attributed to Muslim women being part of a minority community within a majority non-Muslim country but also to their 'visibility' (Imtoual, 2003). According to Alia Imtoual, this is a visibility that 'evokes popular ideas of Muslim women being oppressed and therefore victims, Muslim women bear the brunt of hostility and negativity' (Imtoual, 2003). Discussions surrounding complex matters relating to the hijab are 'reduced to simplistic debates such as "hijab: to ban or not to ban?" or "Muslim women: oppressed or liberated?"' (Dreher and Ho, 2009).

While there is an awareness of the communal solidarity brought about by these reductive expressions of Islamophobia, there is also an underlying tension within the Muslim community between external and intercommunal Islamophobic experiences and a lack of awareness of internalized oppression as a root cause. The physical act of wearing the hijab is at the centre of many of these tensions and is often put forward using rigid dichotomies.

The oral interviews suggest several critical factors when considering the hijab. The first is family and their interaction with the female. The suggestion that Muslim girls and women are 'oppressed' when wearing the veil removes any agency from the subject as well as those around her. It also replicates non-Muslim Islamophobic assumptions and prejudices and shows the extent to which these forms of external Islamophobia have been internalized and subconsciously adopted by Muslims.

The origin of the sentiments against hijab in this particular case is not prejudice but concern in response to the external judgements. One interviewee recounted the conversation she had with her husband when her daughter asked to wear the hijab and he responded:

> Let her do it, I was like too young. Let her do it, she wants it. He was born and raised in Lebanon, so being born and raised in Australia I think my perspective of living is completely different to his, but he was like yep, let her do it if she wants to do it. You do have those odd comments you know, why is she wearing it, she's so young, and you're too young, why you are wearing it?
>
> (Firdaus, 2017)

This Australian-born Muslim woman demonstrates an awareness of the possible effect of non-Muslim Islamophobic reactions on her daughter and is more hesitant to exposing her to it than her overseas-born husband.

The experiences of young girls who decide to wear the hijab can be particularly unnerving and confusing. One interviewee spoke in length about her daughter's desire to wear the veil and the subsequent challenges and questions they both had to negotiate in order to comprehend and work through the experience:

> How come Muslims are telling me to take it off, where non-Muslims are supportive? And I said, 'it's not Muslims who are telling you to take it off.

It's family members. There's a big difference, you can't say because some people in our family that are Muslim want you to take it off, not all Muslims want you to take it off', so I go, 'just be patient, they'll get over it, like, I went through it, you're going to go through it, we'll go through it together'.

(Hanifa, 2017)

What is particularly interesting is the young child's comparison of Muslim and non-Muslim reactions to her wearing of the hijab. The uneasiness with the hijab that is often found in the mainstream media and among non-Muslims is replicated by this child's own Muslim's family. The child is both shocked and disappointed with the reaction of her extended family. Just as interesting are the conversations such experiences spark between family members and between genders. While mainstream studies perceive Muslim women experiencing discrimination because they are 'more in the public eye than their male counterparts' (Jones, 1993b), the experiences of immediate male family members with the act of wearing the hijab is largely overlooked. When the aforementioned young Muslim girl decided to wear the hijab and stood in front of the mirror adjusting it, her mother recalls the words of her older brother who stated, 'well didn't you hear so and so, they said that you didn't have to wear it, so why do you keep wearing it?' This example reflects on the broader impact of non-Muslim Islamophobia within the Muslim family unit and the deeper vulnerabilities it can stir between siblings who begin to subconsciously mimic Islamophobic questions found more commonly in mainstream media. The mother's words to her son regarding 'personal space' are a good example of mending Islamophobic criticism by barrowing Western concepts:

What she does with her body, how she feels with it, you're not allowed to say anything … you can't go into her room and watch her put hijab on and say to her so and so said not to wear it, why are you wearing it, it's none of your business, how she wants to cover up. Leave her alone, let her experience it and if you have any questions come to me, because she is vulnerable right now and it's going to hurt her, to think her brother doesn't want her to wear it.

(Hanifa, 2017)

While such expressions of self-articulation may not conform to mainstream discourses, they are nevertheless influenced by the ripples, and internalization, of their stereotypes. Other examples of Western barrowed concepts can be seen in the idea that, like the hijab and prayers that are forced religious expressions, so too is the act of not driving a car and wearing a niqab. One interviewee explained how her daughter, the 'only one that was wearing hijab from kindergarten', and who attends school by 'carpooling', came home one day and told her that the Muslim woman who dropped her off at home said, 'you're so oppressed because you don't drive' (Asma, 2017). This particular example was a manifestation of a scarfed woman's prejudice to a niqabi woman with very much Western barrowed concept of Islam being backward and discriminating as coined with not allowing women to drive.

The association of the niqab with danger, fear and negative stereotyping within the Muslim community is a pertinent example of adopted Islamophobia. The reaction that the niqab evokes within the Muslim community can be just as scathing, if not more hurtful, than the one expressed by many members of the broader Australian society. For instance, one woman spoke of her fear of losing her job at an Islamic school when she decided to wear the niqab instead of the hijab and the response was no less confronting when her daughter expressed her desire to wear the niqab to school. The reaction of the school administration mirrored the Islamophobic responses to the niqab present in the broader non-Muslim Australian community. She recalls how the school administration 'kicked a fuss, they didn't really like it, the management' (Farkhunda, 2017). It was clearly a traumatic time for her and although she stood her ground and refused to remove it, she felt that her tenuous employment was again under threat when her daughter brought up the subject of wearing the niqab. The school may have seen the daughter's decision as being directly influenced by her now niqabi-wearing mother. Their resistance may have had more to do with their concern about a potential ripple effect among the other students. The mother's anxiety is evident in her response to her adamant daughter who was effectively cornered into leaving her school and missing educational opportunities due to the social pressure of her choosing to wear a niqab:

> 'I wanna go, I wanna put the niqab on, this and that', and I said 'please don't give me a headache, I still needed my job, they're going to kick me out, just leave it until you get out of school'. She said 'nope, I wanna put it on now', and she kept nagging and nagging and I kept refusing her. And then Subhanallah she ended up leaving, and then yeah, she put it on.
>
> (Farkhunda, 2017)

Aside from fearing unemployment, what is significant here is the Islamic school's reluctance to employ Muslim women wearing the niqab. Distancing themselves from what is considered to be 'extreme' covering in the mainstream media and public/political discrimination, this parallel discourse of exclusion reinforces a specific stereotype and thus plays an explicit role in the reproduction of a particular ideology, which in this example is the niqab as the visual embodiment of female oppression (Dijk, 1998). As such, Islamophobic representations are shared by both non-Muslim and certain Muslim individuals as a means of regulating social/religious practices and inclusion/exclusion in/from the work space. The response to such practices by Australian Muslim women who choose to wear the hijab is no doubt varied. In the following instance, the woman experiences anti-Muslim discrimination by her hijabi counterpart and the expression of 'hate' is no different to Western/external displays of Islamophobia:

> You've got your own people that hate it [niqab]. I remember walking past one woman and she's a hijabi, Muslim hijabi, and she walked past me, and she was swearing under her breath. Like really? What am I doing to you?

Really? If I could get that from you like that then what's left for other people that don't even understand it.

(Farkhunda, 2017)

What is striking is the sudden shift in frustration from the discriminating non-Muslim to the sheer disbelief at the reaction of the veiled Muslim woman who hates her niqab. The 'ignorant' judgement of the Muslim woman is seen as more damaging than that of non-Muslims because she should *understand* or at least try to. This lack of empathy from fellow Muslims runs as a theme throughout many of the oral interviews. One Muslim woman spoke of her experiences with her non-Muslim extended family who, after being satisfied that she willingly chose to wear the niqab, embraced her decision and went out in public with her with no hesitation. Once again, the response from the 'Muslim community' is met with disbelief and disappointment:

Whereas the Muslim community, the backlash that I got from wearing it at 19, everybody had a comment to say ... or you'll be walking and someone in hijab will walk past and say 'Astaghfirallah' [As a reaction of disapproval]! Really? Really? (laughs) That I don't understand. I don't get it.

(Alia, 2017)

The responses and the reactions to them are similar and perhaps the reasons for the reactions may be too. What is interesting to note and would require further study is the fact that both distasteful reactions were made by Muslim women who were also veiled. While patriarchy is often cited as the reason for the oppression of Muslim women, the relationships between Muslim women has been largely overshadowed by the adoption of gender dichotomies and will be explored in a separate study. In both these instances there are Muslim women who hesitate about the wearing of the hijab/niqab out of sincere concern for their daughters and Muslim women who actively demonstrate their disapproval. The reactions of all these women are a by-product of the underlying influence of non-Muslim Islamophobia that has permeated the Australian Muslim psyche.

For the purpose of this research, it appears that one of the reasons why these women chose to 'distance' themselves from what may be perceived as a visual adoption of a more conservative form of Islam may be due to external Islamophobic pressures. External Islamophobic pressures can also be seen in an interview with a Muslim teacher who described the awkward distance Muslim students maintained with her:

They just don't want to be identified and they don't want the world to know that they're seeking help of there being favoured by the Muslims. They want to belong to the majority of the community. They don't want to be isolated as Muslims.

(Leila, 2017)

There is a direct link between visibility and association/isolation in many of these instances. The sense of isolation and discrimination through association with Islam is a direct consequence of Islamophobia and its persistent presence in the media and public discourses. Perhaps strong physical and 'closed' manifestations of Islam through the niqab, for instance, increased the distance between mainstream acceptance and rejection for some of these Muslims. While it is an area that requires further investigation, it does suggest a strong causal link between mainstream Islamophobia, Muslim self-identification and intercommunal Muslim relations. For Muslims who have succumbed to the pressures of external Islamophobia, whether actively or subconsciously, looking at the niqab or even hijab may be seen as a hindrance to social acceptance in Australia society. 'Acceptance' appears to manifest itself when shrouded in mainstream rhetoric adopted by Muslims who actively seek to map their integration within the established discourse. The use of expressions like 'Meet some Aussie Mossies' indicates a conscious effort to demonstrate 'similarity'. (Chelebi, 2008).

Religious identification: between the secular and the faithful

In his analysis of the dynamics of 'Australian Islam', Michael Humphrey points out that the 'formulation "Islam and the West" suggests an encounter between two incompatible and homogenising cultures, one religious and the other secular' (Humphrey, 2001). He argues that in a postmodern/late modern reality, they both confront the difficulties associated with a 'porous pluralism' (Humphrey, 2001). Earlier in this chapter, reference was made to the diversity within the first group of Australian Muslim settlers who arrived in the late nineteenth century. This diversity widened as Muslims migrated in growing numbers throughout the twentieth and twenty-first centuries. The countries from which they came differed in terms of levels of nationalism, political stability and religious identification. Some migrated from nations where the shadows of colonialism remained, while others came from newly secularized societies (Jones, 1993a) Their practice and perceptions of religion have been just as diverse and with the growing number of Australian-born Muslims, this has continued to change and develop at differing levels. The differences in religious identification were explicit in several of the interviews conducted. The difference, which is not unusual, becomes a source of prejudice about one another's Islamic perception and practice. For instance, one woman gave a detailed description of the less 'religious' Muslim parents at her daughter's school who refuse to send their children to scripture class. When she questioned them, they explained that it was because the previous teacher they had spoken about 'jahanam' (hell) and they did not want their children listening 'to stuff like that' (Firdaus, 2017). Her description of these parents is judgemental and laments their lack of faith:

> They're not very religious themselves so they don't practice at all, when Ramadan comes, she's not fasting, they don't pray, they don't practice,

they're Islam by name. And she says it, we don't practice, we can't fast because I'm a smoker, or my husband is a smoker, or whatever it may be, but yeah you do see the odd ones, the ones that want to completely move themselves away from Islam, it's very … it hurts.

(Firdaus, 2017)

The prejudice is mutual as the non-practicing parent assumes that the scripture teacher is hard-line and motivated to use fear (i.e. hell) in her religious discourse. Accordingly, although the parent is Muslim, she prefers her child not to study Islam in the scripture class that is voluntarily delivered to Muslim students in public schools in Australia. The Islamophobic image of Islam and Islamic preachers to be intolerant and fearful survive in the perception of non-practicing Muslim towards a practicing Muslim.

The 'strict Islam' prejudice among non-religious or relatively religious Muslims towards more religious ones exists in different forms, including attitudes towards Islamic schools. One woman who considers herself a 'devoted Muslim' recounted memories of growing up in a 'more relaxed' environment before reflecting critically on Islamic schools:

Islamic schools unfortunately they are really, very strict and we don't want that, our kids to have. They live in a western society, they should love their religion, which is Islam, but at the same time, they should be relaxed.

(Hela, 2017)

The differing levels of religious identification and the associated assumptions were a source of tension and frustration for several of the women interviewed. One participant indeed stated that Muslims' prejudice among each other help spreading Islamophobia in the West:

I know most of my family friends, the first thing they want to know is the religion of someone, are you Christian, Muslim? I am opposed to that, I think you have to take people as human regardless of their religion … I think we did a lot of work, a big job to help Islamophobia spreading this way … I know for example that most of these ladies, because I am not scarfed don't say hello to me, my friend is scarfed and they looked at her and said Assalamualaikum sister.

(Noura, 2017)

By choosing to greet her hijabi friend with 'Assalamualaikum' and ignoring her, they were, according to the interviewee, essentially excluding this Muslim woman from a common Islamic practice and discriminating solely on the basis of her dress code. The interviews suggest that Islamophobic behaviours targeted both 'visible' and non-hijabi Muslim women. While one interviewee is critical of intercommunal discrimination based on her niqab, the non-hijabi participant is frustrated with the other Muslim's questioning her faith because she was not covered. In both instances, the Islamic greeting was the tool used to demonstrate disapproval. Coming from a secular country that is also the most diverse in the Middle East where Christians make up approximately one-third of the population, this interviewee was clearly unhappy with the assumptions made because she was not visually identifiable as Muslim.

Although she would be quite aware of the many sects that make up the Lebanese population back in Lebanon and Australia, she chooses to focus on negating their relevance as well the relevance of religious–conservative practices. Instead she focuses on the importance of being a good person and expresses fear of dealing with people who 'don't believe in Allah' because:

> If they don't believe in Allah nothing, they have nothing to respect, nothing to worry about but no I prefer if they believe in Allah, but the way they believe is their right. See if I saw someone praying, does that make them a better person, no.
>
> (Hela, 2017)

The non-hijabi Lebanese participant judges Muslims in the same way the Lebanese scripture teacher who assumes the smoker and non-fasting Muslim parent does not have a faith. Moreover, regardless of the verse 'Indeed, prayer prohibits immorality and wrongdoing (Quran, 29:45), this participant states that performing ritual prayers does not make one a better person. The issue here is not whether prayer is or is not the sole criteria for 'judging' the 'good' of a person but rather the Islamophobic inspired tendency to generalize, discriminate and dichotomize. This concealed criticism of praying Muslims by non-praying Muslims is common among Muslims.

The element of criticism based on religion appears to stem from political instability and social insecurities imported from their respective homelands or a reaction to being 'judged' since the similar participant was frustrated with being constantly asked if she is Sunni or Shia.

Both the Lebanese (Christian/Muslim and Shia/Sunni) as well as the Cypriot Turks (who lived near and interacted with Cypriot Greeks) came from secular homelands and they remained secular for some time even after their migration to Australia (Yucel, 2010). The criticism of religiosity is manifested in the secular Cypriot family's attitude towards the scarfed daughter in law to the extent that when she was asked about the Western modes of Islamophobia, she immediately started speaking about the internal Islamophobia:

> I just want to say that Islamophobia doesn't always come from non-Muslims, it can also come from Muslims and within the family … I started wearing [hijab] just after I got married and my new family, my husband's family they didn't like my scarf … they are always saying don't wear scarf this way etc.… I was afraid to send my kids to her house because of what she might feed them, but she is slowly coming around but she is still picking on things.
>
> (Sakine, 2017)

Although the interviewees expressed intercommunal and even inter-family criticism, there was an element of discomfort when it came to reconciling disagreements with 'other' Muslims and their children's awareness of it. One interviewee who, strive to maintain a meticulous religious life with her family, found her kids confused between their own practice of Islam and that of other Muslims:

> Even my boys, I've had people come tell them to their face 'your dad says this and this and this' [too much religious interpretations] … I said the Easter show was haram. Woah. Woah. I got chewed up for saying that. I don't mind. But I have to talk to my kids all the time … because the kids have an internal battle. When there's the pull from their friends, and the pull from society, and then their religion, and their faith, and they can't reconcile. Yeah very difficult to reconcile.
>
> (Alia, 2017)

Apart from people's conscious choice of not practicing or partially practicing Islam, what is apparent in these narratives from both sides of the religious 'divide' is the implicit impact of colonial and Western constructs and their normalization within differing contexts. At the heart of the heavily 'Westernized' Islamic reform movement of the late nineteenth and early twentieth centuries was, as Clive Christie argues, the 'Islamic version' of the extensive 'cultural revolution' that swept the colonized world prior to the First World War. (Christie, 1998) Liberating Islam from custom and tradition was part of this movement and as nationalism took hold of the Arab world and Turkey following the war, religious identification went through further changes. The remnants of the colonial influence are evident in the relaxed attitudes adopted by many of the first-generation migrants to Australia. One interviewee, an Australian revert, referring to her Turkish in-laws stated:

> The only Islamophobia experience I could recall is from family members that are Muslim … they had an idea that when you live in Australia and you are Muslim, you shouldn't wear the scarf, you don't have to pray … as long as you are Muslim in your heart that's enough.
>
> (Hanifa, 2017)

Another Australian revert interviewee referred to similar resistance with her husband's family who live in Algeria, a 'Muslim country'. She and her daughters experienced Islamophobia in the form of criticizing their religious level and practices at their extended family members' hands for the four years they lived there and recalls telling her daughters that 'Allah is preparing you for when we're going back to Australia because you'll have to defend yourself' (Asma, 2017).

An element of intercommunal racism, a by-product of nationalism, is also evident in the responses of some of the interviewees. While 'racism' continues to be associated with skin colour, the racism referred to in this research also includes current forms of racism that are more 'cultural' (Runnymede Trust, 2017). Speaking of her son's experience in an Islamic school, one woman described students teasing her son 'because I am not Arab because I am from Bangladesh, so our skin colour is a bit different' (Razia, 2017).

She went on to explain the way she contextualized this 'racist bullying' to her son:

> Listen, who has a happy life, and happy memory and everything is going well, they don't say bad things to others. Sometimes, maybe he's having some problem, maybe in himself, or maybe in his family or maybe somewhere, then they, what they do is say bad things to others. So be patient, maybe they are having some problems.
>
> (Razia, 2017)

Her compassionate response to the bullying suggests an awareness of the problems facing many Australian Muslim youth, many of which are a direct result of Islamophobia. In this particular case, the Arab children's bullying of a darker-skinned Bangladeshi boy appears as a replica of the Arab children's same experience with their Anglo peers. The mirroring effect of Islamophobic bullying within the Muslim peer groups is an unraised problem in the literature.

This 'pull', these broader ramifications brought about by the complex relationships between external Islamophobia and internal discrimination stand out as a significant challenge facing Australia's Muslims.

Reflections and ramifications

The by-product of Islamophobia, whether it be mainstream or intercommunal, has broad ramifications for Australia's Muslims regardless of the level of their religious identification. Australia's Muslims belong to multiple socio-cultural and ethnic groups and identify with their Australianness in differing degrees. They are no longer migrants in motion but an established community with a history that predates white settlement. Australia was home for the women interviewed as part of this study and as they and their families seek a sense of place, mainstream Islamophobia has consistently exacerbated their efforts in maintaining constructive relationships with Muslims who identify with Islam in ways that may differ to their own. Their struggle in overcoming the hurdles presented by both ends of the Islamophobic pull has been stifling for many. This has seen the 'insidious consequence of oppression' manifest itself through Muslims making statements that differ very little from those expressed by Islamophobic mainstream media (David, 2013). This is evident in this response:

> One of the reasons I don't want an Islamic school, because they need to be exposed to other faiths and other cultures. Because when you are in an Islamic school and you go to university and you see all this bunch of different culture, you think, whoa. It's a reality check; it's a shock to them, so it's very important for them to mix.
>
> (Firdaus, 2017)

Self-reflection and an awareness of intercommunal racism was also critical. One woman describes her reaction when her son told her he had made a 'slightly racist' comment to another boy:

> They had an argument – and my son was telling me the story and was listing the reasons he'd made the comment. It wasn't really polite, so I brought it back to him and said 'Now if someone said that about me walking in the street', would you just walk away or would you be like 'why is he saying that about my mum?' So, bigotry does exist in Muslims even. Some people have an issue with that and some people have an issue with Asians. Some people have an issue with Indians. Racism exists across the board. This particular thing, being Muslim, some people may have a problem with it, but I don't want it to affect their lives.
>
> (Alia, 2017)

The cyclical nature of Islamophobia as it wreaks havoc within the Australia Muslim community and between its members is not lost on the participants. Nor is the existence of this anti-Muslim discrimination at a global level and within their countries of origin. One participant describes her children's reactions to the 'niqab not being so welcome' in Egypt and their fear for their mother who was travelling through the country to get to Saudi Arabia to perform pilgrimage. The prevalence of Islamophobia and the ways in which both its explicit discourse and implicit forms have penetrated every part of the Australian Muslim experience highlights the dangers it poses for society as a whole.

The research indicates that the criticism present in the interviews operated on two different levels. On the one hand there were the subconscious Islamophobic references that typecast fellow Muslims. There was also constructive criticism and reflection. There was recognition of the fact that as 'as Muslims we are not perfect' (Firdaus, 2017) and that Muslims need to be more conscious of setting positive role models for both their children as well as members of mainstream society.

Conclusion

When the Runnymede Trust Report was first published in 1997, the term Islamophobia became a catchphrase that dominated media outlets and led to numerous mainstream and academic publications. With its focus on experiences of anti-Muslim racism and discrimination, the practice and analyses of Islamophobia cemented the place of the antiquated West versus Islam dichotomy. As this chapter has shown, Islamophobia has traditionally centred on Western and non-Muslim acts of discrimination upon the 'Muslim' other. We have argued that different forms of Islamophobic practice and ideas are not confined to the misleading non-Muslim/Muslim divide. Our data and research show that non-Muslim Islamophobic discourses have influenced, both actively and subconsciously, the anti-Muslim sentiments and experiences *within* the Australian Muslim community. Islamophobic practices within the Australian Muslim community appear to be driven by the fear and anxiety of *being* Muslim in a prejudiced Western environment. In some instances, Islamophobia within the community mirrors, reproduces and amplifies prejudices in order to widen the distance between the acceptable Muslim and the stereotypical 'bad Muslim' who is the subject of public vilification. The literature and interviews referred to in this chapter indicate that the forms of Islamophobia perpetrated through Western colonization, modernization and secularization are present within the discourses of both practicing and non-practicing Muslims within the Australian Muslim community.

The ambiguity of 'internalised oppression' has meant that Australian Muslim women have not been able to confront the source of their oppression. As David's theory suggests, this has led to their frustrations being 'directed inwardly' to those who remind them, 'the oppressed individual of himself – or herself' (David, 2013).

The ramifications of this influence and the resulting Islamophobic behaviours within the community are dangerous and the experiences included in this chapter offer only a small sample of the possible consequences to be found with further studies.

Bibliography

Alia (2017, 23 November). Children Affected by Islamophobia. (D. D. Iner, Interviewer).

Akbarzadeh, S. (2016). The Muslim Question in Australia: Islamophobia and Muslim Alienation. *Journal of Muslim Minority Affairs* 36.

Akbarzadeh, S. and Smith, B. (2005). The Representation of Islam and Muslims in the media. *School of Political and Social Inquiry* 4.

Asma (2017, 10 December). Children Affected by Islamophobia. (D. D. Iner and E. Malas, Interviewers).

Australian Bureau of Statistics (n.d.). *Australian Bureau of Statistics, Australian Government*. Retrieved from www.abs.gov.au/, date of access: 6 May 2018.

Beshara, R. K. (2018). *The Ideology of (Counter) Terrorism-Islamophobia/Islamophilia and the Ethico-Political Subjectivity of US Muslims: From Decolonial Psychoanalysis to Liberation Praxis* (Doctoral dissertation, University of West Georgia).

Bleich, E. (2011). What is Islamophobia and How Much is There? Theorizing and Measuring an Emerging Comparative Concept. *American Behavioral Scientist* 55.

Chelebi, M. (2008). *The Australian Muslim Student*. Terrigal: David Barlow Publishing.

Cheng, J. E. (2017). *Anti-Racist Discourse on Muslims in the Australian Parliament* (Vol. 72). Amsterdam: John Benjamins Publishing Company.

Christie, C. J. (1998). *Race and Nation*. London: I.B. Tauris Publishers.

David, E. J. R. (Ed.) (2013). *Internalized Oppression: The Psychology of Marginalized Groups*. New York: Springer.

Dijk, T. A. (1998). *Ideology: A Multidisciplinary Approach*. London: Sage Publications.

Dreher, T. and Ho, C. (2009). *Beyond the Hijab Debates: New Conversations on Gender, Race and Religion*. Newcastle: Cambridge Scholars Publishing.

Dunn, K. M., Atie, R., Mapedzahama, V., Ozalp, M. and Aydogan, A. F. (2015). The Resilience and Ordinariness of Australian Muslims: Attitudes and Experiences of Muslims Report.

Dunn, K. M., Klocker, N. and Salabay, T. (2007). Contemporary Racism and Islamaphobia in Australia: Racializing Religion. *Ethnicities 7.*

Farkhunda (2017, 18 December). Children Affected by Islamophobia. (D. D. Iner and E. Malas, Interviewers).

Firdaus (2017, 10 December). Children Affected by Islamophobia. (D. D. Iner and E. Malas, Interviewers).

Hanifa (2017, 20 December). Children Affected by Islamophobia. (D. D. Iner, Interviewer).

Hassan, R. and Martin, B. (2015). Islamophobia, Social Distance and Fear of Terrorism in Australia: A Preliminary Report.

Hela (2017, 8 December). Children Affected by Islamophobia. (D. D. Iner and P. L. Briskman, Interviewers).

Humphrey, M. (2001). An Australian Islam? Religion in the Multicultural City. In A. Saeed and S. Akbarzadeh, *Muslim Communities in Australia* (pp. 33–52). Sydney: University of New South Wales Press.

Imtoual, A. (2003). Freedom of Expression. In S. Joseph (Ed.), *Encyclopedia of Women and Islamic Cultures, II* (pp. 175–177). Leiden: Brill Academic Publishers.

Iner, D. (2017). *Islamophobia in Australia 2014–2016.* Sydney: Islamic Sciences and Research Academy of Australia.

Jakubowicz, A., Dunn, K., Mason, G., Paradies, Y., Bliuc, A. M., Bahfen, N., Oboler, A., Atie, R. and Connelly, K. (2017). *Cyber Racism and Community Resilience: Strategies for Combating Online Race Hate.* Switzerland: Springer.

Johns, A., Mansouri, F. and Lobo, M. (2015). Religiosity, Citizenship and Belonging: The Everyday Experiences of Young Australian Muslims. *Journal of Muslim Minority Affairs* 35.

Jones, M. L. (1993a). *An Australian Pilgrimage: Muslims in Australia from the Seventeenth Century to the Present.* Melbourne: The Law Printer.

Jones, M. L. (1993b). Muslim Women: Both Sides of the Veil. In *An Australian Pilgrimage: Muslims in Australia from the Seventeenth Century to the Present* (pp. 117–124). Melbourne: The Law Printer.

Jupp, J. (1998). *Immigration .* Melbourne: Oxford University Press.

Leila. (2017, 26 November). Children Affected by Islamophobia. (D. D. Iner and E. Malas, Interviewers).

Lyng, J. (1927). *Non-Britishers in Australia.* Melbourne: Melbourne University Press.

Markus, A. (1979). *Fear & Hatred: Purifying Australia & California 1850–1901.* Sydney: Hale & Iremonger.

May, M. C. (2013). *Macassan History and Heritage: Journeys, Encounters and Influences.* Canberra; ANU Press.

Noura (2017, 12 December). Children Affected by Islamophobia. (D. D. Iner, Interviewer).

Oboler, A. (2016). The Normalisation of Islamophobia through Social Media: Facebook. In *Islamophobia in Cyberspace* (pp. 55–76). Oxford: Routledge.

Poynting, S. and Noble, G. (2003). 'Dog-Whistle' Journalism and Muslim Australians since 2001. *Media International Australia Iincorporating Culture and Policy* 10.

Pyke, K. D. (2010). What is Internalized Racial Oppression and Why Don't We Study It? Acknowledging Racism's Hidden Injuries. *Sociological Perspectives* 53.

Rane, H. and Ewart, J. (2012). The Framing of Islam and Muslims in the Tenth Anniversary Coverage of 9/11: Implications for Reconciliation and Moving On. *Journal of Muslim Minority Affairs* 32.

Razia (2017). Children Affected by Islamophobia. (D. D. Iner and E. Malas, Interviewers).

Sakine (2017, 12 December). Children Affected by Islamophobia. (D. Iner, Interviewer).

Salman, S. (2014). A Measure of Islamophobia. *Islamophobia Studies Journal* 2.

Sayyid, S. (2014). A Measure of Islamophobia. *Islamophobia Studies Journal* 2.

Stolz, J. (2005). Explaining Islamophobia. A Test of Four Theories Based on the Case of a Swiss City. *Schweizerische Zeitschrift fur Soziologie* 31.

The Runnymede Trust (1997). *Islamophobia: A Challenge to Us All.* London: The Runnymede Trust.

The Runnymede Trust (2017). *Islamophobia: Still a Challenge For Us All.* London: The Runnymede Trust.

Yucel, S. (2010). *The Struggle of Ibrahim: Biography of an Australian Muslim.* Clifton: Tughra Books.

Index